CRITICAL ISSUES, DEVELOPMENTS, AND TRENDS IN PROFESSIONAL PSYCHOLOGY

VOLUME 3

CRITICAL ISSUES, DEVELOPMENTS, AND TRENDS IN PROFESSIONAL PSYCHOLOGY

VOLUME 3

edited by

J. Regis McNamara
Margret A. Appel

PRAEGER

New York
Westport, Connecticut
London

Library of Congress Cataloging in Publication Data
(Revised for volume 3)
Main entry under title:

Critical issues, developments, and trends in professional
  psychology.

  (Professional psychology update)
  Vol. 3 edited by J. Regis McNamara and Margret A. Appel.
  Includes bibliographies and indexes.
  1. Psychology, Applied.   2. Clinical psychology.
3. Psychology – Practice. I. McNamara, John Regis.
II. Barclay, Allan G.   III. Series.
BF636.C74   1982   150   81-15863
ISBN : 0-275-90860-7 (v. 1)
ISBN : 0-275-91227-2 (v. 2: alk. paper)
ISBN: 0-275-92250-2 (v. 3 : alk. paper)
ISSN : 0890-9946

Library of Congress Catalog Card Number: 81-15863
ISBN: 0-275-92250-2
ISSN: 0890-9946

First published in 1987

Praeger Publishers, 521 Fifth Avenue, New York, NY 10175
A division of Greenwood Press, Inc.

Printed in the United States of America

The paper used in this book complies with the Permanent
Paper Standard issued by the National Information Standards
Organization (Z39.48-1984).

10 9 8 7 6 5 4 3 2 1

CONTENTS

LIST OF TABLES

PREFACE

The third volume of *Critical Issues, Developments, and Trends in Professional Psychology* continues to review and update important developments in the field of professional psychology and provide the opportunity for psychologists to receive continuing education credit for their reading by means of a self-assessment examination. The contents selected for the third volume are once again diverse in nature, reflecting the broad knowledge base that underlies professional psychology.

The areas of professional functioning and interest and assessment and intervention provide the broad foci around which the various chapters are organized. The first four chapters concern professional functioning. Chapter 1 critiques the scientist-practitioner model and offers suggestions on how to improve it. The second chapter identifies and analyzes important social and ethical issues associated with women in psychotherapy. The chapter on malpractice sensitizes psychologists to the varying legal liabilities attendant to psychological practice. The final chapter in this section describes practical problems psychologists face in medical settings and how more appropriate professional interaction can be accomplished.

The four remaining chapters focus on assessment and intervention beginning with a chapter that deals with the clinical applications of role playing. This chapter provides useful information about the strengths and limitations of this important technique. A chapter on intervention techniques most appropriate for dealing with the disordered behavior of adolescents is presented next. A chapter with an overview of social learning approaches used to assess and treat child sexual offenders provides an up-to-date understanding of an important area for professionals. The concluding chapter in the book appraises the merits of short-term and time-limited psychotherapies.

The book was prepared to provide a current review of topics that would likely be relevant to the practicing professional psychologist. It could also serve as an ancillary graduate-level text in schools of professional psychology and academic graduate programs in clinical and counseling psychology where a topical overview and issues-oriented text is required. Undergraduates enrolled in upper division courses dealing with professional psychology issues would also find useful material in the text.

We are particularly grateful to Mark Kirschner, Carol Cockrill, and Jane Hamel who assisted with the proofreading and the preparation of the author index.

1

THE SCIENTIST-PRACTITIONER MODEL IN CLINICAL PSYCHOLOGY: SUGGESTIONS FOR IMPLEMENTING AN ALTERNATIVE MODEL

Stephen N. Haynes
Carolyn Lemsky
Kathleen Sexton-Radek

THE ISSUES

There have been frequent discussions, often of an adversarial nature, on the proper role of research in the practice of clinical psychology. The discussions formally began with the Boulder Conference (Raimy, 1950; see review by Barlow, Hayes, & Nelson, 1984). This conference proposed the *scientist-practitioner* model of training and practice in clinical psychology—a model in which clinical psychologists would be trained in both clinical and research skills and function concurrently as practicing clinicians and clinical scientists. The intended outcome of this model was that each practicing clinical psychologist would contribute to the evolution of psychological knowledge as well as provide psychological services.

Although later conferences on training in clinical psychology, at Chicago and Vail, acknowledged greater diversity among programs in the role of research (Barlow et al., 1984), the rhetoric has not abated. The number of recently published articles addressing this issue (for example, Agras & Berkowitz, 1980; Barlow et al., 1984; Emmelkamp, 1981; Fishman, 1981; Goldfried, 1984; Hayes, 1981; Kiesler, 1981; Lehrer, 1981; Levy, 1981; Maletzky, 1981; Ross, 1981; Schover, 1980; Strupp, 1981; Wilson, 1981) is further testament that the desirability, form, and degree of integration of empirical methods into clinical practice remains a contentious issue within the discipline. This issue is not unique to clinical

The authors would like to express their appreciation to Robert Schlesser and Frank Floyd for their helpful comments on an earlier version of this chapter.

psychology; it is representative of the philosophical and methodological disagreements between many academic and applied psychologists in the field.

Basically, two positions have emerged on the appropriate role of empiricism in clinical psychology practice:

1. The *scientist-practitioner model*, which proposes that clinicians[1] evaluate their own interventions using empirically sound methodologies, that clinical practice include controlled investigation (for example, of etiological factors for a particular target problem, of the comparative efficacy of different interventions with a particular target problem, and of predictors of treatment outcome), and that training in clinical research methods be an important part of doctoral training in clinical psychology (Barlow et al., 1984; Garfield, 1966; Hayes, 1981; Proshansky, 1972; Schover, 1980; Sechrest, 1975; Tyler & Speisman, 1967; Wollersheim, 1974).

2. The *clinician model*, which proposes that scientific methodology is basically incompatible with effective clinical practice and that training in research principles and methodology should be weighted significantly less than training in clinical skills in doctoral programs (Peterson, 1976a, 1976b; Stricker, 1973, 1975; Strupp, 1981).

These positions have been dichotomized for purposes of illustration. Many clinical psychologists and clinical psychology training programs have adopted intermediate models. However, advocates of both positions are in agreement that, regardless of the desirability of integrating empiricism in clinical practice, only a small proportion of practicing clinical psychologists have adopted the scientist-practitioner model and are engaged in any type of research concurrently with their clinical practice (Barlow et al., 1984).

Congruent with this assumption are the findings of Garfield and Kurtz (1976) and Peterson, Eaton, Levine, and Snepp (1982). Both studies involved a survey of the professional activities of Ph.D. and Psy.D. clinical psychologists. The mean proportion of time spent in research-related activities (research, research supervision, and scholarly writing) was .14 for respondents with a Ph.D. and .04 for respondents with a Psy.D. These figures were not broken down by major professional affiliation (that is, clinician, administrator, academician) and probably overestimated the proportion of time spent in research by clinicians (25 percent of the Ph.D.s and 6 percent of the Psy.D.s identified themselves primarily as academicians or researchers). These results are consistent with those of an earlier study (Kelly, 1961).

The results of our survey of 79 practicing clinical psychologists in the Chicago area also support these findings.[2] The mean proportion of time spent in research-related activities by our sample was .04. Respondents reported spending, on the average, less than 1.3 hours per week engaged in research related to their clinical activities. Interestingly, 58 percent of the sample reported that the integration of research and clinical practice was moderately or very important; only 4 percent said it was unimportant. These are important findings because they suggest that the low level of research activities by clinicians is due primarily to factors other than the perceived unimportance of research.

It is interesting to note that the authors of this chapter, and 94 percent of the authors cited in the chapter, are primarily affiliated with academic institutions. In essence, there is a lively debate among academicians about the proper role of research in clinical settings with which they have little contact. This is consistent with the statements of some practicing clinical psychologists (reviewed later in this chapter) that academically affiliated clinical researchers tend to be insensitive to the contexts and demands of clinical practice, and that clinical psychology graduate students are frequently trained in research methodologies that are more suited for academic than for clinical situations or populations.

Nowhere are the clashes between these two orientations more evident than in the context of graduate training. Rejection of the traditional Boulder Conference scientist-practitioner model of training has been one stimulus for the development of free-standing professional schools in clinical psychology. Although there is considerable variability across programs, professional schools (which grant Psy.D. degrees) tend to place less emphasis on research training than do programs affiliated with universities. The American Psychological Association has removed itself from any leadership role in this issue by approving both types of programs.

An equally important issue, which is beyond the focus of this chapter, is the consumption and utilization of published research findings by practicing clinical psychologists. Although there are some contradictory data (Lipsey, 1974; McNamara, 1977), a number of authors have suggested that published research findings have little impact on the professional behaviors of practicing psychologists (Barlow et al., 1984; Cohen, 1979; Kiesler, 1981; Lehrer, 1981; Maletsky, 1981). These authors have proposed various causes for the underutilization of research, as well as suggesting mechanisms for addressing this problem (for example, publication of more clinically relevant studies).

The manner in which these issues are resolved is important. They will affect the direction, professional identity, public perception, credibility, and vitality of clinical psychology (Barlow et al., 1984; Perry, 1979).

FOCUS

As indicated, the positive and negative aspects of both models have been addressed numerous times and were articulately summarized by Barlow et al. (1984). This chapter is not designed to reiterate these positions but to: (1) provide a causal model for the low rate of research activities by practicing clinical psychologists, (2) examine the rationale for the scientist-practitioner model and present an alternative model for the role of empiricism in clinical practice, and (3) suggest mechanisms for implementing this alternative model.

Several points will be emphasized:

1. The characterization of a scientist-practitioner model in clinical psychology has been unnecessarily restrictive and there are many behaviors, in addition to the conduct of controlled research, that are congruent with this model.

2. It is important to discriminate between different *types* of clinical research (for example, treatment outcome evaluation versus controlled research designs) when discussing the role of research activities in clinical practice.

3. Some types of research activities can be more easily integrated with clinical practice than can others.

4. There are multiple causes for the low rate of research generated by clinicians, and these causes vary across settings and clinicians.

5. Previously published articles addressing the reasons why so few clinicians adopt the scientist-practitioner model have focused on relatively minor determinants (such as the availability of appropriate research designs) and have invoked univariate rather than multivariate causal models.

6. The number of practicing clinicians who value the scientist-practitioner model is greater than would be expected on the basis of previously published research.

7. An *operant* paradigm (invoking concepts of facilitative stimuli, response cost, and contingencies) provides a useful approach to both understanding and modifying the degree of clinical-empirical integration.

The following section of this chapter addresses the question of why clinicians are infrequently involved in research. The subsequent section presents an alternative model for the integration of research into clinical practice. The last section addresses methods by which the alternative scientist-practitioner model can be implemented.

The authors acknowledge the subjective basis for the concepts presented here. Although a number of articles have been published on this issue, few of them have contained relevant data. Consequently, our causal hypotheses, model, and intervention proposals are based on our clinical experience, informal discussions with other clinical psychologists, the few previously published data-based studies, and the data collected in our survey that was conducted specifically for this chapter. We believe that many of the issues raised in this chapter can be addressed empirically, and we hope that this chapter will stimulate such attempts.

WHY CLINICIANS INFREQUENTLY DO RESEARCH: A CAUSAL ANALYSIS

This section examines the reasons why, despite the Boulder Conference and subsequent imperatives, research occurs only infrequently in conjunction with the practice of clinical psychology. As indicated in the introduction, the determinants of this phenomenon are numerous and vary across clinicians and clinical settings, as well as by the type of research activity addressed. The development of a causal model of the clinical-empirical split is important because any suggestions for intervention must be based on that model (Haynes, 1986).

Several classes of determinants are proposed to account for the low rate of clinical research: (1) beliefs by clinicians that clinical activities and research are incompatible, (2) difficulty in identifying and applying research designs and methods appropriate for clinical situations, (3) selection and

TABLE 1.1 Self-Reported Factors Inhibiting the Integration of Research in Clinical Practice (N = 79)

Inhibiting Factor	Percent of Respondents Indicating That It Moderately or Severely Inhibits	Mean Rating[a]	Rank[b]
Insufficient time	69	2.0	1
No research grants	66	1.9	2/3
No assistants	63	1.9	2/3
Costly	57	1.6	4
Insufficient interest	37	1.2	5-7
Not part of job	43	1.2	5-7
No agency support	42	1.2	5-7
No collaborators	34	1.1	8/9
Insufficient resources	34	1.1	8/9
Inadequate research designs	33	1.0	10
Would interfere with therapy	24	.8	11
Would not improve practice	21	.7	12
Ethics of doing research with clients	21	.7	13
Internal review boards	21	.6	14
Previous negative experience	17	.5	15

[a]0 (does not inhibit), 1 (mildly inhibits), 2 (moderately inhibits), 3 (severely inhibits).

[b]Based on mean rankings.

TABLE 1.2 Pearson Correlation Coefficients between Amount of Time Spent in Research, Proportion of Time Devoted to Research, and Factors Inhibiting Research (N = 79)

Inhibiting Factor	Amount of Time Spent in Research	Proportion of Time Spent in Research
Insufficient time	-.18*	-.16
No research grants	-.18	-.19*
No assistants	-.19*	-.17
Costly	-.12	-.21*
Insufficient interest	-.27**	-.37***
Not part of job	-.21*	-.23*
No agency support	-.18	-.16
No collaborators	-.12	-.23*
Insufficient resources	-.08	-.16
Inadequate research designs	-.17	.07
Would interfere with therapy	-.19*	-.31**
Would not improve practice	-.13	-.17
Ethics of doing research with clients	-.13	-.17
Internal review boards	-.08	-.08
Previous negative experience	-.10	-.06

*p < .05
**p < .01
***p < .001

training factors in graduate education, (4) accrediting and licensing procedures and criteria, and (5) intrinsic and extrinsic contingencies that are not conducive to clinical research.

As noted, these hypothesized determinants were derived from previous publications, clinical experience of the authors, informal feedback from clinicians, and our survey of practicing clinicians.

Table 1.1 summarizes the degree to which subjects in our survey indicated that various factors inhibited their conduct of clinical research. Table 1.2 summarizes the Pearson correlation coefficients between inhibiting factors and two measures of research activity--amount and proportion of time spent in research. These results will be discussed in the following sections.

THE PERCEIVED INCOMPATIBILITY BETWEEN CLINICAL ACTIVITIES AND RESEARCH

A number of authors (Schover, 1980; Strupp, 1981; see reviews by Fishman, 1981; Levy, 1981) have suggested that research, regardless of the methodology employed, is incompatible with clinical practice. For example, Schover (1980), in a view held by many clinicians, stated that therapy is an "art": a creative process that is not amenable to scientific analysis. Strupp (1981), although he did not embrace a "therapy as art" metaphor, stated that the roles of clinician and researcher are each extremely demanding and, therefore, incompatible. It is important to note, however, that while both Schover and Strupp emphasized the basic incompatibility between these two activities, both called for increased knowledge of research principles and methodology by clinicians in order to make them better research *consumers*.

In our survey (see Table 1.1), 24 percent of the clinicians sampled indicated the belief that research activities would significantly interfere with clinical practice, although this factor was ranked only 11th out of 15 possible factors inhibiting the conduct of clinical research. Furthermore, only 21 percent of the clinicians indicated a significant belief that research would not improve clinical practice. However, the belief that research would interfere with therapy was significantly and negatively associated with the amount ($r = -.19$, $p < .05$) and proportion ($r = -.31$, $p < .01$) of time spent in research. These data suggest that perceived incompatibility between research and clinical activities is an important determinant of the low rate of clinical research, but that it is less important than many other determinants.

The perceived incompatibility between clinical and research activities appears to be derived from several additional assumptions:

1. The behavior problems of clients are usually multiple, complex, and interdependent and, therefore, not amenable to empirical analysis, which is necessarily fragmented and reductionistic.

2. Regardless of the methods used, research strategies cannot be imposed on clients without compromising treatment-of-choice: Research necessitates the imposition of no treatment groups, extended baseline periods, treatment reversals or withdrawals, and/or undesirably rigid and inflexible treatment procedures.

3. Research strategies cannot be imposed in clinical situations without modifying the therapy process, and these reactive effects render any findings invalid and devoid of clinical significance.

4. Research activities reduce the time devoted to therapy (within sessions and by clinicians).

In essence, the research process is presumed to be unlikely to be beneficial, and may be detrimental, to the welfare of participating clients (Emmelkamp, 1981; Fishman, 1981; Levy, 1981).

The prevalence of these beliefs is important because it indicates the degree to which the research productivity of clinicians will be facilitated by technological and methodological advances (such as the development of clinically useful research designs and measurement methods) and incentives for doing clinical research. Unfortunately, no empirical data exist that either support or refute many of these beliefs. We do not know, for example, if client perceptions of therapy are affected by their participation in research, if research activities affect the behavior of clinicians during therapy, or if long-term treatment outcome is influenced by the imposition of formal research designs (both single-subject and group factorial) in therapy.

The Issue of Research Designs and Methods

Most discussions of the determinants of the clinician-researcher split have pointed to the dearth of research methodologies appropriate for clinical settings (Adler, 1972; Albee, 1970; Barlow, 1981b; Barlow et al., 1984; Bergin & Strupp, 1972; Emmelkamp, 1981; Fishman, 1981; Hayes, 1981; Kiesler, 1981; Levy, 1981; Raush, 1974; Ross, 1981). This emphasis has been particularly characteristic of essays appearing in the behavior therapy journals and in books written by behavior therapists (Barlow, 1981b; Barlow et al., 1984; Emmelkamp, 1981; Fishman, 1981; Hayes, 1981; Kiesler, 1981; Levy, 1981). These authors have, accurately, noted that the large group factorial designs and many of the measurement procedures traditionally taught to graduate students and used by academically affiliated clinical psychologists are appropriate for analogue research (that is, research with well-functioning college students or in academic settings) but ill-suited for clinical settings and populations. The limitations associated with these methodologies include sample size requirements, mandated no-treatment or placebo treatment conditions, exclusion of subjects who would frequently be treated by clinicians because of the search for highly "homogeneous" groups, constraints on applying individually tailored treatments, and limitations on clinical generalizability associated with nomothetic research strategies.

These critiques of the clinical applicability of traditional group research methodologies frequently have been used to argue for the preferred use of single-subject methodologies in clinical settings (Barlow et al., 1984; Hersen & Barlow, 1976; Kazdin, 1980; 1982; Kratochwill, 1978; Kratochwill, Mott, & Dodson, 1984). For example, all authors of a recently published series of articles in *Behavioral Assessment* (Barlow, 1981a; Emmelkamp, 1981; Fishman, 1981; Kiesler, 1981; Levy, 1981), attributed the low rate of research activities by clinical psychologists primarily to difficulties in using traditional factorial group research designs in clinical settings. Except for Levy's (1981) cautions about unequivocal adoption of single-subject designs, the use of single-subject designs was advocated by all authors as the most appropriate mechanism for increasing the rate of clinical research.

Other clinically useful research strategies, such as focusing on "deviant cases" (subjects who do not respond in expected ways to treatment programs) were suggested by Ross (1981). However, Ross's recommendations emphasized adoption of different research foci rather than different research methods.

We are in agreement with these authors that controlled single-case designs (for example, multiple baseline, reversal, replication, changing criterion, simultaneous treatment) are especially suitable for clinical settings. There are several reasons for this: (1) they can be applied with one or a few subjects; (2) "no-treatment" control groups are not required; (3) they frequently can be invoked with minimal disruption of ongoing treatment; (4) in most cases they do not require statistical analysis; and (5) they provide a mechanism for the therapist to examine client behavior changes and the determinants of those changes. In addition, single-case designs are excellent for use in documenting treatment efficacy, investigating parameters of treatment effects, and deriving and testing causal hypotheses concerning behavior characteristics and change with individual clients (see reviews by Barlow et al., 1984; Hersen & Barlow, 1976; Kazdin, 1980; 1982; Kratochwill, 1978; Kratochwill et al., 1984).

Perhaps most importantly, the integration of single-case designs in clinical practice is congruent with inquisitive, hypotheses-testing, self-evaluation, and accountability orientations toward therapy (Shakow, 1976). They provide a means for a therapist to evaluate and document systematically the outcome of his or her therapy and hypotheses.

Clinical research has also been facilitated by the refinement of valid, efficient, inexpensive, and less obtrusive assessment methods. Assessment procedures such as participant observation, self-monitoring, brief questionnaires, brief structured interviews, computerized psychophysiological assessment, and computer-administered questionnaires (Barlow, 1981a; Cone & Hawkins, 1977; Haynes, 1978; Haynes & Wilson, 1979) allow clinicians to collect relevant data efficiently with minimal interference with therapy.

Further, the adoption of single-subject research strategies would at least partially address one of the difficulties in conducting research in clinical settings. In our survey, it became apparent that a high percentage of practicing clinicians were not educated in the principles or applications of this technology (although knowledge of research methodology was not formally assessed). To the degree that the low rate of clinical research reflects a deficit in exposure to these designs, increasing educational efforts (through books, articles, symposia, and graduate courses) would be expected to be associated with an increase in that rate. However, to have maximum impact on the rates of clinical research, education in these alternative research strategies must occur during graduate school.

The presumption that training in and adoption of single-subject methodologies will be associated with a meaningful increase in research activities by clinicians has not been tested. Furthermore, the supposition that familiarity with single-subject research designs is the variable primarily controlling the rate of research activities of clinicians is unsupported in our survey. As noted in Table 1.1, "inadequate research designs" was ranked only 10th out of 15 possible deterrents to conducting clinical research and was cited as a significant deterrent by only 33 percent of the clinicians in our sample. Furthermore, "inadequate research designs" correlated only .07 with the self-reported proportion of professional time spent on research and -.17 with the number of hours per month spent in research-related activities.

These findings suggest that the availability of and familiarity with appropriate research methodologies is a *necessary but insufficient* condition for increasing the rate of clinical research. They *enable* research to be conducted in clinical settings but do not address the major determinants of the low rate of clinical research.

Selection and Training of Graduate Students

Goldfried (1984), Kiesler (1981), Marwit (1983), and others have emphasized the importance of graduate school training as an impediment to the integration of research in clinical settings. While many training programs emphasize the scientist-practitioner model of professional psychology, significantly fewer appear to train students adequately to implement this model. Students are often exposed to research methods and designs that are ill-suited for clinical settings (Barlow et al., 1984), they are exposed to professional models who exemplify academic rather than applied clinical research skills, and they undergo research training that many students find aversive (Goldfried, 1984; Kiesler, 1981; Peterson et al., 1982). In effect, graduate students are frequently exposed to professional role models who engage in analogue research strategies, with analogue populations, in analogue settings, using clinically inapplicable designs, and who sometimes demean the role of the practitioner.

Graduate admissions criteria may also contribute to low rates of clinical research. Although many university-based clinical psychology training programs use a professed interest in research as one admission criterion, many students enter clinical psychology training programs, particularly Psy.D. programs, with a primary interest in the *practice* of clinical psychology. Although we could locate no data on this topic, it has been our experience that the proportion of entering graduate students primarily interested in the practice of psychology appears to be increasing. Without programs to provide training in appropriate clinical research strategies and, most importantly, to excite these students about doing research in applied clinical settings, further deterioration in the rate of adoption of the scientist-practitioner model is unavoidable. Potentially, clinical psychology graduates with little interest or training in clinical research may assume policymaking roles and perpetuate the "clinician" model.

The Role of the American Psychological Association Committee on Accreditation and Licensing Procedures

The structure and content of clinical psychology training programs is significantly influenced by the criteria for accreditation established by the APA Committee on Accreditation. Because of the impact on training, these criteria ultimately have an important influence on the behavior of practicing clinical psychologists.

The APA has not been an advocate of a scientist-practitioner model in clinical training. In fact, the accreditation criteria and procedures, although allowing for diversity in orientations among programs (APA, 1983), ensure a bias toward clinical rather than research-oriented programs. The criteria reinforce programs for preparation of practitioners more than for preparation of scientist-practitioners. For example, specific courses are required in basic psychology and research methodology, but there is no requirement that the content of research methodology courses be appropriate for clinical settings or populations. Faculty are evaluated on clinical (for example, licensing, American Board of Professional Psychology) more than scientific competencies. Furthermore, the clinical psychologist site visitors are required to have clinical but not research credentials. APA accreditation criteria do include "research training appropriate to professional psychologist" but the weight given this criterion is less than is warranted by its importance.

This degree of paradigmatic unassertiveness probably reflects a political solution to the diverse views of those on the APA accreditation committee. The consequence is an inevitable decrease in the proportion of clinical psychologists who are trained in and interested in clinical research.

State licensing criteria and procedures vary considerably but are also inconsistent with the promotion of a scientist-practitioner model. The national examination contains many items on basic psychology, basic statistics, and psychometric theory, but very few items appear to be devoted specifically to knowledge of clinical research strategies. The personal interviews, required in some states, tend to focus on ethics and case management.

In summary, the criteria used by both the APA and state licensing bodies do little to ensure that graduate training and clinical faculty models foster scientist-practitioner expertise or orientation in students. Further, they do not facilitate knowledge by licensed clinical psychologists of appropriate clinical research strategies and methods.

Contingenices Associated with the Conduct of Clinical Research

A major tenet of this chapter is that the most important factors affecting the research behaviors of practicing clinical psychologists are the intrinsic and extrinsic contingencies associated with those behaviors. In most cases, these contingencies inhibit rather than facilitate clinical research activities. Therefore, the low rate of clinical research is a predictable and rational outcome of the environment in which most clinicians operate.

There are several classes of applicable contingencies; their relevance and impact vary across clinicians and across settings in which clinical activities occur. They include: (1) insufficient impact of research on clinical practice, (2) the high cost of doing research in clinical settings, (3) a decrement in reinforcers associated with the conduct of research in clinical practice, (4) a lack of institutional reinforcement for research, and (5) insufficient intrinsic reinforcement associated with research activities.

The data from Table 1.1 support the contention that intrinsic and extrinsic contingencies are not conducive to the conduct of clinical research. The integration of research in clinical practice was reported to be inhibited by insufficient time by 69 percent of the respondents, by lack of grants by 66 percent, by lack of assistants by 63 percent, by cost by 57 percent, by the fact that research was not a designated part of their job by 43 percent, by a lack of collaborators by 34 percent, and by a lack of agency support by 42 percent. Additionally, many of these factors are significantly correlated with the amount and proportion of time spent in research activities (Table 1.2).

If we assume that reinforcers associated with clinical practice include the interpersonal interaction associated with the therapy process, financial benefits, and functioning as an effective professional "helper," a reduction in all of these reinforcers can be expected when a therapist integrates research into his or her clinical practice. When integrating research into therapy, the therapy focus and process become more structured; intervention foci are sometimes predetermined on the basis of a research protocol and are, therefore, less flexible; and data collection takes a small, but important, amount of time that would normally be allocated to therapy. Furthermore, data collection is less enjoyable than therapy for most clinicians. Although reductions in these interpersonal reinforcers can be minimized, the importance of this aspect of the treatment process to a clinician will influence his or her willingness to engage in clinical research activities.

Research seldom generates and sometimes reduces income for the clinician. Even the simplest outcome evaluations require time for the collection and manipulation of data. Questionnaires must be scored, data plotted, and summary statistics compiled. In many instances, clients are reluctant to pay for time spent in research, and time spent engaging in research activities can reduce time spent in chargeable activities. Furthermore, many institutions and mental health centers receive funding from insurance companies and public funding sources on the basis of client contact hours. In these cases, the costs for time devoted to research activities are seldom recoverable. The reluctance of institutions operating under these financial contingencies to encourage clinical research is understandable. The importance of cost factors in inhibiting clinical research activities is amply documented in Tables 1.1 and 1.2 (for example, grants, assistants, cost, agency support, resources).

The outcome, as well as the process, of clinical research is seldom associated with extrinsic reinforcement for the clinician. Research activities and reports are infrequently reinforced by the clinical community, publication of research results is difficult, feedback through the peer review system of journals is sometimes demeaning, the degree to which scholarly publications enhance a therapist's professional status is unknown, and the impact of research on a clinician's therapy effectiveness has not been demonstrated.

One frequently cited benefit of a scientist-practitioner model is the potential improvement in therapy effectiveness associated with systematic measurement of therapy outcomes and processes (see Barlow et al., 1984). Such a benefit might be sufficient to outweigh the reinforcer deficits associated with clinical research. Although the assumption of improved therapeutic efficacy is certainly reasonable, there is no evidence that a therapist's effectiveness is enhanced by an empirical orientation. Furthermore, the impact of research activities on client satisfaction has not been determined.

The destructive impact of these deficits in extrinsic reinforcement is made stronger by the fact that many therapists do not find research activities intrinsically exciting, stimulating, or enjoyable. As noted in Tables 1.1 and 1.2, 37 percent of the clinicians surveyed indicated a strong lack of interest in doing research. In fact, "insufficient interest" was the variable most highly correlated with the amount ($r = -.27$, p < .01) and proportion (r = .37, p < .001) of time spent in research. This is not surprising as the degree to which psychologists find research activities enjoyable probably influences professional affiliations and activities. Those for whom research is enjoyable are more likely to select professional positions (for example, medical schools and universities) in which research is a designated part of their job.

It is more noteworthy that 63 percent of the clinicians surveyed reported that insufficient interest was not a major hindrance to their research activities. Additionally, only 4 percent of the sample indicated that the integration of research and clinical practice was unimportant to the field. These data suggest that a majority of practicing clinicians have an interest in conducting research—strengthening one of our contentions that contingencies, rather than lack of interest, account for the low rate of clinical research.

Magnifying the effects of the deficits in intrinsic and extrinsic reinforcement associated with clinical research, the effort or response cost required for clinical research is also greater for clinicians than for academically affiliated clinical psychologists. Clinicians are less likely to have grants, research assistants, or research collaborators. As noted in Tables 1.1 and 1.2, these deficits are perceived as significant inhibiting factors and are correlated with the amount and proportion of time spent in clinical research.

In summary, we are suggesting that the most important class of determinants of the low rate of clinical research is the professional environment in which clinicians operate. In this environment, research decreases several sources of reinforcement associated with clinical practice, is associated with insufficient intrinsic or extrinsic payoffs, and is inhibited by the response cost of doing it. As with other determinants, the salience and impact of these contingencies varies across clinical settings and across therapists within those settings. There are examples of clinicians who find research intrinsically reinforcing to the extent that they engage in research activities in professional settings in which such activities are discouraged. Similarly, many therapists are uninvolved in research in settings in which it is actively encouraged.

Summary

The low rate of clinical research was hypothesized to be a function of a number of interacting factors. These included the perceived difficulty of subjecting empirical phenomena and procedures to empirical scrutiny, the availability of and familiarity with appropriate research methodology, factors associated with graduate admissions and education, the role of accrediting and licensing criteria and procedures, and intrinsic and extrinsic contingencies that serve to inhibit the conduct of clinical research. The role of contingencies received particular emphasis. Additionally, it was noted that the relevance and impact of these determinants are expected to vary across clinical settings and across clinicians within settings.

The identification of these determinants provides the basis for recommendations for intervention. However, an alternative scientist-practitioner model for clinical psychology must first be proposed. The next section addresses the importance of clinical research in clinical psychology and proposes an alternative model of clinical research.

AN ALTERNATIVE SCIENTIST-PRACTITIONER MODEL
FOR CLINICAL PSYCHOLOGY

The previous sections introduced the traditional scientist-practitioner model in clinical psychology, documented the low rate of research activities by clinicians, and outlined potential reasons for this low rate of clinical research. In this section we address the desirability, feasibility, and characteristics of a scientist-practitioner model. We present an alternative model that more accurately reflects the contingencies operating in clinical practice. Because it is based on different causal assumptions, this alternative model differs from that traditionally proposed (Barlow et al., 1984).

Several concepts will be emphasized:

1. A strong research orientation is vital to the intervention efficacy, development, and identity of clinical psychology.

2. For these reasons, an increase in empiricism in the practice of clinical psychology would be beneficial.

3. There are many ways, in addition to the application of controlled research designs, in which empiricism can be integrated into clinical practice.

4. Qualitative and quantitative observations by clinicians can provide a rich source for hypotheses and should be communicated.

5. Expecting clinicians to apply controlled research strategies (either traditional group or single-subject) is unreasonable in most clinical settings.

6. In most cases, empiricism in clinical settings is best exemplified by systematic measurement (of dependent and independent variables, outcome, or predictor variables) rather than by controlled manipulation or interventions.

7. An increase in positions in clinical settings in which research is a designated and reinforced component is desirable.

The Role of Empiricism in Clinical Psychology

We are strongly in agreement with other authors (such as Barlow et al., 1984; Garfield, 1966; Perry, 1979; Raimy, 1950; Roe et al., 1959) that empiricism is the quality that most powerfully distinguishes clinical psychology from other applied behavioral science and "mental health" disciplines. Although we were not able to locate data on the degree to which a research orientation enhances the perception of clinical psychology, numerous instances of informal feedback from consumers and other professionals suggest that an empirical orientation has a very positive effect on the perceived status of the field.

While empiricism will always be important, its impact in an applied field is inversely related to the degree of predictive and intervention efficacy of that field. Clinical psychology can provide only an elementary and imprecise understanding of the characteristics and determinants of human behavior and of the principles and methods of its modification. If we understood why individuals sometimes abuse children, rape, become paranoid, or develop hypertension, and if we had effective methods of addressing these problems, the integration of research into clinical practice would be less important. It would then be possible to train clinical psychologists primarily in the application of proven concepts and methods of treatment and decrease the emphasis on empirical-clinical integration. However, given the current state of predictive and intervention efficacy, increasing the rate of clinical research is essential to the development of more powerful conceptual and intervention systems.

We are describing an ideal *cybernetic* discipline in which the empirical characteristics of the system facilitate the evolution of its predictive and intervention efficacy. In the absence of empiricism, the cybernetic quality of clinical psychology ceases and the field is reduced to the technical application of unproven procedures to inadequately understood behavior problems (Roe et al., 1959).

An Alternative Conceptual and Methodological Model
for the Scientist-Practitioner

Because of the weak predictive and intervention efficacy of clinical psychology, the consequent desirability of maintaining a conceptually and methodologically evolving discipline, and the distinctiveness afforded the field by an empirical emphasis, a strong commitment to a scientist-practitioner model is mandatory. However, the issue is the form in which this commitment is best operationalized.

Our position is that the integration of formal research strategies, whether single-subject or group factorial, in clinical practice is desirable but impractical in most clinical settings. We are in agreement with Strupp (1968; 1981) that the factors inhibiting empirical-clinical integration are simply too powerful to expect most clinicians also to function concurrently as researchers. However, there are other methods through which clinicians can make significant contributions to the evolution of clinical constructs and treatment systems.

As Shakow (1976) and Strupp (1976) noted, a scientist-practitioner model of clinical psychology emphasizes more than just the conduct of controlled research in clinical settings. It implies the adoption of an observational, inquisitive, and integrating orientation toward therapy. The scientist-practitioner functions as a participant observer of clients' behavior and the intervention process in addition to adopting an inquisitive stance regarding relationships among behaviors and the causes and mediators of behavior and behavior change. He or she attempts to integrate these observations into a useful model while remaining cognizant of alternative conceptual models. While the adoption of these behaviors is presumed to strongly benefit the treatment efficacy of the therapist, the development of more powerful conceptual and intervention systems is facilitated by publication of the derived inferences.

This expanded characterization of a scientist-practitioner suggests avenues for clinicians to contribute in addition to conducting formal research: the presentation and publication of the observations, hypotheses, and models derived from their clinical experience (Larsen & Nichols, 1972). However, a high rate of publications does not ensure a cybernetic discipline. The utility of these clinical communications will be affected by the same factors that affect the utility of other empirical or theoretical contributions. These include the level of inference and operationalization of constructs, susceptibility of the hypotheses to more rigorous empirical evaluation, and the quality of data upon which they are based—in other words, the degree to which the clinician adopts a scientific stance in regard to clinical phenomena. Violation of these methodological guidelines reduces the impact of hypotheses derived from clinical observations.

In addition to this scientist-practitioner conceptual orientation, an evolving discipline is also served by a more systematic evaluation of treatment effects and predictor variables. Under ideal conditions, the evolution of conceptual and treatment efficacy would be well served if all clinicians concurrently engaged in controlled research. However, such a model is impractical and does not reflect the reality of professional work environments and contingency systems.

Adoption of a scientist-practitioner role does not necessitate the use of single-subject or group designs in clinical practice. A role that is less inconsistent with the operative contingencies for most clinicians involves repeated measurement of predictors, mediators, and dependent and independent variables before, during, and following treatment. For example, a scientist-practitioner treating a depressed client might use daily or weekly short questionnaire measures of depression (a dependent variable), self-monitored quantity and quality of social interaction and negative cognitive self-statements (hypothesized causal and dependent variables), and the client's application of cognitive restructuring strategies (an independent variable). Intervention might be preceded by measures of variables such as the cyclical nature of depressive episodes, the degree of recent losses of social support, and self-reported anxiety in social situations (precipitating and mediating variables).

Applying such assessment methods across a number of depressed clients would significantly increase the amount of data available on the effects of specific treatments on specific behaviors and the variables associated with those effects. Importantly, these scientific activities could be carried out with minimal cost to the clinician, would be minimally incongruent with most institutional contingency systems, and would not require modification of treatment. Such systems would be particularly useful for clinicians who see many clients with the same behavior problems or who apply similar interventions across many clients.

Equally important, such an assessment-based treatment paradigm aids the practitioner in evaluating his or her intervention effects more validly than is possible with less systematic, more subjective methods (Haynes, 1978). Consequently, the adoption of the scientist-practitioner model aids the evolution of the therapist's efficacy.

We have outlined what we believe to be research behaviors that are consistent with a scientist-practitioner model and that are reasonable given the professional contingencies affecting most clinicians. Our preference, as outlined in the next section, is also for a modification of those contingencies to facilitate more systematic research efforts by practicing clinicians using single-subject and group designs.

The Need for Controlled Clinical Research

A scientist-practitioner model based on systematic assessment, rather than manipulation, can be a rich source of hypotheses, but such a model can provide only weak support for causal hypotheses and intervention effects. More systematic research efforts are still necessary to confirm causal and treatment hypotheses.

Given that clinicians cannot be expected to engage in systematic research of the type proposed by many authors and given that controlled clinical research is important to the continued development of the field, the evolution of a subset of clinicians who are designated as researchers seems unavoidable and heuristic. This dichotomy would approximate the methodological paradigm that has evolved in the medical sciences in which basic research on etiologies and treatments is frequently conducted by a subgroup of researcher-physicians or scientists. Intervention strategies developed by these researchers are then applied by physicians who collect data on effects, side-effects, and so on.

While this model is at variance with the traditional scientist-practitioner model, given the current constraints, the field would be well served by its adoption. However, its adoption and impact are affected by many of the factors outlined in the section on "Why Clinicians Infrequently Do Research." The next section proposes strategies for implementing this dichotomous model and for modifying the factors affecting the research behaviors and empirical orientation of clinicians.

Summary

In summary, the importance of an empirical orientation in clinical psychology was reaffirmed but an alternative scientist-practitioner model was offered. This model recognizes the current environmental constraints on the research behavior of clinicians and proposes a more limited role for formal research but a strengthening of the empirical orientation in clinical practice. Contributions may occur through careful report of hypotheses and observations and through systematic measurement of dependent and independent variables. Concurrently, the need for controlled clinical research involving careful manipulation of variables remains and should be satisfied by a greater number of designated research clinicians.

INCREASING EMPIRICISM IN CLINICAL SETTINGS

In this section, we propose specific methods of encouraging empiricism and increasing the rate of research in clinical settings. All of the suggestions are derived from the causal model delineated in previous sections and involve a realignment of the contingencies affecting the conduct of clinical research or modification of other hypothesized determinants. The suggestions target the selection and training of graduate students, the criteria used by accrediting and licensing bodies, extrinsic and intrinsic contingencies for research, client education, and the communication of clinical research findings. The intended impact of these recommendations is that a higher proportion of clinical psychology graduate students would be interested in clinical research, these students would be well trained in scientist-practitioner principles, and methods and contingencies affecting professional psychologists would facilitate the application of a scientist-practitioner model. Specific recommendations are outlined below.

Increase the emphasis on the scientist-practitioner model in graduate training. The scientist-practitioner model in clinical psychology can be strengthened through course work in clinically relevant principles of empiricism, research design (for example, single-subject designs and program evaluation), clinically useful assessment methods, and alternative statistical procedures such as time-series, LISREL, and causal analyses. These didactic courses should be complemented with experiential training by scientist-practitioner models in clinical settings (Goldfried, 1984). Training experiences might include research practica in the community, research collaboration with practicing clinicians, or research affiliations with mental health agencies. Research training can include, but should not be confined to, traditional experimental designs and methods. More importantly, students should be encouraged to adopt an empirical, skeptical, and inquisitive attitude toward clinical phenomena and therapy.

Change contingencies in universities to reward scientist-practitioner behaviors. Academic psychologists also respond to contingencies, and universities should reinforce clinical research that involves longitudinal time-series designs with a small number of subjects and the publication of less formally derived inferences (Kiesler, 1981). In the authors' experience, research using clinical populations is significantly more time-consuming and generates more problems than analogue research with university students. It is important that promotion and raise criteria acknowledge the importance of research with clinical populations and that the rate of publication of such research may be lower than that for analogue research. Similarly, single-subject designs and work with clinical populations should be encouraged in dissertations and theses.

Increase the emphasis on scientist-practitioner training in APA criteria for approval of clinical training programs. APA accrediting criteria should be changed to emphasize the concepts and methods of clinical-empirical integration. Criteria should focus on the didactic and experiential dimensions and contingencies outlined in the previous section: course work in clinically applicable research designs, statistics and assessment methods, exposure of students to research in clinical settings, involvement in clinical research by faculty members, and acknowledgment of clinical research in tenure and promotion criteria and in dissertation and thesis topics.

Increase the weight given to interest in research when evaluating candidates for graduate admission. The impact of training in clinical research strategies and philosophy is likely to be mediated by the level of research interests of students. Although the degree of interest in empiricism can be affected by graduate training, doctoral candidates who have an initial interest in clinical research are more likely to adopt a scientist-practitioner model. Therefore, empirical interest should be evaluated and considered in admissions procedures.

Make third-party payments contingent on systematic measurement of therapy process and outcome. In concert with the recent emphasis on accountability (Barlow, 1981b; Fishman, 1981), third-party payers should reserve payment for those clinicians who provide systematic data on their interventions and treatment outcomes. This would increase the number of clinicians practicing systematic data collection. Although monitoring assessment procedures used by clinicians initially will require added effort by third-party payers, it is in the long-term interest of the payers because the data acquired eventually will help identify more cost-efficient interventions for behavior problems and more effective therapists. It is in the interest of clients and clinicians because it provides some evaluation of treatment outcome and facilitates the evolution of the therapist's effectiveness.

Include knowledge of clinically relevant measurement procedures as a criterion for licensure. Criteria for state licensure should include knowledge of clinically applicable research designs, statistics and assessment methods, and the epistemology underlying their use. Although a greater emphasis on methods of clinical measurement in licensing exams cannot ensure their application, it would ensure some familiarity with this technology by practicing clinicians and increase the probability of their application.

Change contingencies in service-delivery systems to reinforce clinical research and a scientific approach to therapy. This is potentially the most powerful intervention but also one of the most complex recommendations to implement because it involves intervention at the systems level. Financial resources, personnel, and time should be allocated to facilitate empiricism in agencies. Job descriptions should include research and other behaviors consistent with a scientist-practitioner model and the reinforcement system at agencies (recognition, promotion, increased responsibility, and salary increases) should recognize empirical contributions. The adoption of an empirical orientation can also be facilitated by seminars, workshops, and interchanges within agencies.

Because research-incentive policies at agencies would often be incompatible with the policies of their financial sources and governing boards (such as state mental health departments, private funding agencies, and boards of directors), intervention must also occur, concurrently or antecedently, at higher systems levels in order to change contingencies placed on service delivey agencies for the conduct of research. For example, state mental health departments should be educated to the benefits of encouraging more systematic documentation of treatment effects.

Establish positions for clinical research at service-delivery agencies. Service delivery agencies should establish designated positions for clinical researchers. These individuals would be evaluated and reinforced primarily on the basis of their research ability and productivity and consultative contributions to other staff. This suggestion recognizes the improbability of most psychologists engaging in formal clinical research and the importance of such efforts.

Modify client expectancies. Prior to therapy, clients should understand that systematic measurement is consistent with and facilitates good clinical practice. Clients can be educated through information provided by therapists before therapy or, on a larger scale, through public information efforts (for example, newspaper and magazine articles and TV interviews). If clients viewed research efforts as an important part of the therapy process, one source of some therapists' reluctance to integrate empiricism into their clinical practice would be reduced. Obviously, some clients (such as some autistic children) are not capable of such understanding, and educational efforts should be extended to others in the client's environment.

Increase the intrinsic reinforcement associated with the conduct of research. The easiest, and perhaps most effective, method of increasing the intrinsic reinforcement associated with the research process is to decrease the isolation of clinical researchers by facilitating collaboration among researchers. Working with others on research can be interpersonally enjoyable and intellectually stimulating. Research conducted in isolation is not only less enjoyable, it is less efficient and subject to more conceptual and methodological errors. Collaboration among practitioners, or the formation of research "support groups" among clinicians, can also increase the available subject pools and allows each clinician-researcher to capitalize on the skills of the others.

Increase collaboration between academicians and clinicians. One method of increasing the reinforcing nature of clinical research, and of capitalizing on the divergent strengths of clinicians and academicians, is for academicians and clinicians to collaborate on research projects (Fishman, 1981). Of all the recommendations noted in this section, this one offers the most exciting opportunities for both the clinician and academician. One academician can bring expertise and resources such as computer access, statistical familiarity, financial support, knowledge of research methodology, as well as graduate and undergraduate assistants; the clinician can provide hypotheses, insight into clinical processes, and an opportunity for the conduct of research on clinical subjects in a clinical setting.

Promote affiliation between graduate students and clinicians interested in research. The research activities of clinicians and the training of graduate students would be enhanced by placing graduate students with clinicians for the purposes of clinical research. This provides an excellent field experience in the benefits and problems of clinical research for the students and addresses a number of the difficulties (among them, time and access to computers) that clinicians have in doing research. This could be accomplished through the establishment of a "clearinghouse" for interested clinicians and students.

The academic-clinical collaboration outlined in the previous two proposals can also be of benefit to agencies by facilitating program evaluation, staff training, and accountability. The educational benefits for faculty and students participating in such collaborative efforts include the provision of scientist-practitioner role models and experiences in addition to direct exposure to the link between theory, research, and practice.

Increase the recognition of clinical research by Division 12 of APA. Division 12 (Clinical) of APA exemplifies the clinical-academic split. For example, the section in Division 12 focusing on experimental clinical psychology is composed mostly of academicians, has officers primarily from academia, features primarily academic speakers, and gives awards for research mostly to academicians. Although the goals of the section are laudable, it could more assertively promote the scientist-practitioner model through actively recruiting clinicians interested in research, integrating them into the section, and providing formal recognition of clinicians who exemplify clinical-empirical integration.

Facilitate the publication of research articles by practicing clinicians. Journals should be more receptive to articles that use single-subject designs (Hayes, 1981), articles by clinicians that do not use factorial or single-subject designs, articles that are well controlled but reflect constraints imposed by clinical settings, and review articles that are particularly useful to clinicians. A report by a clinician on a particular intervention, using careful process and outcome measurement and appropriate follow-up, with a moderate number of agoraphobics, is an example of research that does not meet traditional standards but which, if carefully conducted and reported, might provide clinically useful information. Several journals, particularly *Behavior Therapy* and *Clinical Psychology Review*, have adopted this policy by publicizing their interest in clinically relevant articles or reviewing them in the context of limitations imposed by clinical settings. We are not suggesting that poorly conceptualized, conducted, or written studies should be published. We are suggesting that good research, conducted in a setting with methodological constraints, should be given careful consideration.

Summary

In summary, it is not presumed that the adoption of the intervention strategies outlined above will render all pure clinicians into scientist-practitioners. Many of the hypothesized causal variables (for example, the perceived incompatibility of research and clinical practice, the modification of the clinical process that sometimes accompanies the superimposition of research strategies, and disinterest in research by clinicians) are not readily amenable to modification. However, the adoption of these suggestions would increase the quantity of clinically relevant research generated in the discipline and, more importantly, the empirical orientation of clinicians. The consequence of this would be an increase in the cybernetic quality of clinical psychology and of the participating clinical researchers, thereby insuring a pattern of increasingly effective interventions.

Adoption of the suggested interventions would also generate two *types* of clinical researchers: (1) clinicians whose research activities are primarily confined to systematic measurement and (2) designated "clinical researchers" who engage in clinical research involving treatment manipulation (within-group factorial or single-subject designs). The two-class system of clinical researchers inherent in these proposals is unavoidable and perhaps desirable (Strupp, 1981) because there is no reasonable set of contingencies that would result in more than a minuscule percentage of practicing clinicians applying controlled research designs.

It should also be noted that many of these recommendations have already been adopted. For example, many hospitals and mental health centers have designated positions for researchers, many agencies provide time for staff to engage in research, some service-delivery centers inform clients that data acquisition and assessment is an expected part of the therapy process, some private and public funding agencies require program evaluation as a prerequisite to continued funding, some academicians collaborate with private practitioners on research, and some journals actively encourage submissions from practicing clinicians.

CONCLUSION

Empiricism is an essential characteristic of clinical psychology but has not been readily adopted by clinicians. Suggestions that clinicians adopt a traditional scientist-practitioner approach to therapy have been infrequently heeded. Additionally, the availability of clinically useful research designs is only a minor determinant of this phenomenon.

There are multiple, interacting determinants for the low rate of empiricism and research in clinical settings. Most of these revolve around contingencies affecting the conduct of research, graduate training, and the intrinsic value of and interest in research. An operant analysis was stressed emphasizing environmental contingencies as powerful determinants of clinical research activities.

Based on this causal analysis, an alternative scientist-practitioner model was proposed that is broader and involves dichotomous roles. Most clinicians would adopt an empirically based orientation toward therapy and systematically measure dependent and independent variables. Others would be designated as "clinical researchers" and carry out controlled research studies on the hypotheses developed in less structured clinical research.

Specific recommendations were provided for implementing the alternative scientist-practitioner model. These included modification of contingencies by institutions, accrediting and licensing boards, the APA, and third-party payers, as well as increased emphasis on scientist-practitioner training, and increased collaboration between clinicians, academicians, and students.

NOTES

1. In this chapter, "clinician" refers to a clinical psychologist whose primary professional activity is the practice of psychotherapy. "Clinical research" refers to research, primarily psychotherapy research, that occurs in the context of clinical practice.

2. The primary goal of this survey was to identify the factors that affected the integration of research in clinical practice. Subjects for this survey were 79 practicing clinical psychologists from the Chicago area. Names were obtained from phone book listings and the APA directory.

Potential subjects were first called to determine their eligibility (practicing clinical psychologists with Ph.D.s or Psy.D.s). Eligible subjects were then given a brief explanation of the goals and methods of the study and asked if they would be willing to participate. Those who answered affirmatively were mailed a cover letter reexplaining the goals of the study and a 1½-page questionnaire containing items on professional affiliation, proportion of time spent in various professional activities (for example, research, direct service), hours per month spent in various professional activities, their rating of the importance of integrating research and clinical practice, and a rating of the degree to which various factors (such as insufficient time or resources) inhibited the conduct of research in their clinical practice.

Of 113 individuals who originally were identified as appropriate for the study and who agreed to participate, 79 (70 percent) returned a completed questionnaire; 82 percent of the sample reported that their primary professional affiliation was with an individual private practice or with private or nonprivate psychological service agencies; 61 percent reported that they were "primarily" in private practice; and 39 percent reported that private practice was their secondary professional affiliation. Respondents reported that 73 percent of their time was spent in direct service or clinical supervision (other time was spent in administration, professional development, and research). Thus one goal of the study, to acquire a sample composed of practicing clinical psychologists, was met.

REFERENCES

Adler, P. T. (1972). Will the Ph.D. be the death of professional psychology? *Professional Psychology, 3,* 69-72.

Agras, W. S., & Berkowitz, R. (1980). Clinical research in behavior therapy: Halfway there? *Behavior Therapy, 11,* 472-488.

Albee, G. W. (1970). The uncertain future of clinical psychology. *American Psychologist, 225,* 1071-1080.

American Psychological Association. (1983). *Accreditation handbook.* Washington, D.C.

Barlow, D. H. (1981a). A role for clinicians in the research process. *Behavioral Assessment, 3,* 227-233.

Barlow, D. H. (1981b). On the relation of clinical research to clinical practice: Current issues, new directions. *Journal of Consulting and Clinical Psychology, 49,* 147-156.

Barlow, D. H., Hayes, S. C., & Nelson, R. O. (1984). *The scientist practitioner: Research and accountability in clinical and educational settings.* New York: Pergamon Press.

Bergin, A., & Strupp, H. (1972). *Changing frontiers in the science of psychotherapy.* Chicago: Aldine.

Cohen, L. H. (1979). The research leadership and information source reliance of clinical psychologists. *Professional Psychology, 10,* 780-786.

Cone, J. D., & Hawkins, R. P. (1977). *Behavioral assessment: New directions in clinical psychology.* New York: Brunner/Mazel.

Emmelkamp, P. M. G. (1981). The current and future status of clinical research. *Behavioral Assessment, 3,* 249-253.

Fishman, S. T. (1981). Narrowing the generalization gap in clinical research. *Behavioral Assessment, 3,* 243-248.

Garfield, S. L. (1966). Clinical psychology and the search for identity. *American Psychologist, 21,* 353-362.

Garfield, S. L., & Kurtz, R. M. (1976). Clinical psychologists in the 1970s. *American Psychologist, 31,* 1-9.

Goldfried, M. R. (1984). Training the clinician as scientist professional. *Professional Psychology: Research and Practice, 15,* 477-481.

Hayes, S. C. (1981). Single case experimental design and empirical clinical practice. *Journal of Consulting and Clinical Psychology, 29,* 193-211.

Haynes, S. N. (1978). *Principles of behavioral assessment.* New York: Gardner Press.

Haynes, S. N. (1986). The design of intervention programs. In R. Nelson and S. C. Hayes (Eds.), *Conceptual foundations of behavioral assessment.* New York: Guilford Press.

Haynes, S. N., & Wilson, C. C. (1979). *Behavioral assessment: Recent advances in concepts and methods.* San Francisco: Jossey-Bass.

Hersen, M., & Barlow, D. H. (1976). *Single case experimental designs: Strategies for studying behavior change.* New York: Pergamon Press.

Kazdin, A. E. (1980). *Research design in clinical psychology.* New York: Harper & Row.

Kazdin, A. E. (1982). *Single-case research designs: Methods for clinical and applied settings.* New York: Oxford University Press.

Kelly, E. (1961). Report of survey findings. *Newsletter: Division of Clinical Psychology of the American Psychological Association, 14,* 1-11.

Kiesler, D. (1981). Empirical clinical psychology: Myth or reality? *Journal of Consulting and Clinical Psychology, 49,* 212-215.

Kratochwill, T. R. (Ed.). (1978). *Single-subject research: Strategies for evaluating change.* New York: Academic Press.

Kratochwill, T. R., Mott, S. E., & Dodson, C. L. (1984). Case study and single-case research in clinical and applied psychology. In A. S. Bellack & M. Hersen (Eds.), *Research methods in clinical psychology* (pp. 55-99). New York: Pergamon Press.

Larsen, J., & Nichols, D. (1972). If nobody knows you've done it, have you? *Evaluation, 1,* 39-44.

Lehrer, A. (1981). Not a science. *American Psychological Association Monitor, 12,* 42.

Levy, R. L. (1981). On the nature of the clinical-research gap: The problems with some solutions. *Behavioral Assessment, 3,* 235-242.

Lipsey, M. W. (1974). Research and relevance: A survey of graduate students and faculty in psychology. *American Psychologist, 29,* 541-553.

Maletzky, B. M. (1981). Clinical relevance and clinical research. *Behavioral Assessment, 3,* 283-288.

Marwit, S. J. (1983). Doctoral candidates' attitudes toward models of professional training. *Professional Psychology: Research and Practice, 14,* 105-111.

McNamara, J. R. (1977). Patterns of continuing education for Ohio psychologists: A survey of interests and activities (1972-1974). *Professional Psychology, 8,* 368-376.

Perry, N. W. (1979). Why clinical psychology does not need alternative training models. *American Psychologist, 34,* 602-611.

Peterson, D. R. (1976a). Is psychology a profession? *American Psychologist, 31,* 572-581.

Peterson, D. R. (1976b). Need for the Doctor of Psychology degree in professional psychology. *American Psychologist, 31,* 792-798.

Peterson, D. R., Eaton, M., Levine, R., & Snepp, F. (1982). Career experiences of doctors of psychology. *Professional Psychology, 13,* 274-285.

Proshansky, H. M. (1972). For what are we training our graduate students? *American Psychologist, 27,* 205-212.

Raimy, V. C. (Ed.). (1950). *Training in clinical psychology (Boulder Conference).* New York: Prentice-Hall.

Raush, H. L. (1974). Research, practice, and accountability. *American Psychologist, 29,* 678-681.

Roe, A., Gustad, J. W., Moore, B. V., Ross, S., & Skodak, M. (1959). *Graduate education in psychology.* (Report of the conference sponsored by the Education and Training Board.) Washington, D.C.: American Psychological Association.

Ross, A. O. (1981). Of rigor and relevance. *Professional Psychology, 12,* 319-327.

Schover, L. R. (1980). Clinical practice and scientific psychology: Can this marriage be saved? *Professional Psychology, 11,* 268-275.

Sechrest, L. (1975). Research contributions of practicing clinical psychologists. *Professional Psychology, 8,* 413-419.

Shakow, D. (1976). What is clinical psychology? *American Psychologist, 31,* 553-560.

Stricker, G. (1973). The doctoral dissertation in clinical psychology. *Professional Psychology, 4,* 72-78.

Stricker, G. (1975). On professional schools and professional degrees. *American Psychologist, 30,* 1062-1066.

Strupp, H. H. (1968). Psychotherapists and (or versus) researchers. *Voices, 4,* 28-32.

Strupp, H. H. (1976). Clinical psychology, irrationalism, and the erosion of excellence. *American Psychologist, 31,* 561-571.

Strupp, H. H. (1981). Clinical research, practice, and the crisis of confidence. *Journal of Consulting and Clinical Psychology, 49,* 216-220.

Tyler, F. B., & Speisman, J. C. (1967). An emerging scientist-professional role in psychology. *American Psychologist, 22,* 839-847.

Wilson, T. G. (1981). Some thoughts about clinical research. *Behavioral Assessment, 3,* 217-255.

Wollersheim, J. P. (1974). Bewail the Vail, or love is not enough. *American Psychologist, 29,* 717-718.

2

SEX, GENDER, AND PSYCHOTHERAPY

Lucia Albino Gilbert

Psychotherapy invariably reflects the culture in which it is embedded—and for those of us living in the Western world, gender is a salient aspect of that culture. All therapists in the course of treatment express their values and visions for women and men; psychotherapy is not gender-free.

This chapter first defines sex and gender and other terms used to refer to gender-related phenomena. A brief review of sex bias in psychotherapy is presented next, together with an explanation of why the focus here is on gender effects rather than on sex bias. Three specific gender issues are then addressed: dependency, power, and beauty and attractiveness. Each of these is related to the therapeutic setting and recommendations are made to enhance therapeutic effectiveness. The final section discusses broader approaches to education and treatment.

DEFINITION OF SEX AND GENDER
AND RELATED TERMS

Psychologists have only recently begun to recognize the pervasive effects of gender. The term "sex," which by definition refers to the biologically based categories of female and male, refers, in actuality, to social categories as well (Deaux, 1985; Eagly & Steffen, 1984; Lott, 1985). Examples abound: Tasks typically performed by females are generally judged to be simpler than those typically performed by males (Hansen & O'Leary, 1985). The behaviors of women and men change depending on the sex composition of the work group (Kanter, 1977). Within the context of the psychotherapy situation, a therapist or client expecting to meet with a female for an initial session is startled when a male walks in; in supervision one of the first questions asked of supervisees is the client's sex (Gilbert, 1985a). The term "gender" acknowledges the broader meaning that has become associated with biological sex and refers to the psychological, social, and cultural features and characteristics frequently associated with the biological categories of female and male.

What about sexuality? According to Webster (1959), sexuality is a quality or state of being sexual and relates to the sexual functions of a person. In our society, however, sexuality and gender often get blended and lose their distinction. Thus, a man's sexual functioning often becomes associated with his self-esteem, privileged position, and need for dominance over women. Alcoholic men, for example, often deny their sexual dysfunctioning. We also see this blending of sexuality and gender in conceptions of homosexuality. Individuals whose sexual preference is for the same sex are attributed the "gender" characteristics of the other sex: Gay men are viewed as taking on the characteristics of women and lesbian women as taking on the characteristics of men.

Another commonly used term is sex (gender) roles. The construct of roles refers to a person's position in an organized social structure and to the rules of conduct governing interactions between individuals in various positions. Sex roles are those roles assigned to individuals on the basis of their biological sex and, in essence, refer to normative expectations about the division of labor between the sexes and to gender-related rules about social interactions that exist within a particular culture or historical context (Angrist, 1969). These prescribed behaviors are accompanied by social sanctions that serve to encourage desired or appropriate behaviors (such as dominance behavior in males) and discourage those considered inappropriate (such as dominance behavior in females). The prescribed sex roles for women typically include a primary focus on marriage and family, a reliance on a male provider, a stress on beauty, and a lack of direct expression of aggression and power-striving (Schaffer, 1980). For males the prescribed sex roles emphasize physical strength, achievement, emotional control and alienation from feelings, and providing for and protecting women and children.

Sex-role identification involves acquisition of an identification with sex roles. Spence (1985), for example, described sex-role identification as the process by which children learn society's role standards and related expectations and acquire the characteristics, attitudes, values, and behaviors that society considers appropriate to their gender, so that they can function effectively in the adult roles assigned to women and men.

It is important to note that conventional thinking often causes practitioners and lay people alike to confuse these role-related phenomena with personality traits that refer to general response dispositions (Gilbert, 1985b). The various masculinity and femininity scales available, for example, despite their names, are measures of specific personality traits—*not* sex-role attitudes or behaviors or sex-role identity. The specific traits they reliably assess are expressive (warm) and instrumental (assertive) personality characteristics. Thus the knowledge that a person is warm and expressive does not predict whether that person is a mother, able to cook, or a supporter of the Equal Rights Amendment. Finally, sex-role stereotypes refer to consensual beliefs and assumptions about the behaviors, characteristics, and personality traits of women and men.

One reason for presenting these definitions is to provide a common vocabulary for the remainder of this chapter. A second reason is to recognize the conceptual clarity provided by recent theory and research that aids greatly in our understanding of the different gender-related phenomena (Spence, 1984; Spence, Deaux, & Helmreich, in press). In the past, psychologists assumed that by knowing a person's biological sex they could accurately predict his or her personality characteristics, life roles, interests, and sexual preference. If they could not, something was amiss. That is, a one-to-one relationship among biological sex, personality characteristics, sex roles, and sexual preference was implicit (for example, this person is female, therefore she is warm and nurturing, dedicates her life to men and children, and desires sexual relationships with men). Although we know this is not the case—for example, neither women nor men are necessarily nurturing, power-seeking, or dominant—conventional thinking is difficult to change; as will be seen throughout this chapter, forcing clients into Procrustean beds may still occur more often than we would like.

SEX BIAS AND SEX-ROLE STEREOTYPING IN PSYCHOTHERAPY: AN OVERVIEW

Albee (1981) defines sexism as a social condition grounded in false beliefs that in turn are rooted in emotional and personal needs. In 1974 The Board of Professional Affairs of the American Psychological Association (APA) established a task force to examine sexism in psychotherapy. The Task Force (American Psychological Association, 1975) identified two underlying problems central to sexism in psychotherapy: values in psychotherapy and therapists' knowledge of psychological processes in women. Four general areas of bias were also identified: fostering traditional sex roles; bias in expectations and devaluation of women; sexist use of psychoanalytic concepts; and responding to women as sex objects, including seduction of female clients. The Task Force recommended that specific educational efforts be undertaken with both graduate students and practicing professionals, that theories be examined for sexism, and that sanctions against sexist practice be enforced. A few years later the Task Force published a set of guidelines for therapy with women (American Psychological Association, 1978) in which it was again stressed that therapists should be knowledgeable about current research on sex roles and sex-related phenomena, that therapy should not be constricted by sexism or sex-role stereotypes, and that therapists should recognize the situational and societal conditions that cause psychological difficulties for women.

Since that time, numerous articles and books on therapy with women have further clarified the separate needs and unique struggles of women who are clients (for example, Hare-Mustin, 1983a; Harmon, Birk, Fitzgerald, & Tanney, 1978; Rawlings & Carter, 1977; Sobel & Russo, 1981; Worrell, 1981), including a state-of-the-art assessment of research on women and psychotherapy sponsored by a contract from the National Institute of Mental Health to the American Psychological Association (Brodsky & Hare-Mustin, 1980). Division 17 (Counseling Psychology) of APA published a set of "Principles Concerning the Counseling and Psychotherapy of Women" (1979), which were subsequently endorsed by other divisions concerned with psychotherapeutic treatment.

This work has had a modest impact on the practice of psychotherapy and somewhat less influence on educational practices (Brodsky, 1982; Hare-Mustin, 1983b). Of the 1975 APA Task force recommendations, the one concerning sanctions against sexist practices has been implemented to the greatest extent. Sexual intimacies with clients and other forms of sexist practice are specifically described as unethical conduct in the principles of psychologists. As we shall see later, however, sexual contact with clients remains a problem for many psychologists, particularly male therapists who treat female clients. The Task Force recommendations related to educational reform have not fared as well; there is resistance to the fundamental changes implicit in the concept and practice of gender-fair psychotherapy.

THE CASE FOR GENDER

Research has moved beyond the very critical demonstrations of discrimination against women to sophisticated analyses of gender belief systems and information coding and retrieval (Wallston, 1985). Gender is a principle of social organization—not just a property of individuals (Sherif, 1982). There is a gendered basis to social organization and institutions, which in turn shapes women's and men's lives. For example, gender beliefs and stereotypes and their concomitant behavioral expectations create self-fulfilling prophecies in interactions such that individuals modify their behavior in response to certain situational cues (Spence et al., in press). A study reported by Klein and Willerman (1979) provides a clear illustration of behavioral modification in response to cues associated with gender: Women instructed to be as dominant as possible showed no differences in their behavior toward a male or female partner. However, when specific "dominance" instructions were absent, women's behavior differed: Lower displays of dominance occurred toward a male partner than a female. Thus, although individuals may differ in their tendency to stereotype or define themselves in traditional gender-specific ways (for example, Deaux & Lewis, 1984), sex and gender persist as pervasive organizers in our culture.

Many of the problems women and men face today are sociocultural in origin and result from the traditional imbalance of power between the sexes and the rigid roles and institutional sanctions and practices that maintain this imbalance. No one doubts that many feminist battles have been fought and won over the past two decades. With increasing frequency, men and women are dealing with one another on equal, enlightened terms. However, open a magazine, enter a theatre, or attend a graduate seminar where the author or instructor is male, and the reality of the gender gap becomes obvious. Ads continue to depict women, and men increasingly so, in sex-object terms. The language of the women's movement has been used pejoratively to sell everything from cigarettes to panties. Moreover, a woman "dresses for success," but "every man [dresses] for himself—while they are not indifferent to the opinions of wives and bosses, in the end, the vast majority of men dress according to their own tastes" (New York *Times*, March 24, 1985, p. 94). In some current hits on Broadway, according to Rich (1984), sexual equality is nonexistent:

> These men can take heart in the fact that they are part of a long chain of male American writers, whether playwrights or not, who have been flummoxed by the demands of creating adult male-female bonds. Old myths die hard. . . . Arthur Miller's best play contains a bevy of B-movie tarts and a wanly characterized wife who is more mother than spouse. . . . the last great Eugene O'Neill heroine was an almost mystical amalgam of mother, daughter, and virgin whore (p. 4).

Finally, only a select minority of APA-approved programs in counseling and clinical psychology include, seek out, or are receptive to training on sex-role issues in mental health. When workshops are presented, students are generally enthusiastic but the male faculty is largely absent (Brodsky, 1982). These phenomena, to varying degrees, reflect the continued reality of women and men in our society, and thus provide insights into the issues with which men and women in the psychotherapeutic situation—client and therapist—must also struggle.

SPECIFIC GENDER ISSUES

Dependency

Dependency conjures up views of women. The female way of being social involves bonds, affiliation, attachment, and commitment (Gilligan, 1982). Because girls are expected eventually to assume the woman's expressive role, the emphasis on instrumental behaviors and attitudes in their child-rearing is less than for boys (Block 1984; Hoffman, 1977). Instead, women are socialized to attract men as life partners and to direct their achievement through their affiliations with others. Being competent and personally ambitious is often not consistent with traditional views of what makes women desirable.

Two aspects of female dependency must be recognized. First is their oversocialization to "assume" dependent stances vis-a-vis men and the functionality of this underfunctioning in relationships with men. Such pervasive, deeply ingrained societal views are related to what Lerner (1983) calls the protective aspects of female dependency. According to Lerner, women traditionally have been encouraged to cultivate an "underfunctioning" that primarily serves to protect men. Women were expected to, and often did, subordinate themselves to men in both physical and intellectual contexts.

The notion that women must strengthen men by relinquishing or hiding their own strength is not new. We see poignant examples in fairy tales, movies, and real life. A vivid illustration of female underfunctioning occurs in the short story "Barcelona" by Alice Adams (1985).

The story describes Persis Fox, a fairly successful illustrator, who is beginning to be sought after by New York publishers but who sees herself as cowardly and fearful. Her husband Thad, in contrast, is a self-assured, self-directed, confident man who teaches at Harvard. The couple is on vacation in Barcelona and on their way to a remote restaurant when a thief suddenly snatches Persis's purse. Thad, who has been quite unattentive to Persis, suddenly springs into action and runs after the thief despite the darkness, danger, and unfamiliar terrain. Persis thinks, "He is not doing this [the chase] for her; it is something between men." The purse is recovered on the cobbles and the couple returns to the restaurant. The story continues:

Thad asks, "Aren't you going to check it? See what's still there?" ". . . Oh good, my passport's still here," she tells Thad.

"That's great." He is genuinely pleased with himself—and why should he not be, having behaved with such courage? Then he frowns, "He got all your money?"

"Well, no, actually there wasn't any money. I
keep it in my pocket. Always when I go to New
York, that's what I do."

Why does Thad look so confused just then? A
confusion of emotions is spread across his fair,
lined face. He is disappointed, somehow? Upset that
he ran after a thief who had stolen a bag containing
so little? Upset that Persis, who now goes down to
New York on publishing business by herself, has
tricks for self-preservation?

"And your passport." Stern, judicious Thad.

"Oh yes, of course," Persis babbles. "That
would have been terrible. We could have spent days
in offices."

Gratified, sipping at his wine, Thad says, "I
wonder why he didn't take it, actually." Persis does
not say, Because it's hidden inside my address
book—although quite possibly that was the case.
Instead, she says what is also surely true: "Because
you scared him. The last thing he expected was
someone running after him, and that *whistle*."

Thad smiles and his face settles into a familiar
expression: that of a generally secure, intelligent
man, a lucky person, for whom things happen more
or less as he would expect them to (From *Return
Trips*, copyright by Alfred A. Knopf, reprinted
by permission).

Thus Persis protects Thad from the knowledge that his motivations for protecting her against worldly dangers are
unfounded and that, in essence, she knows how to take care
of herself. Thad, on the other hand, assumes he needs to
protect her despite evidence that she can take care of herself. Thus they both collude to maintain a system that shelters
the male ego from the threat of female competence and that
continues an illusion of female dependency. Such collusion
also serves to maintain the status quo and to perpetuate traditional views about gender.

The second aspect of female dependency that must be
understood is that women's human emotional needs are often
not met in their relationships with men, although they are
socialized to believe that they will be. In contrast to the
female role, the male role has fostered an alienation from
emotions and expressivity, an alienation that is not conducive
to intimacy, communion, and attachment. Thus, should women
depend on men to meet their needs for affiliation and intimacy,
which women often do, their needs are likely to go unmet. This
situation is exacerbated by societal norms that lead women to
believe that the preferred and most desirable way to meet
their normal interdependency needs is through relationships

with the other sex (for different reasons, the same is true for men, as we will see later).

As Bernard (1976) points out, the attachment and bonding with other women that was a valued and accepted part of the social order in previous centuries became less available for twentieth-century women. The focus on the nuclear family and the shift from a rural to an urban economy, among other factors, tended to isolate women from each other. The impact of this "relational deficit," which inhibits women's ability to fulfill their normal dependency needs, is further intensified by limitations on female independence strivings in our society and by the fear many women have, perhaps realistically, of being less desired as women should they be capable of earning their way and thinking their own thoughts. They are typically socialized to believe that, unlike men, having a life-long career and a family is difficult, and having career aspirations jeopardizes the likelihood of having a family.

Thus the structure of marriage and society encourages unrealistic dependency needs in women while at the same time discouraging adaptive independency needs. Women, for example, often tolerate emotional and physical abuse or dissatisfying relationships with spouses or therapists because the internalized belief that they are dependent on men inhibits them from taking care of themselves or meeting their needs in other ways.

Power

To discuss dependency in men we need to focus on the concept of power. Because of society's need to keep women weak and men strong, the experiences and needs of women fall under the rubric of dependency and those of men under the rubric of power. A case in point is Pleck's (1981) description of the "psychological sources of men's needs for power over women" (p. 235). There are three—and each relates to dependency *but* is stated as a power that men attribute to women, which in turn causes men to oppress women.

The first power that men perceive women to have over them is what Pleck calls "masculine-validating power": that is, through sexual relations with women a man seeks validation of himself as a man. For men in our society, sexuality and gender are highly intercorrelated. Men are socialized to believe in penis power, and unfortunately the expression of this power requires a female partner or victim. Women who are virgins are often admired; men who are virgins are suspect. Homosexual men are viewed as wimps, fags, or weaklings, in part because they do not desire power through sexual intercourse with women.

In his description of the ten myths of masculinity, Zilbergeld (1978) illustrates the close association between sexual power (functioning) and a man's sense of self: A man always wants and is always ready to have sex (myth #4). All physical contact must lead to sex (myth #5). In sex, as elsewhere, it is performance that counts (myth #2). The man must take charge of and orchestrate sex (myth #3).

We see many examples of men's need for power over women, a power that, in effect, illuminates their dependency. To some degree it is present in violence against women—rape and battering, in particular. Men who are abusive of women often experience intense feelings of social and personal (masculine) inadequacy and feel especially dependent on women to make them feel better about themselves. Their extreme sense of dependency is often reflected in strong feelings of jealousy and possessiveness of their sexual partners (Donzetti, Cate, & Koval, 1983; Sonkin, Martin, & Walker, 1985; Telch & Lindquist, 1984). This same pattern is illustrated in noted literary works. In Tennessee Williams's play *A Streetcar Named Desire*, Blanche, who disapproves of her brother-in-law's crude behavior, is raped by him in order to destroy her power over him. Similarly, in Bizet's opera *Carmen*, Don Jose is devastated by Carmen's rejection of him as a lover and in a jealous rage murders her.

This aspect of male dependency is often shrouded in silence because men rarely discuss their sexuality or sexual functioning with other men. Instead, sexuality is used as a vehicle by which men gain status with other men—a status or position that would be endangered by honest self-disclosure.

A second power that men attribute to women involves what Pleck calls "expressive power" or the power to express emotions. Women often express men's feelings for them or have the power to bring or draw out their feelings. It is all right for men to be "soft" with women—they are safe havens for male emotion. Women, however, are also blamed for male expressivity, particularly if such expressivity is socially undesirable or violent. Thus men view women as bringing out both their positive and negative emotions and as causing them to do things that are beyond their control.

This situation relates to the third way in which men are dependent on women and are thus motivated to have power over them. Women have a role or part in men's power vis-a-vis other men: They are symbols of success in men's competition with each other and are a refuge for men. They also reduce the stress of competition between men by serving as an underclass (Pleck, 1981). In a patriarchal society, women represent the lowest status, a status to which men can fall only under the most exceptional circumstance. Still, today, among the most insulting things to call a man is an adjective associated with being female, particularly a female sexual organ.

The hidden nature of male dependency has been recognized by other writers. Baumrind (1980), for example, sees boys as being bribed by promises of power and domination and prematurely relinquishing aspects of their dependency strivings. Because boys are often separated prematurely from their home environment and asked to behave as "little men" before they comfortably can do so, they may depend more than they realize on unconditional acceptance and nurturance from a woman to sustain their pseudo independent stance. Girls, on the other hand, are bribed by promises of love and approval and prematurely relinquish aspects of their independency strivings. Thus, as Pogrebin (1983) points out, wives in patriarchal families conventionally give the care that husbands take: "Contrary to the popular belief that women have the greater dependency needs, men's [noneconomic] dependency needs are far more insatiable. . . . Sex specialization in caring atrophies men's capacity to give comfort" (p. 197).

Beauty and Attractiveness

Interestingly, both dependency and power are related to a third prevalent gender issue: concepts of beauty and its relation to self-esteem, personal functioning, and role behavior. Social psychologists have long known that "what is beautiful is good," especially for women. Traditional sex-role definitions specify different sources of power for women and men. Men derive status and power from wealth, ability, and possessions; women, who are dependent on the men they attract for their status, derive power from physical beauty. Through beauty, women gain access to a man's resources and to a man's heart. The importance of physical attractiveness for women is seen daily in advertisements and in the profits earned from cosmetics and other products guaranteed to beautify. One danger of this aspect of female sex-role socialization is becoming increasingly more apparent in the form of eating disorders.

Rodin, Silberstein, and Striegel-Moore's (1985) review of the literature indicates that women more than men spend a great deal of time worrying about their appearance and about being too fat. As they aptly note, the society that heralds women's diversifying professional accomplishments also presents fashion models chosen to match a template of abnormal thinness, along with new diets to attain it. The message given to women is that they must undertake new beauty treatments, new exercise programs, and new diets to hide physical flaws and conceal aging. On the basis of their review, Rodin et al. propose that women's concerns about weight and thinness are so normative that, in addition to the large number of women already diagnosed as anorexic and bulimic, a large majority are at risk for developing an eating disorder.

Polivy and Herman (1985) concur and predict that the sociocultural pressures to diet that made anorexia nervosa the disorder of the 1970s is making bulimia the disorder of the 1980s. Self-reports of college women indicate that 13 to

67 percent of them engage in binge eating. Moreover, both these groups of researchers view dieting and societal views of women as the disorder psychologists should be attempting to cure; that is, dieting is a causal factor and may cause binging by promoting the adoption of a cognitively regulated, rather than a metabolically regulated, eating style.

The psychological consequences of women's preoccupation with weight and beauty are well documented (Garner & Garfinkel, 1985; Rodin et al., 1985; Wooley, 1985; Wooley & Wooley, 1980). They include decreased self-esteem for failure to meet societal standards of beauty, distorted body image, feelings of helplessness and frustration in response to unsuccessful efforts to attain societal ideals of attractiveness, and depression related to a chronic dissatisfaction with one's body and physical appearance. Also crucial here is the victimization of women by consumerism. Stereotypic female (and male) ideals sell products and profit the status quo. Sexism, the present economic structure, and the oppression of women and men are inextricably related.

Men's and women's difficulties with dependency, power, and standards of beauty are recognized in the contemporary women's and men's movements. The men's movement has emphasized the importance of men's recognizing their own dependency and positively valuing it as an integral part of male development. Moreover, men are being helped to learn how to express and experience their emotions in intimate relationships and to validate themselves and other men instead of needing women to do this. Similarly, the women's consciousness-raising groups of the 1960s and 1970s assisted women in recognizing how they had internalized societal views of female attributes and roles and, as a result, had to some degree come to devalue themselves and other women in their quest for the "right" and "superior" male. These groups, and the women's movement in general, emphasize the importance of women nurturing and sustaining themselves and each other and of developing a sense of self separate from their affiliative relationships with men.

Society changes slowly, however, and the well-established patterns and myths remain in operation to a greater degree than we often care to admit. The increasing incidence of reported sexual intimacies between male therapists and female patients, despite the clearly unethical nature of such sexual relations, is one obvious reminder of how slow the change is.

APPLICATION TO THE PSYCHOTHERAPEUTIC SITUATION

Sexual Contact with Clients—A Problem Area

Among psychologists approximately 1 in 10 men and 1 in 100 women have had self-reported erotic contact with clients, nearly all of whom were female (Holroyd & Brodsky, 1977).[1]

The number of violations of principle 6A (which says that
sexual intimacies with clients are unethical) reported to the
Ethics Committee of APA has increased each year since 1979
when sexual intimacies with clients were specifically defined
as unethical (American Psychological Association, 1979). Many
times the psychologists involved feel very remorseful and
regretful (Hall & Hare-Mustin, 1983; Hare-Mustin & Hall, 1981)
and view such behavior as harmful to the client and to the
therapeutic relationship (Bouhoutsos, Holroyd, Lerman, Forer,
& Greenberg, 1983; Edelwich & Brodsky, 1982; Holroyd &
Brodsky, 1977).

Research findings corroborate the negative psychological
impact on clients of sexual intimacies in the therapeutic setting. Feldman-Summers and Jones (1984), for example, report
that female clients who had had sexual contact with therapists
revealed greater mistrust of and anger toward men and therapists, and a greater number of psychological and psychosomatic symptoms following the termination of therapy than did
women who had not experienced sexual contact with their
therapists. Brodsky (1984) studied the psychological functioning of clients who had had sexual contact with their therapists
by assessing them at several intervals following termination of
therapy; evidence of harmful effects on personal functioning
were evident as long as three years (the length of the study)
after termination of the sexual relationship.

In the past such unethical behavior caused little concern.
It was consistent with traditional views of women and the pre-
rogatives of men—a manifestation of a broader male and female
role structure in which men were omniscient and women were
naive. When such behavior began to be questioned, the situation was often studied from the viewpoint of the client's
motivations. What made her do it? Thus, rather than looking
at therapists' attitudes and behaviors, the profession adopted
the self-serving view that men are vulnerable to women's
sexual power over them, and therapists are no exception.
Today we realize that we can no longer blame the female victim; regardless of the client's motives, such behavior is
unethical and as such requires us to go beyond blaming the
client for what happens under the guise of therapy.

Several aspects of gender issues may help to explain why
sexual contact between male therapists and female clients
occurs. One involves the strong connection between emotional
closeness and female dependency, on the one hand, and sexual
expression and male dominance, on the other. Women who come
to therapy are often experiencing a "relational deficit" and
are seeking intimacy with a man. The man who is trained as
the therapist, however, has been socialized to view women as
having the power to bring out men's feelings (and not vice
versa) as well as to validate their masculinity through sexual
relations. They may also share the universal male fear of
women's fantasied power and rage that, if unleashed, would

cause massive destructiveness (Carmen & Driver, 1982). Thus when the client feels distressed and emotionally intense, the male therapist may feel afraid of her intensity and yet feel compelled to "help" her because of her assumed dependency on him as a man. The feeling of needing to help her, and yet experiencing the client as both overwhelming and weak, can leave the therapist feeling paralyzed and impotent. One deeply ingrained way of reestablishing potency with women is through sexual expression. Hence the therapist responds to the client's needs for intimacy with his needs for male validation and dominance.

A second possibility is that male therapists lack sufficient awareness and understanding of their own dependency needs, particularly their need to be validated by women, and the close association between their sexual functioning and their sense of self. According to the data available, 75 percent of male therapists who self-reported sexual intimacies with one client repeated sexual contact with other clients (Holroyd & Brodsky, 1977). Thus the therapist's needs were such that despite ethical violations and harm to the client, they had to be met. Similarly, Bouhoutsos et al. (1983) report that in their sample of psychologists who reported incidents of clients' sexual intimacies with previous therapists, sexual intimacies (usually intercourse) began within the first few sessions for 30 percent of the clients, after three months for 25 percent, after six months for 22 percent, and after a year for 19 percent. (Both therapy and the sexual relationship ended simultaneously for 55 percent of the cases; termination of therapy was usually initiated by the clients.) These results, which indicate that sexual intimacies with clients are more apt to occur in the early stages of therapy than in later stages, also support the view that some male therapists are unable to establish effective working alliances with female clients because of their unresolved personal needs vis-a-vis women.

A third, and related, possibility is that many men have learned the language of intimacy, but not the accompanying emotional feelings and behavior (Rubin, 1983), and thus are uncomfortable about being emotionally close to and intimate with women in a nonsexual way. Moreover, men have little experience relating to women in a truly egalitarian manner. In order to avoid this inability to be genuinely intimate with another human being, and because he is socialized to feel superior to women, the therapist keeps the relationship sexually charged and, in essence, patronizes the client by not directly encountering who she is. These kinds of strategies work well in social situations, but are harmful and unproductive in the therapeutic situation.

In his book *Male Sexuality*, Zilbergeld (1978) lists as the ninth myth that sex should be natural and spontaneous. Perhaps the first myth of eroticism in the psychotherapeutic setting, as with sexual intercourse, is that the male therapist should naturally know what to do. The second myth is that, as long as it is unethical, it will not happen. And the third is that educated consumers will keep the profession honest. Such myths perpetuate the problem.

Conformity to Stereotypic Views of Gender

A woman needs to be loved; she also needs space to grow independently. These dual needs, highlighted in the women's liberation movement, are at the center of the conflict in many relationships, including those between clients and therapists. Some feminist therapists question whether therapy in which a woman works with a male therapist can truly benefit the client because of the potential reenactment of traditional male-female relationship patterns extant in the culture at large (Gilbert, 1980; Lerner, 1982). The therapeutic relationship may foster dependency without facilitating autonomous solutions (Lerner, 1982). Male therapists, more than female, may have difficulty recognizing and confronting neurotic or defensive behavior on the part of a female client, which is related to unquestioned internalized definitions of femaleness or femininity or conformity to socially prescribed views of women. Carmen and Driver (1982), for example, reported that males avoided acknowledging women's anger and attended to their helplessness. Schover (1981) found that female therapists were more comfortable than males with clients' sexual material and more accurate in reporting the content of this material.

Other traditional male-female dynamics can easily be played out in the therapeutic situation if therapists do not recognize these tendencies in themselves and if they do not struggle with the client to prevent them from becoming established. As was mentioned earlier, contemporary women are overly socialized to depend on men to meet their emotional needs and often enter therapy for help in this area. Therapists, also trapped to some degree in their own socialization, may lack the vision or objectivity needed to assist women in moving beyond their own societally imposed limits. Hence they too focus on the women's dependency and covertly and unwittingly encourage compliant behaviors rather than independent, self-defining behaviors. The female client's ability to underfunction with men serves to enhance the male therapist's ego and to collude with him in continuing her dependency in the therapeutic relationship. (Further fostering female dependency is unlikely to be a desired or positive therapeutic goal for women.) Separating oneself from one's own socialization is difficult in the best of circumstances and is made even more difficult when individuals enter a relationship in which one person (the therapist) is the expert who helps the other (the client).

There is also evidence that male therapists may have greater difficulty than female therapists in understanding career-oriented or professional women (Myers, 1982). Marriage and motherhood, even love and sex, more often than not can erode a woman's ambitions, energy, and sense of self-definition and direction. Many women still fear that a separate self will be submerged in the roles of wife and mother—as has been the case for many women in our society, more so in earlier times than now. We are headed toward a time when such integration is possible, and therapists can be helpful only if they understand contemporary women's lives. Parallel issues emerge for men who wish to broaden their self-concept beyond the traditional good provider role to include active parenting; intimate, loving relationships; and communal concerns.

Men's attempts to fit themselves to definitions of masculinity and to mask their dependency and emotionality are also implicitly communicated to therapists and may go unrecognized by both the therapist and the client. For males, a crucial area that must be recognized both by clients and therapists is the strong interconnection between sexuality and gender. Too often men define their sense of self in terms of their sexual functioning and their ability to make it with women. Male clients need to be encouraged to discuss their sexuality and helped to understand how it might be related to their self-esteem, concepts of intimacy, and manliness. Recognizing and owning their own dependency needs in general and vis-a-vis real and imagined relationships with women are crucial to effective therapeutic treatment with men.

Generally speaking, both male and female clients need help from the therapist in differentiating what they have been taught and have accepted as socially desirable and appropriate from what actually might be desirable and appropriate for them. Thus therapists should encourage clients to evaluate the influence of social roles and norms on their personal experiences and to see the relationship between sociological and psychological factors. Also, through therapy, the client will be in a better position to understand the role of society in shaping all individuals and, in particular, its role in shaping the behavior of women and men.

In addition, therapists themselves must constantly explore their own values and attitudes about women and men and confront tendencies within themselves to limit their clients with gendered and sexist views. They need to be aware of the theories that support their therapeutic interventions and of how the development of women and men are described. They need to be aware of their use of language. For example, do they describe female patients but not males as seductive; do they view female patients who disagree as being difficult but such male patients as challenging. Do they tend to touch female patients more than males. Are they uncomfortable in

working with lesbian and gay male clients because of homophobia or lack of knowledge (Graham, Rawlings, Halpern, &
Hermes, 1984). Female therapists who work with men must
learn to recognize and effectively respond to demands for
unconditional nurturance and to attempts to dominate the therapeutic relationship. Female therapists must be particularly
mindful of their tendencies to protect the male ego and to
offer unconditional support and nurturance in order to avoid
direct competition and issues of control and power. Many
male clients will unconsciously attempt to place a female therapist in her traditional role be it through flirtatiousness,
excessive dependency, or questioning of her professional
skills. As mentioned earlier, male therapists who work with
female clients may find themselves in therapeutic relationships
that unwittingly reinforce dependent, nonthreatening behaviors.

Supervision

The supervisee-supervisor relationship must also be looked
at with regard to sexism and gender issues. Robinson and
Reid (1985) report that clinical psychology students experienced more sexual seduction (flirting and excessive attention)
and sexual contact during their training than did psychology
students in other areas of graduate study. Most experiences
of sexual seduction and contact involved professors in graduate programs and, to a somewhat lesser extent, supervisors
and administrators. Nearly all of the respondents in the study
indicated that these relationships were detrimental to one or
both parties.

The APA code of ethics specifically states that psychologists should not exploit their professional relationship with
supervisees or students, sexually or otherwise. They are to
be mindful of relationships in which the power differential
may result in compliance on the part of students, supervisees,
and clients. Clearly, sexual attraction can influence the nature
of student-professor and supervisor-supervisee relationships
and inhibit establishment of mentoring and role modeling relationships. Interestingly, male students rarely have to spend
time and energy counteracting potential sexual overtures from
female teachers and supervisors. Yet such behavior on the
part of male teachers and supervisors is often considered *as
part of the social order* rather than a factor that may compli-
cate, even hinder, women's educational and professional
development.

Teaching supervisors how to deal with inappropriate sexual
desires and behaviors should be part of an educational process.
Agencies and institutions should incorporate appropriate pro-
grams in their on-going staff development (see Vasquez and
Grenard-Moore [1985] for an example of a training model).
Furthermore, both trainees and staff should be informed of

the unprofessional nature of such relationships and steps should be taken to enforce compliance with this stance.

As Scher (1981) aptly notes, psychologists who supervise (most of whom are male) rarely question their adequacy to do so—regardless of their knowledge of the psychology of women and of men's and women's changing self-concepts and roles. Supervisors often demand compliance from female supervisees and risk-taking from male supervisees. Often greater attention is given to the intellectual concerns of male supervisees and to the emotional difficulties of female supervisees. Challenges from female supervisees may not be viewed positively and may be prejudicial to women when evaluations and recommendations are made. Male supervisees who hold feminist belief systems or who do not identify with traditional male values may be viewed with distrust.

Clearly these possible difficulties, which parallel societal expectations with regard to sex and gender, often occur unwittingly and need to be brought out in the open and confronted both by supervisees and other members of the staff and faculty. An atmosphere in which gender issues are fair game for discussion and understanding will bring immeasurable growth to the individuals involved in that work or educational environment.

EDUCATION OF THE PROFESSION

Education with regard to sex and gender effects in psychotherapy needs to occur at many levels and in many forms. Several factors need attention for change to occur (Gilbert, 1985a; Hare-Mustin, 1983b). *First*, therapists need to evaluate their own attitudes, values, and behaviors with regard to women and men and become educated about the psychology of women, men's and women's changing roles, and the gendered nature of our society. Such education does not come about simply by being married to a woman or treating female patients. A rich body of literature has accumulated in the past 20 years, and these theories and findings need to be incorporated into one's knowledge as a psychologist. In fact, lack of information about women (Sherman, Koufacos, & Kenworthy, 1978) and holding traditional views of women and men (for example, Kabacoff, Marwit, & Orlofsky, 1985) are associated with greater sex-role stereotyping in the treatment provided to clients.

Second, training needs to be broadened so that psychologists recognize and understand topics such as those discussed in this chapter. The restrictive effects of gender socialization on the lives of individual women and men must be understood by therapists if they are to work successfully with individuals who are suffering as a consequence of sexism and want help dealing with their emotional reactions to the internalized restrictiveness of their own sex-role socialization and the injustices of their day-to-day patriarchal environment. The pervasiveness of sexism and how it is maintained by our social institutions must be recognized. The dynamics of power and how this operates at both individual and societal levels to perpetuate a male-dominant structure must be reckoned with.

Third, the training of therapists should seek to inculcate a set of beliefs, attitudes, and values that are conducive to a high level of personal and professional responsibility in the treatment of women and men. Such training, of course, requires programs to hire professionals who are qualified to teach in these areas. Other avenues are also possible. Projects such as the Western States Project on Women in the Curriculum offer a service in which matching funds are provided to college presidents and deans who bring consultants to their campuses to help faculty integrate materials on women into the general curriculum. Relevant continuing education programs are offered by the American Psychological Association and other accredited providers of continuing education. The APA also has available bibliographies and other materials that can help instructors incorporate new and existing knowledge about gender and the psychology of women into their course content and teaching practices. A handbook on women and psychotherapy is available from the Federation of Professional Women (1982). Excellent films such as *Killing Us Softly: Advertising's Images of Women* and *Pink Triangles* (concerns homophobia) are available from Cambridge Documentary Films as is a videotape, *Sex Fair Psychotherapy*, developed by Brodsky (1979) and distributed by the University of Alabama. Resources abound.

Finally, it is important to recognize the apparent collusion between current educational practices and the social system. What we do as educators and practitioners reflects the social practices of the culture and society in which we live. Thus in therapy, as in the real world, we nourish ourselves on female dependency and go to great lengths to protect men from their strong dependency needs. Moreover, our training programs engage in this same collusion. Rarely is male sexuality discussed or studied. Rarely are male students given the opportunity to understand their own sexuality and how it relates to their sense of self and developing ego. Little, if any, attention is given to the social construction of gender and how it relates to therapist-client dynamics and the process and goals of therapy.

Clearly, psychologists must first deal with their own sexism and gender socialization—as individuals and as educators. They and the students they educate will then be in the position to more effectively do what therapists typically do—secondary and tertiary prevention and treatment—as well as what Hare-Mustin (1983b) identifies as a *third* crucial factor—interventions that are geared toward systemic change and the prevention or amelioration of social conditions that foster sexism and reinforce traditional social learning processes.

Change at this primary prevention level is in many ways political. As Albee (1981) notes, psychologists need to support each other in making sexism and gender issues visible, in making recent psychological knowledge available to decision-makers, and in advocating changes in social institutions and laws. Psychologists can influence policymakers to recognize that the root of many social and individual problems resides in the system and not in the individual who is the identified patient.

Specific areas in which psychologists can influence public policy are discussed in a recent issue of the *American Psychologist* (Russo & Denmark, 1984), a publication of the American Psychological Association. Russo and Denmark note that the ability of psychologists to identify and critique sex-biased practices can help eliminate the disparity between current policy and the realities of women's and men's lives. Women's issues are often ignored or made light of by policymakers and such practices need to be monitored and reported. Public policy regarding domestic violence and pay equity, for example, has significantly changed in the past decade, and psychologists have played an active role in this transformation (Huston, 1984; Walker, 1984). Testimony by expert witnesses has rebutted myths that prevented battered women from receiving fair treatment by the law. The dramatic changes in women's work and family roles have profound implications for employment and family policy. Psychologists are well aware of the need for quality, affordable childcare and for changes in the structure of work that would allow both men and women to responsibly parent their children.

CONCLUSION

This chapter has described aspects of male and female socialization that need to be understood to provide effective therapeutic treatment to clients. Society has insisted on viewing men and women as "opposite sexes" and on attributing characteristics to one sex and not the other. Women are stereotypically viewed as intuitive, emotional, and dependent, and men as intelligent, independent, and rational, although for the most part, few meaningful and consistent differences are found in women's and men's cognitive skills and social behavior. Moreover, such differences, when they do occur, are often dependent on contextual and structural factors such as those described in this chapter (for example, attitudes about men's and women's abilities and roles, and the behavior of the therapist). Understanding the gendered basis of social organization and institutions, which in turn shapes women's and men's lives, is essential to effective therapeutic treatment.

As a profession we are deeply concerned about negative effects in psychotherapeutic treatment that are related to gender, such as the continuing problem of sexual relations between therapists and clients. Yet as educators we appear reluctant to look at the broader and deeper psychosociological issues, and the social structure in which they are embedded, that give rise to unacceptable and harmful behavior on the part of therapists. Specific courses and material should be made available in graduate programs and continuing education offerings so that practitioners have sufficient self-awareness and knowledge to live by the code of ethics of their profession. Although we can influence society only in relatively small, incremental ways, we surely can change our behavior so as to make the therapeutic environment more conducive to positive emotional functioning and less confined by the happenstance of gender.

NOTE

1. Not all erotic contact occurs between male therapists and female clients. Of the licensed psychologists surveyed by Holroyd and Brodsky (1977), 5.6 percent of the males and 0.6 percent of the females reported having had sexual intercourse with clients. The Bouhoutsos et al. (1983) survey of licensed California psychologists who were asked to report on their clients' sexual intimacies with previous therapists indicated that the preponderance of such incidents occurred with male therapists and female clients (93 percent of those reported, as compared to 1.7 percent for female therapists and female clients, .03 percent for male therapists and male clients, and .02 percent for female therapists and male clients). The numbers are small for these other gender pairings, but the problem is serious and requires our attention. Many of the comments and recommendations made in this chapter are directly applicable to these situations, particularly those in the earlier section on power and the section on supervision.

REFERENCES

Adams, A. (1985). "Barcelona," in *Return Trips*. New York: Alfred A. Knopf.

Albee, G. W. (1981). The prevention of sexism. *Professional Psychology, 12,* 20-28.

American Psychological Association. (1975). Report of the task force on sex bias and sex-role stereotyping in psychotherapeutic practice. *American Psychologist, 30,* 1169-1175.

American Psychological Association, Task Force on Sex Bias and Sex Role Stereotyping in Psychotherapeutic Practice. (1978). Guildelines for therapy with women. *American Psychologist, 33,* 1122-1123.

American Psychological Association. (1979). *Ethical standards of psychologists.* Washington, D.C.

Angrist, S. A. (1969). The study of sex roles. *Journal of Social Issues, 15,* 215-232.

Baumrind, D. (1980). New directions in socialization research. *American Psychologist, 35,* 639-652.

Bernard, J. (1976). Homosociality and female depression. *Journal of Social Issues, 32,* 213-238.

Block, J. H. (1984). *Sex role identity and ego development.* San Francisco: Jossey-Bass.

Bouhoutsos, J., Holroyd, J., Lerman, H., Forer, B. R., & Greenberg, M. (1983). Sexual intimacy between psychotherapists and patients. *Professional Psychology: Research and Practice, 14,* 185-196.

Brodsky, A. (1979). *Sex fair psychotherapy* (Videotape). Available from the University of Alabama.

——. (1982). *Sex bias in psychotherapy: An update.* Paper presented at the meeting of the American Psychological Association, August, Washington, D.C.

——. (1984). *Issues in the litigation of a sexually abusive therapist: The expert witness' perspective.* Paper presented at the meeting of the American Psychological Association, August, Toronto.

Brodsky, A. M., & Hare-Mustin, R. T. (1980). *Women and psychotherapy: An assessment of research and practice.* New York: Guilford.

Carmen, E. H., & Driver, F. (1982). Teaching women's studies: Values in conflict. *Psychology of Women Quarterly, 7,* 81-95.

Deaux, K. (1985). Sex and gender. In L. Porter & M. Rosenzweig (Eds.), *Annual review of psychology 1985* (Vol. 36, pp. 49-81). Palo Alto, Calif.: Annual Reviews.

Deaux, K., & Lewis, L. L. (1984). Structure of gender stereotypes: Interrelationships among components and gender label. *Journal of Personality and Social Psychology, 46,* 991-1004.

Donzetti, J. J., Jr., Cate, R. M., & Koval, J. E. (1983). Violence between couples: Profiling the male abuser. *The Personnel and Guidance Journal, 62,* 222-224.

Eagly, A. H., & Steffen, V. J. (1984). *The social structural basis of beliefs about gender.* Paper presented at the meeting of the American Psychological Association, August, Anaheim, Calif.

Edelwich, J., & Brodsky, A. (1982). *Sexual dilemmas for the helping professional.* New York: Brunner/Mazel.

Federation of Professional Women. (1982). *Women and psychotherapy: A consumer handbook.* (Available from FOPW, 1825 Connecticut Ave., NW, Suite 403, Washington, D.C. 20009.)

Feldman-Summers, S., & Jones, G. (1984). Psychological impacts of sexual contact between therapists or other health care practitioners and their clients. *Journal of Consulting and Clinical Psychology, 52,* 1054-1061.

Garner, D. M., & Garfinkel, P. E. (1985). *Handbook of psychotherapy for anorexia nervosa and bulimia.* New York: Guilford.

Gilbert, L. A. (1980). Feminist therapy. In A. M. Brodsky & R. T. Hare-Mustin (Eds.), *Women and psychotherapy: An assessment of research and practice* (pp. 245-265). New York: Guilford.

——. (1985a). *Gender and sexuality issues in perspective: The case of female and male emotional dependency and its implications for the therapist-client relationship.* Paper presented at the meeting of the American Psychological Association, August, Los Angeles.

——. (1985b). Measures of psychological masculinity and femininity. *Journal of Counseling Psychology, 32,* 163-166.

Gilligan, C. (1982). *In a different voice: Psychological theory and women's development.* Cambridge, Mass.: Harvard University Press.

Graham, D. L. R., Rawlings, E. I., Halpern, H. S., & Hermes, J. (1984). Therapists' needs for training in counseling lesbians and gay men. *Professional Psychology, 15,* 482-496.

Hall, J., & Hare-Mustin, R. (1983). Sanctions and the diversity of ethical complaints against psychologists. *American Psychologist, 38,* 714-729.

Hansen, R. D., & O'Leary, V. E. (1985). Sex-determined attributes. In V. E. O'Leary, R. K. Unger, & B. S. Wallston (Eds.), *Women, gender, and social psychology* (pp. 67-100). Hillsdale, N.J.: Lawrence Erlbaum.

Hare-Mustin, R. T. (1983a). An appraisal of the relationship between women and psychotherapy: 80 years after the case of Dora. *American Psychologist, 38,* 593-601.

——. (1983b). *Educating for counseling and psychotherapy with women*. Paper presented at the meeting of the American Psychological Association, August, Anaheim, Calif.

Hare-Mustin, R. T., & Hall, J. E. (1981). Procedures for responding to ethics complaints against psychologists. *American Psychologist, 36*, 1494-1505.

Harmon, L. W., Birk, J. M., Fitzgerald, L. E., & Tanney, M. F. (Eds.). (1978). *Counseling women*. Monterey, Calif.: Brooks/Cole.

Hoffman, L. W. (1977). Changes in family roles, socialization, and sex differences. *American Psychologist, 32*, 644-657.

Holroyd, J. C., & Brodsky, A. M. (1977). Psychologists' attitudes and practices regarding erotic and nonerotic physical contact with patients. *American Psychologist, 32*, 843-849.

Huston, K. (1984). Ethical issues in treating battered women. *Professional Psychology: Research and Practice, 15*, 822-832.

Kabacoff, R. I., Marwit, S. J., & Orlofsky, J. L. (1985). Correlates of sex role stereotyping among mental health professionals. *Professional Psychology: Research and Practice, 16*, 98-105.

Kanter, M. (1977). *Men and women of the corporation*. New York: Basic Books.

Klein, H. M., & Willerman, L. (1979). Psychological masculinity and femininity and typical and maximal dominance expression in women. *Journal of Personality and Social Psychology, 37*, 2059-2070.

Lerner, H. E. (1982). Special issues for women in psychotherapy. In M. T. Notman & C. C. Nadelson (Eds.), *The woman patient: Vol. 3. Aggression, adaptations, and psychotherapy* (pp. 273-286). New York: Plenum Press.

Lerner, H. E. (1983). Female dependency in context: Some theoretical and technical considerations. *American Journal of Orthopsychiatry, 53*, 697-705.

Lott, B. (1985). The potential enrichment of social/personality psychology through feminist research and vice versa. *American Psychologist, 40*, 155-164.

Myers, M. F. (1982). The professional woman as patient: A review and an appeal. *Canadian Journal of Psychiatry, 27*, 236-240.

Pleck, J. H. (1981). Men's power with women, other men, and society: A men's movement analysis. In R. A. Lewis (Ed.), *Men in difficult times: Masculinity today and tomorrow* (pp. 234-245). Englewood Cliffs, N.J.: Prentice-Hall.

Pogrebin, L. C. (1983). *Family politics: Love and power on an intimate frontier.* New York: McGraw-Hill.

Polivy, J., & Herman, C. P. (1985). Dieting and binging: A causal analysis. *American Psychologist, 40,* 193-201.

Principles concerning the counseling and therapy of women. (1979). *The Counseling Psychologist, 8,* 21.

Rawlings, E. I., & Carter, D. K. (1977). *Psychotherapy for women.* Springfield, Ill.: C. C. Thomas.

Rich, F. (1984). Theater's gender gap is a chasm. New York *Times,* September 30, pp. 1; 4.

Robinson, W. L., & Reid, P. T. (1985). Sexual intimacies in psychology revisited. *Professional Psychology: Research and Practice, 16,* 512-520.

Rodin, J., Silberstein, L., & Striegel-Moore, R. (1985). Women and weight: A normative discontent. In T. B. Sonderegger (Ed.), *Nebraska symposium on motivation* (pp. 267-307). Lincoln: University of Nebraska Press.

Rubin, L. (1983). *Intimate strangers.* New York: Harper & Row.

Russo, N. F., & Denmark, F. L. (1984). Women, psychology, and public policy: Selected issues. *American Psychologist, 39,* 1161-1165.

Schaffer, K. (1980). *Sex-role issues in mental health.* Reading, Mass.: Addison Wesley.

Scher, M. (1981). Gender issues in psychiatric supervision. *Comprehensive Psychiatry, 22,* 179-183.

Schover, L. R. (1981). Male and female therapists' responses to male and female client sexual material: An analogue study. *Archives of Sexual Behavior, 10,* 477-491.

Sherif, C. W. (1982). Needed concepts in the study of gender identity. *Psychology of Women Quarterly, 6,* 375-398.

Sherman, J. A., Koufacos, C., & Kenworthy, J. A. (1978). Therapists: Their attitudes and information about women. *Psychology of Women Quarterly, 2,* 299-313.

Sobel, S. B., & Russo, N. F. (Eds.). (1981). Sex roles, equality, and mental health (special issue). *Professional Psychology, 12*(1).

Sonkin, D. J., Martin, D., & Walker, L. E. A. (1985). *The male batterer: A treatment approach.* New York: Springer.

Spence, J. T. (1984). Masculinity, femininity, and gender-related traits: A conceptual analysis and critique of current research. In B. A. Maker (Ed.), *Progress in experimental personality research* (Vol. 13, pp. 2-97). New York: Academic Press.

——. (1985). Gender identity and its implications for concepts of masculinity and femininity. In T. B. Sonderegger (Ed.), *Nebraska symposium on motivation: Psychology and gender* (Vol. 32). Lincoln: University of Nebraska Press.

Spence, J. T., Deaux, K., & Helmreich, R. L. (in press). Sex roles in contemporary American society. In G. Lindzey & E. Aronson (Eds.), *Handbook of social psychology* (3rd ed.). Hillsdale, N.J.: Laurence Erlbaum.

Telch, C. F., & Lindquist, C. U. (1984). Violent versus nonviolent couples: A comparison of patterns. *Psychotherapy, 21,* 242-248.

Vasquez, M. J. T., & Grenard-Moore, S. J. (1985). *Exploring gender issues at a university counseling center: A training model.* Paper presented at the meeting of the American Psychological Association, August, Los Angeles.

Walker, L. E. A. (1984). Battered women, psychology, and public policy. *American Psychologist, 39,* 1178-1182.

Wallston, B. S. (1985). Social psychology of women and gender. *Journal of Applied Social Psychology* (Special Anniversary Issue), July.

Webster. (1959). *New collegiate dictionary.* Springfield, Mass.: G. & C. Merriam.

Wooley, S. C. (1985). *Body images and eating disorders.* Symposium presented at the meeting of the American Psychological Association, August, Los Angeles.

Wooley, S. C., & Wooley, O. W. (1980). Eating disorders: Obesity and anorexia. In A. M. Brodsky & R. T. Hare-Mustin (Eds.), *Women and psychotherapy: An assessment of research and practice* (pp. 135-158). New York: Guilford.

Worrell, J. (1981). New directions in counseling women. In E. Howell & M. Bayes (Eds.), *Women and mental health* (pp. 620-637). New York: Basic Books.

Zilbergeld, B. (1978). *Male sexuality.* Boston: Little, Brown.

3

MALPRACTICE IN PSYCHOTHERAPY AND PSYCHOLOGICAL EVALUATION

Herbert J. Cross
William W. Deardorff

Malpractice has become a familiar term in the last few years. Medical costs have risen steadily as malpractice insurance rates have skyrocketed. In April 1985, *Newsweek* reported that medical malpractice costs rose from $0.5 billion to $2.5 billion between 1975 and 1984. In some places, physicians are refusing to treat patients; and at least 35 states have considered legislation to control lawsuits, jury awards, and attorneys' fees. Dr. James Sammons, executive director of the American Medical Association, has called the difficulty physicians are having a "nationwide crisis" (Hornblower, 1985).

The cost for insurance is high and roughly estimable, but the hidden costs that come from defensive medicine and refusal to treat some patients are incalculable. Some of this propensity to sue physicians is probably associated with the consumerism movement and the idea of accountability. There is also a tendency to question authority and a great public interest in medical and health-related issues.

Psychologists have not been threatened in the same proportions, or to the same degree, as physicians, but they are now beginning to notice increased insurance premiums, and increased public sensitivity to their behavior. For instance, in the first ten years (1955-65) of the American Psychological Association's (APA) malpractice program, no claims were filed (Fisher, 1985; Wright, 1981) and insurance premiums were at low, stable rates. During the years 1976 to 1981, an average of 44 claims per year were filed. During the years 1982 to 1984 there was an annual rate of 153 claims. Concomitant with these increases, malpractice premiums for psychologists have risen 600 percent in the period 1984 to 1985 (from $50 to $300 for $1 million worth of coverage [American Psychological Association, 1985; Fisher, 1985]). Of course, fees for psychological services might be expected to increase to absorb these new professional costs. Thus, similar trends can be seen in medicine and psychology.

In one sense, the threat of malpractice is useful to the profession because it helps to regulate the behavior of practitioners and thereby serves the public. It is difficult to determine the precise effect, because if increased practitioner vigilance prevents malpractice, there is no way to measure its absence. However, it seems reasonable that increased attention in the professional literature to the issues associated with malpractice will aid both the profession and the public.

Malpractice law accomplishes three important social functions (Klein & Glover, 1983, p. 131): First, it deters socially undesirable conduct by establishing aversive consequences for professional wrongdoing. Such contingencies seek to protect the public from injustice and injury. Second, it transfers the loss of one party onto another who more "deserves" to pay the loss. Third, it generally serves as a "cost-distribution" mechanism such that the costs of a negligent professional's actions are borne by all malpractice insurance policyholders and not just the individual. Also, beyond actual professional negligence, there is another variable to the malpractice cost formula: consumers' propensity to initiate legal action where no negligence is subsequently determined. Of course, the cost to policyholders is ultimately passed on to consumers.

PSYCHOLOGICAL MALPRACTICE

Malpractice is a professional error of commission or omission. In order to sue a psychologist successfully, the plaintiff-client must prove the following four basic facts (Feldman & Ward, 1979; Furrow, 1980; Harris, 1973):

1. It must be shown that the practitioner owed a duty to the patient. This duty is related to the contract between the practitioner and patient. The patient comes with some malady or deficiency that he or she wishes to correct. By taking the case, the practitioner implies that he or she can help. The professional owes a duty to possess the skill and learning possessed by the average member of the profession when he or she practices, and this knowledge must be applied with reasonable care (Deardorff, Cross, & Hupprich, 1984; "Professional Negligence," 1973).

2. It must be established that the practitioner breached the duty to the patient. The patient's attorney must show that the proper knowledge was absent from the practitioner's repertoire, or that the proper knowledge was misapplied. In other words, the practitioner clearly did something wrong. In an ambiguous endeavor such as psychotherapy, it can be exceptionally difficult to prove breach of duty. Flagrant

actions, such as engaging in sexual intercourse with a patient under the guise of "treatment" (*Roy* v. *Hartogs*, 1975) or beating a patient (*Hammer* v. *Rosen*, 1960), are readily identifiable and can make a prima facie case of malpractice (the practice is such a grossly inappropriate act that it falls within the common knowledge of laypersons; Knapp, 1980). Aside from professionally negligent behavior that falls into this category, proving a breach of duty can be exceptionally difficult. Generally, negligence from a proper standard of care must be established by expert witnesses and it is frequently hard to get a colleague to testify against a "guild" member (Markus, 1965). This is much less of a problem at present as courts have abandoned the "locality rule," which required the expert witness to be of the same regional area as the defendant-practitioner. Currently, in a malpractice action, a reasonable standard of care for psychological practice would be set according to national standards; in fact in some states, adhering to local standards of care that are below national standards may subject the professional to malpractice liability (Pope, Simpson, & Myron, 1978).

3. The plaintiff-patient must prove that his or her injury was "proximately caused" by the defendant-practitioner's breach of duty. Cause is a difficult concept in science, and most scientists are content to show relationships between variables or the influence of one variable over another. In psychotherapy malpractice suits, injury is often emotional/mental and constitutes an aggravation of a preexisting disorder. Thus, proving the essential "causal link" between the defendant's behavior and the plaintiff's mental injury can be a significant obstacle to a successful malpractice suit (Tarshis, 1972), especially when this injury must be shown not to have been caused by other environmental pressures (for example, relationship or financial stressors) unrelated to the therapeutic situation.

4. Once proximate cause is established, the plaintiff-patient must still prove that he or she suffered harm. Proof is easier if the harm is physical, but the harm from a psychologist practitioner is likely to be mental or psychological. Therefore, it is usually quite difficult to specify amount of harm, in order that the court can set damages. If the plaintiff-patient can successfully make a case for lost wages, or costs for corrective treatment, or specify the amount of injury in some way, the court is more likely to award damages. Ordinarily, damages are awarded only to compensate for the harm caused by the practitioner. Tort law has not generally provided restitution for emotional or mental injury (Klein & Glover, 1983). Several states do allow punitive damages to be awarded in civil cases, but only when the defendant-practitioner's conduct is so outrageous that it shocks the conscience of the public (Deardorff et al., 1984).

It should be noted that all four of these basic allegations must be proved for a malpractice suit to be successful, but they need not be proved beyond the shadow of a doubt, which is frequently the standard in a criminal case. In a civil case, the standard of proof is by the preponderance of evidence, which is an easier standard to meet.

SOURCES OF MALPRACTICE CLAIMS

In a recent article it was suggested that there are no good models of malpractice or good theories about why it occurs (Fisher, 1985), although one survey suggested that physicians are sued more frequently because plaintiff-patients believe they have been slighted or insulted, not because physicians fail to cure them. Aspects of the dynamics of the doctor-patient relationship may help to explain this further. Gutheil, Bursztajn, and Brodsky (1984) conclude that "patients invoke wishful or magical thinking as a defense against feelings of helplessness" and that "when illness presents a threat to one's well-being—to one's very being, in fact—one attempts to resolve the discrepancy between the perception of powerlessness and the wish for omnipotence by transferring the latter to the physician" (p.50). When the health care professional does not measure up to this projected image, which is often fostered by the physician, the patient may seek recompense by forcing the physician to share in the suffering via malpractice action.

It would be most useful to better understand how practitioners contribute to "causing" malpractice actions. The lack of malpractice litigation against mental health professionals in the past has been attributed to tort law's approach to emotional injuries (Klein & Glover, 1983). Also the nature of the therapist-patient relationship tends to inhibit legal action by the patient. However, there is no guarantee that a long-term relationship will be protection against legal action, especially with increased public scrutiny of psychologists' professional behavior. It seems reasonable that if a psychotherapy patient feels dissatisfied with treatment or believes that a negligent action has occurred, the intensity with which malpractice action is pursued might be proportional to the level of investment the patient had in the therapeutic relationship. An empirical test of this speculation has yet to be made but a qualitative analysis of malpractice claims does offer support for it.

It would be useful to develop an understanding of patient dissatisfaction with psychotherapy treatment in attempting to delineate what factors contribute to the initiation of malpractice claims.

ORIGINS OF PATIENT DISSATISFACTION

Malpractice always involves patient dissatisfaction. We believe that the source of this feeling comes from three variables: psychologist incompetence, psychologist exploitativeness, and patient psychopathology.

Psychologist incompetence seems inexcusable, but it is not rare. Graduate schools are often reluctant to terminate poor students (Biaggio, Gasparikova-Krasnec, & Bauer, 1983); and once psychologists have graduated, there is little impetus for remediation other than licensing regulations, which are sometimes difficult to enforce. Furthermore, licensing boards must operate according to state laws, some of which allow graduates from unaccredited schools to apply. Even the best of licensing procedures can enforce only a minimal standard of competence. When the early licensing laws were written, the psychologists who helped to frame them seemed to believe that graduate school did not adequately prepare young psychologists for immediate independent practice. Therefore, all states require at least one year of supervised internship training and many require a supervised postdoctoral year as well, before licensing. Preparation to function as a lone practitioner, then, comes from a blend of university work and supervised practical work—an enormously complex set of skills and attitudes to be mastered in at least two independent settings. Regarded in these terms, it is easy to see how the education system for psychologists occasionally fails. Incompetent practitioners, then, cause malpractice suits to be filed.

Exploitativeness is perhaps a more serious matter because it attracts public interest and seems less likely to be forgiven than incompetence. In the main, there are two kinds of exploitativeness: financial and sexual (Mills, 1984). Both are clear violations of the American Psychological Association's code of ethics (American Psychological Association, 1981). Financial exploitation occurs when the psychologist treats a patient who should be referred or terminated. Many patients are willing to pay the psychologist's fee long after progress has ceased. For the ethical therapist this is frequently a dilemma because the patient may believe the therapy is beneficial when it is not. Of course, therapies that are salable to the public, but whose value lags far behind their cost, are financially exploitative. Financial exploitation also entails filing fraudulent insurance claims or charging exorbitant fees; complaints in these areas are among the most common heard by the American Psychological Association Ethics Committee (Mills, 1984).

While financial exploitativeness has been relatively ignored in the literature, sexual exploitativeness is well known (Edelwich & Brodsky, 1982). Holroyd and Brodsky's (1977) widely quoted study found that 5.5 percent of male psychologists and 0.6 percent of female psychologists had intercourse with their patients. In 1976 the American Psychological Association made sex with patients explicitly unethical, and the American Psychiatric Association did the same in 1977 (Edelwich & Brodsky, 1982, p. 198). Sex between a therapist and patient within the context of a professional relationship is grounds for malpractice. The fact that the patient may have consented to sexual involvement is not a viable defense. The courts have found that a psychotherapy patient cannot give true informed consent to such an act or that consent cannot be given to a professionally unacceptable form of "treatment" (Klein & Glover, 1983). There are a number of well-known malpractice cases that have awarded on the basis of sex between therapists and patients, the most famous of which is *Roy* v. *Hartogs* (1975), which inspired the book *Betrayal* (Freeman & Roy, 1976) and a television drama. Ms. Roy had been diagnosed as schizophrenic and had difficulties in some sex-role behaviors. Her attorneys held that Dr. Hartogs represented sex as part of his treatment. His attorneys did not deny that such behavior is unethical, but defended on the grounds of impotence due to a penile tumor. Other female patients testified (a procedure ordinarily not allowed) that Dr. Hartogs had intercourse with them also, thereby weakening his defense. In finding Dr. Hartogs guilty of malpractice, the court held that he had breached a fiduciary relationship and had not done his best to obtain a cure for his patient. The APA's Task Force on Sex Bias and Sex Role Stereotyping in Psychotherapeutic Practice views any therapist-patient sex as exploitative. Taking an even stronger position, William Masters states forcefully that therapists who have sex with patients should be charged with rape (Masters & Johnson, 1976).

Sexual exploitativeness and harassment are much less likely to go undetected than ever before so that malpractice will continue to result from exploitative sex in the therapeutic setting. One might speculate about why a therapist would be sexually indiscreet with a patient, knowing that he might come under legal and professional scrutiny. It seems likely that people who are drawn to a profession where the chief activity is persuading others to change are somewhat likely to be manipulative themselves. Both the challenge of psychotherapy and the ambiguities of it might attract sensation seekers who are unlikely to be controlled by rules and principles. In her Western Psychological Association presidential address, Patricia Keith-Spiegal (1982) noted that ethical issues would be more difficult once the "me" generation became psychotherapists. The implication of her statement is that there are more self-aggrandizing people who are becoming therapists. These people are more likely to be exploitative of patients than the generation of primarily self-sacrificing therapists who preceded them.

Sexual exploitation probably can never be totally controlled, but the threat of malpractice, disciplinary board scrutiny, and education will help to minimize its occurrence.

TEACHING ETHICAL BEHAVIOR

The public is becoming educated about professional ethical issues by books such as *Betrayal* (Freeman & Roy, 1976), other feminist works, and consumer advocacy literature. Thus the public is better able to recognize professional negligence and unethical behavior when it occurs and do something about it. Psychologists and other therapists should be trained with a strong emphasis on ethics in their programs, although there is some evidence this has not been the case in the past. Pharis and Hill (1983) reported the results of a survey questionnaire that assessed graduate training emphasis on promoting professional and ethical principles. Data were gathered from accredited graduate psychology and social work programs (N = 85, an unprompted return rate of 42 percent; the authors concluded that results were probably obtained from the more "conscientious" programs). The study found that in a majority of the programs (72 percent) ethical training had only an average or lower priority ranking in the teaching curriculum, with very few programs (less than 10 percent) doing anything innovative in the way of teaching in this area. Other data collected in the same survey revealed several interesting beliefs among training programs about the teaching of ethical behavior. These included beliefs that ethical behaviors are unteachable in any structured manner, that ethical behavior is a function of individual character and not of training, and that all coursework implicitly included the teaching of ethical behavior but in an indirect and unstructured way. Pharis and Hill (1983) posit that the teaching of ethical behavior deserves the highest priority and that a direct and systematic approach to teaching ethics is necessary.

We agree with this position. More recent survey data (Wood, Klein, Cross, Lammers, & Elliot, 1985) suggest that ethics courses do have a favorable impact on psychologists. Wood et al. reported the results of a survey that assessed psychologists' attitudes and experiences with unethical behavior and "burnout" in impaired practitioners (defined as psychologists whose work is adversely affected by physical, emotional, legal, or job-related problems). A total of 380 questionnaires was sent to training directors of APA-approved psychology programs and a random selection of practitioners from the National Register of Health Service Providers, with 49 percent of these being returned. Results showed only 42 percent of the sample had a graduate course in professional ethics. These psychologists were more aware of their colleagues who were impaired or "burned out" than psychologists who had not had a graduate ethics course. Also, they were more likely to seek help themselves, offer help to an impaired colleague, and report an impaired colleague to a regulatory agency (consistent with APA ethical principles). These data support Pharis and Hill's position that teaching structured graduate ethics courses does indeed have positive effects.

MALPRACTICE IN PSYCHOLOGICAL EVALUATIONS

There are several differences between clinical evaluations and psychotherapy, some of which contribute to less likelihood of malpractice, and some to more likelihood. Psychological assessment is more specifiable than psychotherapy. Psychologists have been taught (Tallent, 1976) that a specific referral question should be asked, and that the evaluator should answer that question. Further, many consider it good practice to specify the confidence the psychologist has in the answer provided. There are many psychological tests available, and a great literature on assessment that would give a serious student of testing quite an armamentarium to answer referral questions. This is especially true if he or she has specialized in one area, such as forensics or psychosomatic disorders.

If assessment can be so well learned and so well done, then why do evaluations generate such a high proportion (Wright, 1981) of malpractice suits? We believe that it is because the subject of the evaluation is often not just the client, and frequently the client does not understand the evaluation process. Since evaluations are often requested by a third party (for example, the court, an insurance company, an attorney), they are more likely to serve that party than the subject. Further, since psychologists evaluate mainly for some prediction of behavior (for example, sanity, stability, ability to parent), it seems likely that the third party requesting evaluation suspects that the subject will show a negative outcome. For instance, in custody struggles, attorneys frequently send their stable clients for evaluations, hoping to put pressure on the more unstable opposing parent to get an evaluation, which might turn out negatively.

Occasionally individuals request evaluations because they wish to answer a specific question about their personality or ability. In these instances it seems more likely that individuals requesting evaluation believe they will be able to use the results because they will do well, that is, "pass the test." In these cases, the subject's attitude toward the evaluation is likely to be more positive. Of course, when anyone is forced to get a psychological evaluation, he or she is likely to be uncomfortable, or even belligerent—attitudes that may contribute to a less positive evaluation.

The subject of any psychological evaluation should be fully informed about the purpose and the use that will be made of the results. In an adversarial situation, or court-ordered evaluation, the psychologist should inform the subject regarding who requested the evaluation and who will pay for it. Deception in these matters is proscribed by the APA (1981) code of ethics.

In their article, "On being ethical in legal places," Anderten, Staulcup, and Grisso (1980) delineate several issues relevant to psychological evaluation in the forensic arena. First, the psychologist must be careful to provide an objective and impartial evaluation consistent with the APA's ethical standards. This may be in the face of pressure to be facilitative of the goals of the attorney or the party requesting services. Second, the psychologist should be aware that doing a thorough evaluation does not mean that all aspects of the results and their interpretation will be heard in court. This depends on the expertise of the attorney and the psychologist, and on the collaborative relationship between the two. The legal proceedings may induce defensiveness in the psychologist expert witness, resulting in testimony being made that goes beyond the scope of the test data. Third, as alluded to above, the psychologist must always keep in mind the client's psychological well-being. There may be a tendency to evaluate insensitively and provide feedback to the retaining attorney or agency to the exclusion of full involvement of the client in an informed way.

Duty to Maintain the Subject's Right of Privacy

A psychologist who uses tests in any situation where personal, or possibly damaging, information will be revealed should inform the subject about the nature, and especially the purpose, of the testing. Otherwise, the subject should have the option to deny scrutiny by psychological tests. The subject has a right to privacy, which should not be infringed, except by the subject's consent.

Informed consent is most often applied to research and to medicine. It means that the participant in a procedure should be informed about the procedure, especially with regard to any hazards and the likely outcome. Informed consent always involves *capacity, information,* and *voluntariness. Capacity* means that the person in question must be able to understand the situation and make a rational decision in his or her best interests. *Information* is not just detailing facts, but should involve some idea of how the test was constructed and how the results will be used. It is imperative not only that essential information is imparted to the subject, but also that it is determined that the subject understands the procedure. *Voluntariness* is the idea that the subject is acting freely. Opinion is divided (Schwitzgebel & Schwitzgebel, 1980; Sheldon-Wildgen, 1982; Wright, 1981) about the usefulness of written informed consent contracts as protection against malpractice claims. Of the more pessimistic views, Foster (1978, p. 72) states that "experienced trial lawyers are adept at overcoming the obstacle of tightly or loosely drawn releases and tend to regard them as minor irritants, if not with disdain."

Data from studies on communication of medical information present another problem in obtaining true informed consent. These results show that patients may understand and retain less than 60 percent of information presented in informed consent forms (Cassileth, Zupkis, Sutton-Smith, & March, 1980; Grunder, 1980; Ley, 1982). These studies suggest that a patient's understanding of what consent is being given for should be carefully assessed, certainly beyond simply handing out a standard form to be signed and filed away.

Regardless of whether or not the psychologist uses a written form, he or she must elicit the subject's cooperation without deception or violating the subject's right to privacy. Therefore, the psychologist must inform the subject of all aspects of the testing situation that the subject needs to know. Psychologists who do a good deal of assessment for forensic purposes would occasionally be unable to assess unwilling subjects. Such events are likely to be frustrating, but are preferable to disgruntled subjects who may sue for malpractice.

Many professionals view informed consent with contempt. The feeling is that it is more "red tape" made necessary by the threat of legal action and serves no therapeutic purpose. In fact, it is often felt to bring about unnecessary or even deleterious anxiety in patients because it must point out explicitly the risks and ramifications of a procedure (Gutheil et al., 1984). This has been more the experience in medicine but certainly a similar situation exists in the practice of psychotherapy. We, as well as other authors (Gutheil et al., 1984), feel that the informed consent procedure need not be aversive, but can be used in a therapeutic manner. Sharing information about the evaluation or treatment process with the patient and involving him or her in a collaborative way serves not only to satisfy the legal aspects of informed consent but also seeks to facilitate a therapeutic alliance by engendering the patient's trust. Further, the process provides the opportunity to elicit the patient's fears or erroneous beliefs about the evaluation or treatment. When this is not adequately addressed, the therapist and patient may be working at cross-purposes as a result of holding discrepant conceptual models regarding evaluation or interventions.

MALPRACTICE IN PSYCHOLOGICAL TREATMENT

The duties owed to a patient are perhaps more complicated for psychotherapy than for evaluation. Many of the ethical responsibilities inherent in doing psychological evaluations discussed above, such as informed consent, are applicable to treatment also. Further, some of the duties to be discussed subsequently apply to doing evaluations.

Duty of Neutrality

Furrow (1980) lists a duty of neutrality by the practitioner as of exceptional importance. Novice psychologists are fre-

quently cautioned by supervisors to maintain an objective attitude toward their patients. A situation where neutrality is lost
and one that frequently starts a malpractice action is a sexual
relationship between practitioner and patient. As we have
already discussed, the impropriety of practitioner-patient sex
is now well recognized and is highly likely to be punished by
regulatory agencies or by a malpractice suit.

Courts (*Anclote Manor* v. *Wilkinson*, 1972, and *Roy* v.
Hartogs, 1975) and attorneys (Furrow, 1980) tend to discuss
practitioner-patient sex in terms of transference-countertrans-
ference. They seem to make the assumption, as does classical
psychoanalysis, that a patient will transfer strong emotions to
the therapist, which the therapist must be able to manage
properly, allegedly because of his or her self-awareness and
ability to be objective, or neutral. Thus, the duty of neutrality is breached when a therapist, acting to fulfill his or her
own needs, engages in behavior not in the best interests of
the patient.

Duty to Consult

The duty to consult may be looked upon as a corollary of
neutrality (Furrow, 1980), especially if the therapist is having
difficulty with a patient so that his or her emotions are aroused.
Aggressive, seductive, or dangerously suicidal patients are
all examples of those who might trigger therapists' emotional
reactions. An experienced colleague's judgment could be beneficial in dealing with such patients.

Practitioners should also consult former therapists and
could be held liable in court if such information is not obtained
and it adversely affects treatment outcome. In a recent California case (*Jablonski* v. *United States*, 1983, as cited in
George, 1985), a psychiatrist was held liable for not warning
a patient's girlfriend of the patient's possible violent behavior
toward women with whom he was close. Even though no specific threat was made toward a specific individual, the court
ruled the psychiatrist "should have known" of the possibility
if previous records had been consulted (see George, 1985).
Beyond consulting these sources, nonmedical therapists should
consult with a physician if there is any medical question. In
general, practitioners protect themselves from malpractice by
a readiness to consult with a colleague whenever they have
doubts about their conceptualization of a case or its treatment.

Duty of Nonabandonment

It would seem that termination of a psychotherapeutic
relationship would be a relatively simple matter, and it is, as
long as both parties agree on the termination. Occasionally,

however, the therapist wishes to terminate and the patient does not. A therapist must exercise caution in deciding to terminate, because a vulnerable and disturbed patient may interpret the termination as a serious rejection. Suicide attempts and gesturing are not unheard of in such situations, and the temptation is to regard an attempt as a message that the patient is too disturbed to terminate, or the therapist should be punished for the premature termination.

To help prevent the above occurrence, the patient must always be given reasonable notice of termination and may need help with a referral and transition to other therapy. There is no easy way to terminate a dependent and needy patient. Therapists should consider a patient's neediness when structuring the developing relationship. It is sometimes easy to promise too much and give too much support so that the needy recipient begins to look to the therapy as the source of all gratification. Termination issues should be handled explicitly and often need to be addressed from early on in the treatment.

Psychotherapists should recognize that a psychotherapy contract does put them in jeopardy of being obliged to aid some not-so-likeable patients through crises at some inconvenient times. When a psychotherapist terminates because of his or her inability to deal with a needy patient, or out of his or her own selfishness, then the therapist may be inviting a malpractice suit.

One phenomenon that occurs more frequently in psychotherapy than probably any other form of treatment is long-term therapy by residents, interns, and trainees. It is standard practice for psychiatrists and psychologists in training to treat patients under supervision. When the training programs are completed, the therapists generally leave the geographic area and cease to treat the patients. Occasionally, patients are assigned to other therapists or are referred to other facilities, but they are mainly terminated at the end of their therapist's program. Certainly, this comes close to the con - cept of abandonment. No suits, to our knowledge, have been brought on this basis. Some patients may have been dissatisfied, but none were dissatisfied enough to sue. We expect that one reason for the therapists escaping litigation is that they prepared the patient for termination by warning them far in advance of the termination date. Since there is no specified amount of time to treat or to cure any particular disorder, psychotherapy could conceivably go on forever, in some cases. Perhaps it is useful to have a set date beyond which one must see another therapist, take a psychotherapy "holiday" to assess achievements, or at least specify time intervals for periodic renegotiation of the therapy contract. Previous work (Budman, 1981) suggests that time-limited therapy can be quite effective. We expect that the time limitation leads to effective goal setting, reasonable expectations, and general satisfaction in the process. In turn, the probability of a malpractice claim being filed would be decreased.

Duty to Terminate Treatment

Furrow (1980) specifically states that duty to terminate is a corollary of nonabandonment, and we have mentioned lack of timely termination as financial exploitation. The decision to terminate is a frequent dilemma, especially for practitioners who are not well established. Often it is less difficult to treat an established patient than a new one and the payment contract already exists with the established patient. There is no clarity about the natural course of most disorders for which psychotherapy is used (Frank, 1961); therefore, in every case that is not terminated for reasons of geography, a decision to terminate must be made on the basis of insufficient data.

The dilemma for recently established practitioners is that they are trying to recover costs from beginning a business, and they are not likely to have a large or profitable caseload. Consequently, they might find it exceptionally difficult to terminate patients who pay and who are not difficult to treat. However, under Principle 6 of the code of ethics, psychologists are reminded to terminate a clinical or consulting relationship when it is reasonably clear that the consumer is not benefiting from it (APA, 1981, p. 636).

From the patient's point of view, it can be especially hard to make a termination decision. The therapist must be relied upon to be decisive even though the data may be equivocal.

An issue related to this is attempting to treat a patient's disorder that is clearly out of one's area of competence. For the young independent practitioner, the tendency is to treat everyone who walks through the door. This stems from the pressures outlined above. It can be a difficult ethical dilemma when professional self-examination and self-scrutiny are required to determine the bounds of one's competence, especially when the results of this process may result in the turning away of potential clients.

Duty to Prevent Patients from Harming Themselves

We have alluded to the ambiguities in psychotherapy and noted that therapists must act on insufficient data. Patients occasionally harm themselves. The most clear and definable harm is suicide, which may not have been preventable, but which may cause the therapist great anguish. Therapists must do all that is in their power to prevent suicide. Whenever it is clear to a therapist that a patient may commit suicide, the therapist must take appropriate preventive measures. However, prevention and precaution are always limited in an outpatient

setting. Therapists who fear suicide must frequently hospitalize their patients as a preventive measure, and they must
never ignore the threat of suicide. It is regrettable that a
determinedly suicidal patient is difficult to thwart, and that
a therapist can do so little short of hospitalization. But a
therapist can be alert to clues to suicide, and he or she can
attend properly to any clear communication of suicidal intent.
For the competent therapist, it is a given that any suicidal
message must be taken seriously. This situation sometimes
gives rise to a dilemma when a manipulative patient makes
frequent inconvenient phone calls to a therapist. The therapist's need to deal effectively with such patients cannot super-
sede the duty to protect suicidal patients from self-inflicted
harm. If the end result is inconvenience or difficulty treating
needy patients, that is preferable to precipitating a suicide.
Being a psychotherapist carries a burden of duty to prevent
patients harming themselves, even at the therapist's inconvenience or cost.

In a recent series of articles (Bursztajn, Gutheil, Hamm,
& Brodsky, 1983; Gutheil, Bursztajn, Hamm, & Brodsky, 1983),
the legal ramifications of suicide assessment are discussed.
The authors' analyses are lengthy and can only be summarized
here. Basically, they state that a practitioner's professional
behavior will be judged by three criteria: the professional
community's standard of care, what a reasonable and prudent
practitioner would do under similar circumstances, and the
"Learned Hand" rule. The first two of these criteria are identical to facts (1) and (2) of malpractice action discussed earlier. The "Learned Hand" rule states that "negligent behavior
is failure to invest resources up to a level that [is commensurate with] the anticipated savings in damages" (as cited in
Gutheil et al., 1983, p. 321). This is a cost-benefit analysis
in making treatment decisions. Related to the suicidal patient,
the courts have not made it an ultimate goal that all suicides
be prevented at any cost. Rather, the risks of certain treatment decisions (such as loosening the restraints on a suicidal
patient or deciding to treat a suicidal patient on an outpatient
basis) must be weighed against the therapeutic benefits to be
gained (such as an increase in functioning). Thus a practitioner does not have to be proved "right" by outcome, but
rather that clinical judgment and decisionmaking fell within
the three standards of care. This underscores the necessity
of careful documentation and consultation when these types of
treatment decisions are being made.

As a useful guide to clinicians, Bursztajn et al. (1983)
present questions a therapist should be contemplating when
treating a suicidal patient, and these derive from the three
standards of care. Examples include: "Would one of my colleagues or, particularly, supervisors, remind me of other considerations that I am overlooking?" (community standard); "Is
this a situation where it is relatively safe to rely on subjective

data?," "Am I overlooking objective data such as the statistical probability that someone with this patient's diagnosis will attempt suicide?", "What if I am right (or wrong) about the consequences?" (Learned Hand); "What is my implicit philosophy of science, the set of standards by which I judge my clinical reasoning to be 'scientific'?" (reasonable and prudent practitioner). As Bursztajn et al. (1983) conclude, "the awareness that one's clinical reasoning must be supportable by the three standards of due care in negligence law can guide the clinician in finding the right questions to ask" (p. 348). Thus this awareness provides not only protection against a successful malpractice action, but also is consistent with sound clinical practice.

Duties to Others

Since the Tarasoff decision, psychotherapists have become aware that psychotherapy is not as protected from public or legal scrutiny as it once was (*Tarasoff* v. *Regents of University of California*, 1976). The Tarasoff decision came from a case at the University of California at Berkeley where a student named Poddar was being treated by a psychologist at the university hospital. Poddar confided to his therapist, Dr. Moore, that he planned to kill Tatinia Tarasoff, a young woman who had rejected him. The psychologist conferred with a psychiatrist who had examined Poddar and with the chief of service. They decided to commit Poddar for observation and reported to the campus police who took him into custody. Poddar promised to stay away from Miss Tarasoff, and was subsequently released by the police. Two months later he killed Miss Tarasoff. Her parents sued the University of California and its employees for failure to hospitalize Poddar and to warn their daughter. The court did not hold the defendants liable for failure to commit, but did hold the defendants liable for failure to protect the victim. The court ruled that because the therapist had a special relationship with Poddar, a dangerous person, the therapist had a duty to protect the victim from the culprit. The court acknowledged the difficulty of predicting dangerousness and the need for confidentiality in psychotherapy but noted that "the protective privilege ends where the public peril begins." The court said in summary:

> Our current crowded and computerized society compels the interdependence of its members. In this risk-infested society we can hardly tolerate the further exposure to danger that would result from concealed knowledge of the therapist that his patient was lethal. If the exercise of reasonable care to protect the threatened victim requires the therapist to warn the endangered party or those who can

reasonably be expected to notify him, we see no sufficient societal interest that would protect and justify
concealment. The containment of such risks lies in
the public interest (pp. 347-348).

The case is often cited as a duty to warn, since warning an
intended victim is the behavior required by the court. The
principle of warning a known likely victim has been incorporated into the code of ethics of the American Psychological
Association (1981). Duty to warn has been expanded in the
case of *McIntosh* v. *Milano* (1979), wherein the psychiatrist
was held liable for failure to warn the next door neighbor of
his violent adolescent patient, who killed her. In effect, the
court decided that the psychiatrist should have concluded
that his patient was dangerous to the intended victim, even
though the patient had made no specific threat toward her.
Based on these two cases, Furrow (1980) notes that the following factors should be considered in duty-to-warn cases:
the control the doctor has over the patient, the doctor's
knowledge of the patient's propensities, and the specific identity of the threatened victim.
  The duty-to-warn doctrine obviously changes the nature
of the confidential relationship between therapist and patient.
A study of California psychologists and psychiatrists (*Stanford Law Review*, 1978) found that since the Tarasoff decision
therapists were more anxious about dangerousness, more
likely to discuss confidentiality, and more likely to give warn-
ings to third parties. Furrow (1980) optimistically states that
the final outcome of Tarasoff will be positive because "it puts
pressure on each therapist to inform himself of certain research findings on dangerousness, correlations between personality disorders and the likelihood of violence, and other
emerging evidence" (p. 56). Furrow's statement implies that
there is a good deal of useful information on predicting dangerousness and that it can be mastered and utilized. Since the
actual knowledge on dangerousness is much less useful (Monahan, 1981) than this, therapists can only react to the pressure
of the Tarasoff decision by conceptualizing their cases as well
as possible and by being exceptionally cautious about threats
to third parties. As a result of the Tarasoff decision, therapists are more vulnerable to malpractice suits, not only from
their patients, but from third parties whom their patients
may harm.

BEHAVIORAL MEDICINE/HEALTH PSYCHOLOGY

A special area of malpractice risk for psychologists lies in
the area of behavioral medicine and/or stress management
(Knapp & Vandecreek, 1981a). Psychologists have discovered
that the public will seek their services if they are labeled

stress management, that physicians do not treat stress disorders especially well, and that the greatest number of health problems are caused by life-style, not infectious disease. Because of this, many psychologists and other clinicians are practicing in the health psychology area. The division of health psychology is the fastest growing in the American Psychological Association, and the majority of continuing education workshops advertised in APA publications have some behavioral medicine application. There is some likelihood that health psychology or behavioral medicine will soon have a specialty status equivalent to clinical, industrial, and school psychology.

Special risks are associated with this practice because nonmedical practitioners run the risk of practicing medicine without a license. Organized medicine has a tradition of conflict with "drugless healers," and several court decisions (see Cohen 1979, p. 39) have gone against such practitioners. Also, a good deal of expertise is required to practice in an area that overlaps another discipline, and defining one's professional role and knowledge base becomes particularly important. Furthermore, patients are often already suspicious of practitioners by the time they are referred, and they want specific answers for questions.

Practice in this area tends to be more behavioral and specific, and patients seem less worried about being stigmatized as a mental patient (Knapp & Vandecreek, 1981a). For all these reasons, practitioners of behavioral medicine are vulnerable to suit. Nonphysicians can protect themselves best by practicing in concert with physicians, consulting with physicians, and accepting referrals from and referring back to physicians. Perhaps this does not resemble the autonomous profession that psychologists proclaim, but behavioral medicine is not the arena to assert independence. Cooperation among physicians and psychologists is essential. Probably more than any other area, the health psychologist needs to be acutely aware of self-competence and take a nondefensive posture in working with other health care professionals. Otherwise, the malpractice risks will outweigh opportunities in this specialty.

THE MALPRACTICE PALL

Several health care professionals have described the painful process of fighting a malpractice suit (for example, Charles, 1985). The suspicion of incompetence by the public or by colleagues is difficult for independent practitioners because they are private businesses that advertise mainly by reputation. Therefore, an accusation of malpractice is costly whether or not the suit is lost or the accusation is true. Furthermore, mental health practitioners deal in behaviors and concepts that are hard to define, and this vagueness enhances the importance of a good reputation. It behooves every independent practitioner to avoid a malpractice suit.

There are other factors operating, aside from all those discussed previously, that influence the frequency with which malpractice lawsuits are being filed. In the United States, lawsuits have increased greatly and the cost of liability insurance has escalated in the last few years. In December 1983, *U.S. News & World Report* stated that in a recent four-year period, the number of lawsuits increased by 23 percent, and the number of lawyers had been increasing by 35,000 per year. There is a great deal of competition among attorneys, and now that advertising is legal, there is open solicitation of business. The Lewiston (Idaho) *Morning Tribune*, a newspaper that serves an area where major industries are wood products and agriculture, ran the following advertisement in June 1985: "What is disease? Many physical and mental conditions caused by your job may qualify for benefits. If your job caused or added to your problems, you may be wise to seek legal advice. No recovery, no fee." Such an advertisement suggests that workers might reconceptualize their ills and use attorneys to discover whether or not their employer can be held responsible. If advertising affects and persuades people, it seems that some people would be persuaded to blame their employers unfairly, and if the attorneys cannot recover in the final outcome, there would be no cost. In an even more serious and dramatic example, on March 7, 1985, the New York *Times* reported that a former attorney testified before a state senate committee that he had bribed judges, court clerks, and physicians in malpractice cases. Also, he had developed cases with illicit access to hospital files, and had illegally sold approximately 100 cases for about $15,000 each to other attorneys.

These facts suggest that health care professionals are vulnerable to accusations that are always difficult to defend against, even though they may be outright fabrications or impossible to prove. Anyone can be sued at any time, and there is a plethora of attorneys seeking work. Thus, clinicians must not only be sure they are practicing competently, but also they should be aware of how to decrease the probability of a patient initiating a malpractice suit where no aberrant professional behavior has actually occurred.

AVOIDING MALPRACTICE SUITS

Since lawsuits have become ordinary, there is no certain method of protecting oneself from the horrors of malpractice litigation. However, competent and ethical practice will minimize the risk, and there are specific precautions that can be taken.

We encourage psychologists to read and discuss periodically with a colleague the APA code of ethics (1981) and Standards for Providers of Psychological Services (1985). Psychologists would be well served by reflecting on the ethical problems in their practices as well as those of others, for sensitivity to ethical problems is one outcome of realizing that they are common. Other professionals should understand their own codes and the most frequently encountered problems for their professions. This kind of awareness should result in protecting oneself not by defensive practice, but by proper attention to the details of one's work.

Of course, "defensive practice" is derogatory only in that it is costly, for it mainly refers to physicians ordering unnecessary medical tests to protect themselves. In psychotherapy it has no real parallel because good defensive measures, such as maintaining strict confidentiality and keeping complete records, are simply useful procedures in any practice.

Informed consent is an especially important area to be aware of in avoiding malpractice, as we have discussed previously in relation to psychological evaluations. With respect to psychotherapy, we perceive informed consent to be a part of the contract or even the rapport between the patient and therapist. It seems likely that the better the patient understands the therapist's overall plans, goals, and techniques, the more he or she is likely to cooperate. The therapist should also inform the patient of any danger in the procedures and the general likelihood of harm from psychotherapy. Psychotherapists immediately recognize the awkwardness of informing a beginning client of the limits of confidentiality and the possible harmful effects of therapy. One group of therapists (Hare-Mustin, Marecek, Kaplan, & Liss-Levinson, 1979) has suggested carefully written office policy statements that give all necessary information to prospective patients, but Wright (1981) notes that specific written statements may be misinterpreted and are sometimes awkward. We recommend the use of written office policy statements regarding fees, hours, telephone numbers, and so on, but suggest that specifics of the therapist-patient interaction be discussed face-to-face so that all ambiguities can be addressed and the patient's reactions to any portion of the policy can be explicitly dealt with. Further, beyond the content of the informed consent form, a written contract can be evidence that the costs and benefits of treatment were discussed with the patient. This would show professional behavior consistent with the "Learned Hand" standard of care discussed previously. This evidence would certainly be advantageous should malpractice action ever become a reality (Bursztajn et al., 1983; Gutheil et al., 1983).

Practitioners must be able to manage the attractiveness of using charisma as a therapeutic tool versus using information. It has been known for some years that nonspecific variables affect psychotherapy outcome (Frank, 1961) and that many people are helped by placebo techniques. However, behavior therapy and consumerism have affected psychotherapy, so that charisma and therapist superiority should now be tempered with a willingness to communicate honestly about the limits of one's knowledge. A promised cure, or even the implication of one, is more likely to leave a dissatisfied patient than is a more accurate probability statement about the therapist's experience with the proposed treatment. Of course, charisma and authority are part of any persuasive healer's armamentarium, but if specific knowledge is necessary in a given situation, authority used as a substitute is likely to be perceived as arrogance, and the seeds of consumer irritation may be sown. The standard for liability probably increases markedly whenever the healer promises a cure.

Humility and the willingness to admit one's limitations do not seem to be a salient characteristic of bright young adults in our society. Those who have done well enough in tough educational competition to get into and to graduate from select professional programs are less likely to be humble than their peers. While their clients come from the public at large, their own values are similar to those of the intelligentsia. Such social differences were useful for Bernheim to cure by suggestion at the turn of the century (Dauven, 1980), but they are now more likely to stimulate antiauthority feelings from consumers who are already suspicious of professionals. Part of the process of professionalization is accreditation and specification of curricula. Curricula can be specified and required only if a body of knowledge exists, and the professional gatekeepers can require that aspirants have assimilated that knowledge. This being the case, and a professional license reflecting that knowledge, the public expects the knowledge to be applied correctly.

Cohen (1979) gives an excellent set of specific suggestions on avoiding malpractice, as does Knapp (1980). Another excellent guideline is the APA code of ethics (1981). A clear understanding and thoughtful debate about each principle is strongly recommended. Especially important are principles 2 and 6, which relate to protecting the welfare of the consumer and to competence. If practitioners always keep the welfare of their patients uppermost in mind, and if they are competent, malpractice litigation will certainly be minimized.

Further, it is quite useful for practitioners to be aware of the impact of their behavior. They must maintain higher standards than the general public because they are privileged to share confidential information, and their own pronouncements about others may be misinterpreted as diagnostic statements that could be damaging and invite litigation. Practitioners should bear in mind that the privileged communication they enjoy is for the patient and not for themselves. Whatever is said in a consultation session can be talked about incessantly by the patient and even reported directly to any person the practitioner may have denigrated.

With respect to behavior toward consumers of services, we suggest that the practitioner bear in mind the possibility of defending his or her behavior in court. Asking themselves how they would feel about defending a proposed action on the witness stand is likely to induce a reflective attitude that could be helpful in planning many aspects of practice.

We further suggest that all practitioners understand the patients they deal with as completely as possible. This understanding could come from an emphasis on the process of classification and conceptualization. In fact, expert conceptualization and diagnosis will aid the practitioner whenever difficult decisions are to be made. It is exceptionally helpful, though no panacea (Monahan, 1981), in the question of violence.

Furthermore, the process of conceptualization and classification leads to the kind of probabilistic predictions (for example, Marks, Seeman, & Haller, 1974) that courts are able to understand and utilize. Therefore, it would be useful for practitioners to be able to frame their concepts in communicable, behavioral, and probabilistic statements in order to be well received in court.

A practitioner can be ethical and still be held liable if there is no record of his ethical practice (Deardorff et al, 1984). Good written summaries, documented consultations, and documented phone contacts cannot be overemphasized as good practice policy that can protect from suit.

Finally, psychologists should recognize that their public and official recognition as an established profession has led to their malpractice vulnerability (Knapp & Vandecreek, 1981b). It is ironic that lawsuits are, in one sense, the mark of maturity of a profession. We choose to regard them as a mark of professional adolescence, and hope that full maturity will show fewer disgruntled customers and fewer court actions against psychologists.

CONCLUSION

The malpractice phenomenon has seemed to alert professional psychologists to many issues related to the development and independent practice of psychotherapy and psychological evaluations. In the past decade, incompetence, ethical insensitivity, and greed have combined with a glut of attorneys and consumer sensitivity so that lawsuits against practitioners are no longer rare. The result has been a number of judgments against practitioners, which have clarified the courts' conceptualization of professional practice. It behooves individual psychologists to examine the malpractice literature and to understand their own practices and vulnerability to suit.

If psychology does not police itself, and if ethics are not valued above profits, the profession as a whole as well as the public will suffer. The process of licensing and maintaining professional status depends upon public acceptance and reputation. Successful malpractice litigation draws media attention and erodes the reputation of the profession. The consequences of poor public acceptance could be drastic where licensing laws are up for sunset review or where insurance companies are scrutinizing their malpractice rates. Further, in states without freedom-of-choice legislation, insurers may tighten third-party payment regulations to limit psychotherapy benefits. Any of these actions that are detrimental to professional psychology ultimately limit psychology's ability to serve the public, because competition with lay practitioners is increased as professional status is lost. In the expressive jargon of the 1960s, "It is time to clean up our act."

REFERENCES

American Psychological Association. (1981). Ethical standards of psychologists. *American Psychologist, 36*, 633-638.

American Psychological Association (1985). *Standards for providers of psychological services* (Draft), January. Washington, D.C.

Anclote Manor Foundation v. *Wilkinson*, 263 So.2d 256 (Fla. App., 1972).

Anderten, P., Staulcup, V., & Grisso, T. (1980). On being ethical in legal places. *Professional Psychology, 11*, 764-773.

Biaggio, M. K., Gasparikova-Krasnec, M., & Bauer, L. (1983). Evaluation of clinical psychology graduate students: The problem of the unsuitable student. *Professional Practice of Psychology, 4*, 9-20.

Budman, S. H. (Ed.). (1981). *Forms of brief therapy.* New York: Guilford Press.

Bursztajn, H., Gutheil, T. G., Hamm, R. M., & Brodsky, A. (1983). Subjective data and suicide assessment in the light of recent legal developments. Part II: Clinical uses of legal standards in the interpretations of subjective data. *International Journal of Law and Psychiatry, 6*, 331-350.

Cassileth, B. R., Zupkis, R. V., Sutton-Smith, K., & March, V. (1980). Informed consent—why are its goals imperfectly realized? *The New England Journal of Medicine, 302*, 896-900.

Charles, S. C. (1985). Doctors and the litigation process: Going against the grain. *Child and Adolescent Psychotherapy, 3*, 219-222.

Cohen, R. J. (1979). *Malpractice: A guide for mental health professionals.* New York: Free Press.

Dauven, J. (1980). *The powers of hypnosis.* New York: Stein & Day.

Deardorff, W., Cross, H., & Hupprich, W. (1984). Malpractice liability in psychotherapy: Client and practitioner perspectives. *Professional Psychology: Research and Practice, 15,* 590-600.

Edelwich, J., & Brodsky, A. (1982). *Sexual dilemmas for the helping professional.* New York: Brunner/Mazel.

Feldman, S. R., & Ward, T. M. (1979). *Psychotherapeutic injury: Reshaping the implied contract as an alternative to malpractice,* North Carolina Law Review, *58,* 63-96.

Fisher, K. (1985). Malpractice: Charges catch clinicians in cycle of shame, slip-ups. *American Psychological Association Monitor, 16,* 6-7.

Foster, H. H. (1978). Informed consent of mental patients. In W. E. Barton & C. J. Sanborn (Eds.). *Law and the mental health professions.* New York: International Universities Press.

Frank, J. (1961). *Persuasion and healing: A comparative study of psychotherapy.* Baltimore: Johns Hopkins University Press.

Freeman, L., & Roy, J. (1976). *Betrayal.* New York: Stein & Day.

Furrow, B. (1980). *Malpractice in psychotherapy.* Lexington, Mass.: D. C. Heath.

George, J. C. (1985). Hedlund paranoia. *Journal of Clinical Psychology, 41,* 291-294.

Grunder, T. M. (1980). On the readability of surgical consent forms. *The New England Journal of Medicine, 302,* 900-902.

Gutheil, T. G., Bursztajn, H., Hamm, R. M., & Brodsky, A. (1983). Subjective data and suicide assessment in the light of recent legal developments: Part I. Malpractice prevention and the use of subjective data. *International Journal of Law and Psychiatry, 6,* 317-329.

Gutheil, T. G., Bursztajn, H., & Brodsky, A. (1984). Malpractice prevention through the sharing of uncertainty. *The New England Journal of Medicine, 311,* 49-51.

Hammer v. *Rosen,* 7 N.Y.2d 376, 165 N.E.2d 756, 198 N.Y.S.2d (1960).

Hare-Mustin, R., Marecek, J., Kaplan, A., & Liss-Levinson, N. (1979). Rights of clients, responsibilities of therapists. *American Psychologist, 34,* 3-16.

Harris, M. (1973). Tort liability of the psychotherapist. *University of San Francisco Law Review, 8,* 405-436.

Holroyd, J. C., & Brodsky, A. M. (1977). Psychologists' attitudes and practices regarding erotic and nonerotic physical contact with patients. *American Psychologist, 32,* 843-849.

Hornblower, M. (1985). Hospitals, doctors grope for cure to high cost of insurance. Lewiston (Idaho) *Morning Tribune,* June 17, pp. 1; 3A.

Keith-Spiegal, P. (1982). *Moral conundrums, shibboleths & Gordian knots.* Presidential address of the Western Psychological Association, April, Sacramento, Calif.

Klein, J. I., & Glover, S. I. (1983). Psychiatric malpractice. *International Journal of Law and Psychiatry, 6,* 131-157.

Knapp, S. (1980). A primer on malpractice for psychologists. *Professional Psychology, 11,* 606-612.

Knapp, S., & Vandecreek, L. (1981a). Behavioral medicine: Its malpractice risks for psychologists. *Professional Psychology, 12,* 677-683.

Knapp, S., & Vandecreek, L. (1981b). Malpractice as a regulator of psychotherapy. *Psychotherapy: Theory, Research, and Practice, 18,* 354-357.

Ley, P. (1982). Studies of recall in medical settings. *Human Learning, 1,* 223-233.

Marks, P., Seeman, W., & Haller, D. (1974). *The actuarial use of the MMPI with adolescents and adults.* Baltimore: Williams & Wilkins.

Markus, R. M. (1965). Conspiracy of silence. *Cleveland Law Review, 14,* 520-533.

Masters, W. H., & Johnson, V. E. (1976). Principles of the new sex therapy. *American Journal of Psychiatry, 133,* 548-554.

McIntosh v. *Milano,* 403, A2d 500 (N.J. 1979).

Mills, D. H. (1984). Ethics education and adjudication within psychology. *American Psychologist, 39,* 669-675.

Monahan, J. (1981). *The clinical prediction of violent behavior.* DHHS Pub #(ADAM) 18-921. Rockville, Md.: U.S. Government Printing Service.

New York *Times.* (1985). Former lawyer says he paid off judges in medical lawsuits. March 7, pp. A1; B7.

Newsweek. (1985). Malpractice insurers are ill. April 29, p. 58.

Pharis, M., & Hill, K. (1983). Training for responsible professional behavior in psychology and social work. *Clinical Social Work Journal, 10,* 178-183.

Pope, K. S., Simpson, H. J., & Myron, M. F. (1978). Malpractice in outpatient psychotherapy. *American Journal of Psychotherapy, 32,* 593-600.

Professional Negligence (1973). *University of Pennsylvania Law Review, 121,* 627.

Roy v. *Hartogs,* 85 Misc.2d 891, 381 N.Y.S.2d 587 (1975).

Schwitzgebel, R. L., & Schwitzgebel, R. K. (1980). *Law and psychological practice.* New York: John Wiley.

Sheldon-Wildgen, J. (1982). Avoiding legal liability: The rights and responsibilities of therapists. *The Behavior Therapist, 5,* 165-169.

Stanford Law Review. (1978). Where the public peril begins: A survey of psychotherapists to determine the effects of *Tarasoff. 35,* 165.

Tallent, N. (1976). *Psychological report writing.* Englewood Cliffs, N.J.: Prentice-Hall.

Tarasoff v. *Regents of University of California,* 131 Cal. Rptr. 14, 551 P.2d 334 (1976).

Tarshis, C. B. (1972). Liability for psychotherapy. *University of Toronto Faculty Law Review, 30,* 75-96.

U.S. News and World Report. (1983). A glut of lawyers—Impact on U.S. December 19, pp. 59-61.

Wood, B., Klein, S., Cross, H. Lammers, C., & Elliott, J. (1985). Impaired practitioners: Psychologists' opinions about prevalence and proposals for intervention. *Professional Psychology: Research and Practice, 16,* 843-850.

Wright, R. H. (1981). Psychologists and professional liability (malpractice) insurance. *American Psychologist, 36,* 1485-1493.

4

PSYCHOLOGICAL CONSULTATION IN MEDICAL SETTINGS: CHALLENGES AND CONSTRAINTS

Dennis Drotar

In recent years, career opportunities for psychologists in medical settings have expanded significantly (Matarazzo, 1980; Nathan, Lubin, Matarazzo, & Persely, 1979). Psychologists collaborate with physicians and health care professionals in a wide range of settings including general and specialized ambulatory services, hospital inpatient units, and centers for the treatment of chronic and acute conditions (Gabinet & Friedson, 1980; Linton, 1981; Routh, Schroeder, & Koocher, 1983; Wright, 1979). Following the recent development of specialized technologies in behavioral medicine (Davidson & Davidson, 1980; Degood, 1979; Russo & Varni, 1982) and health promotion (Matarazzo, Weiss, Herd, Miller, & Weiss, 1984), psychologists who practice in medical settings employ a range of clinical and research methods with varied clinical problems. It is now well recognized that the practice of psychology in medical settings has extended the knowledge base and influence of psychology as a health profession (Schofield, 1969) and stimulated research and practice innovations concerning the interrelationship between physical and psychological health (Schwartz, 1982). Although the opportunities for psychologists in medical settings are undeniable, the professional practice of psychology in such settings remains a combination of challenge and threat: Special advantages of medical settings as work environments include stimulating and varied patient populations, the opportunity to conduct research and clinical practice in areas of interest, and autonomy of functioning. On the other hand, clinical work in medical settings is demanding and stressful (Cartwright, 1979; Kushner & Asken, 1980). Psychologists must work within complex hospital environments in which interprofessional collaboration inevitably raises tensions as each profession negotiates its connection and autonomy with respect to the other (Drotar, 1982; McNamara, 1981).

Unless the psychologist understands the needs of medical practitioners as well as the special problems of psychological practice in medical settings, his or her success and work satisfaction will be compromised. However, knowledge of physicians and their settings is difficult to come by within current patterns of psychological training. Despite an increasing emphasis on medical and health psychology in graduate training, the overwhelming majority of psychologists do not receive substantial formal training in medical settings. Academic education in psychology is generally insulated from medical concepts and practices and from the pressures faced by physicians, nurses, and other health care professionals. Moreover, the complex forces that drive the practice of modern medicine in the United States are difficult to comprehend (Starr, 1982). As a consequence, there is a salient gap between psychological knowledge that is potentially applicable to medical problems and the practice of psychology in hospital settings. Skills in psychological consultation are an important means to facilitate the application of psychological knowledge to the clinical problems encountered in hospital settings. The purpose of this chapter is to describe the practice of psychological consultation-liaison in medical settings and the implications for psychology as a profession.

VARIETIES OF CONSULTATION
IN MEDICAL SETTINGS

Patient-Centered Consultation

Consultation refers to the interaction between one professional, a consultant, and another, a consultee, who asks for help concerning a problem with a client (patient) that falls within the consultant's area of interest and competence (Caplan, 1970). (See Gallesich [1982] for a comprehensive discussion of consultation in a variety of settings.) Among medical subspecialties, physicians frequently consult with others to request information such as a diagnosis or suggestions for management. However, psychological consultation is much broader than medical consultation in scope and follows different models. Caplan's (1970) distinctions among types of consultation are applicable to medical settings. In client-centered consultation, which is the closest to the medical tradition, a physician consultee who has difficulty dealing with the management of one of his patients calls a psychological consultant for advice concerning the patient's difficulties (Caplan, 1970). The psychological consultant examines the patient and makes recommendations for management. For example, a patient who is being followed for a chronic illness, asthma, troubles his physician because he is not taking his medication. The physician requests a psychological evaluation to determine the factors that are contributing to the patient's noncompliance and for suggestions concerning management. The psychologist provides information to help the physician manage his or her patient more effectively.

Consultee-Centered Consultation

Another form of consultation, which Caplan (1970) terms consultee-centered consultation, focuses on the physician's functioning to enhance his or her capacity to care for the patient and to benefit similar patients in the future. The advantages of consultee-centered consultation, which has also been described as process-educative consultation (Stabler, 1979), include dialogue between the physician and psychologist and greater potential for the physician's acquisition of psychological skill and knowledge. This consultation model has different implications for the psychologist's functioning than patient-centered consultation. For example, in the case of the chronically ill patient with asthma described earlier, the psychologist who works in accord with a consultee-centered model of consultation would not necessarily see the patient. Alternatively, the psychologist would help the physician find ways of understanding the source of the patient's compliance problem and develop methods to help the patient cope more effectively with the illness. Although this consultation model has much to recommend it, it is difficult to implement in practice because of time constraints and because it differs from the precedent set by medical consultation.

Systems Consultation

Psychological consultation can productively involve groups of professionals. Systems-oriented consultation is useful because patient care activities take place in a complex social structure (Miller, 1973). Factors such as work-related pressures or interpersonal conflicts between staff and patients often influence the kinds of problems referred to the psychological consultant (Bates, 1970; Drotar, 1976a, 1977b). For this reason, it may be difficult to effectively implement patient-centered consultation unless one addresses issues that relate to the social context of medical care. In addition, a systems orientation also can open up exciting opportunities for psychological consultants to participate in the planning of health care practices rather than be compelled to react to the considerable pressures of problematic hospital structures (Ack, 1974; Tefft & Simeonsson, 1979). Despite the undeniable attractiveness and importance of systems-oriented consultation, it is probably the most difficult of consultation models to implement in medical settings for a number of reasons: The participants in a problematic clinic or hospital structure are not always aware of the forces that shape their behavior. Even when problematic aspects of hospital structure and organization are obvious, psychological consultation is not necessarily the route that is chosen to ameliorate these problems. Yet, even though a systems consultation may not always be necessary or possible, a thorough understanding of the impact of health care settings on practitioners, patient care, and psychological services is one of the most valuable tools of the psychological consultant (Miller, 1973).

Liaison and Program Development

Although consultation-liaison is often considered to be a unit, it is useful to make a working distinction between these two activities. Consultation refers to the specific activities of working with other professions, whereas liaison refers more generally to interprofessional relationships and program development involving psychology and medicine. The level of program development of psychological services in medical settings depends upon a complex set of factors, including mutual collaborative interests, hospital budgetary constraints, and the degree to which medical programs and individual medical practitioners are supportive of psychological services. Issues related to program development in psychological consultation are described in subsequent sections.

SETTING DIFFERENCES IN CONSULTATION

The nature of the medical setting determines the patient populations seen by physicians and the consultation requests made to psychologists. Medical settings are heterogeneous and differ with respect to populations served, size and structure, physician specialty, academic or training emphasis, and ambulatory versus inpatient focus. Psychologists consult to physicians in a remarkable array of settings such as group medical practices, prepaid ambulatory practices, general community hospitals, academic teaching hospitals, subspecialty clinics, and rehabilitation hospitals. Specific requests for psychological consultation vary with demographic and developmental characteristics of patient populations (for example, whether one is dealing with adults, adolescents, or pediatric patients). However, common referral problems include management of psychological aspects of chronic illness, differential diagnosis of somatic symptoms, management of pain, psychosomatic disorders, suicidal behavior, problems with compliance, family adaptation to acute or chronic disease, patient psychological reactions to acute medical problems, and assessment of intellectual or neuropsychological functioning (Degood, 1979; Drotar, 1976b,

1977a; Epstein & Cluss, 1982; LeBaron & Zeltzer, 1985; Lipowski, 1967a,b; Magrab, 1978; Schubert & Friedson, 1980).

Teaching Hospitals

University-based teaching hospitals are a common site for the practice of psychological consultation. Such settings emphasize inpatient consultation and are characterized by a large number of physicians, including physicians-in-training (house staff) and subspecialists, as well as high patient volume. In addition, like his or her physician counterparts, the psychologist in a teaching hospital usually has multiple responsibilities such as teaching and research that extend beyond patient care. The psychologist in a large teaching hospital is often part of a psychology department, which is only one of a number of professional disciplines that care for the behavioral or mental health needs of patients.

In many large teaching hospitals, medical care is centered around specialized wards such as a surgical ward or adolescent unit. Focusing psychological consultation on specialty wards has a number of advantages: The consulting psychologist can establish ongoing relationships with medical and nursing staff, be visible and available to the staff, and develop structures of group problem solving and management that transcend the efficacy of case-by-case consultation (Drotar, 1975, 1982; Geist, 1977). Geist's (1977) eloquent description of consultation on a pediatric surgical ward presents an interesting, practical account of setting-specific consultation.

Subspecialty-Oriented Settings

One of the most salient characteristics of modern medicine is its highly specialized nature (Mechanic, 1972). Many physicians concentrate their activities on populations that may relate to a specific organ system (such as cardiology) or type of care (such as intensive care). In subspecialty consultation, the psychologist works with a specific patient population and the medical subspecialists who care for them. Subspecialty-oriented psychological consultation has now been described for a number of specialties such as spinal cord injury (Linton, 1981), neurology (Harper, Wiens, & Hammerstad, 1981), renal disease (Drotar, Ganofsky, Makker, & DeMaio, 1981), oncology (Koocher, Sourkes, & Keane, 1979), cardiology (Bloom, 1979), multiple sclerosis (Pavlou, Johnson, Davis, & Lefebvre, 1979), and neonatology (Magrab & Davitt, 1975). Subspecialty-oriented psychological consultation has a number of advantages: Given the specialized nature of their work, many physicians wish to have their "own" psychologist who can meet the unique service, teaching, and research needs of their patient population. In addition, collaborative research and practice is an efficient way to generate new knowledge concerning the etiology and management of medical disorders, especially those (for example, asthma, headaches, hypertension, diabetes, and obesity) that involve interrelationships between medical and psychological influences (Blanchard & Andrasik, 1982; Brownell, 1982; Creer, 1982; Whitehead & Bosmajian, 1982). Finally, subspecialty-oriented consultation can develop comprehensive care approaches that involve more efficient care, advocacy for patients and their families, and open intrastaff communication (Drotar et al., 1981; Harper et al., 1981; Koocher et al., 1979).

Ambulatory Settings

The ambulatory setting offers the psychological consultant a congenial opportunity for focusing on prevention (Wertlieb, 1979), a goal that is all too often lost in the heat of the frenetic pace and emphasis on disease management that characterizes inpatient settings. Although the clinical problems encountered in ambulatory settings overlap with those encountered in inpatient settings, they are generally less emergent (Griswold, 1980; Schroeder, 1979). In addition, because psychologists in ambulatory settings work with a smaller group of physicians, they may have a greater opportunity to impact upon medical practice (Smith, Rome, & Freedheim, 1967).

A number of interesting models of psychological liaison have been described in ambulatory settings, including joint practice arrangements in which psychologists work closely with a number of physicians. Schroeder's (1979) consultation with a pediatric practice is a model program that has generated innovative models of psychological service and training (Routh et al., 1983; Schroeder, Goolsby, & Strangler, 1975). At the other end of the spectrum, it should also be noted that psychological consultation in ambulatory clinic settings can be fraught with frustrations related to the problematic structure of clinic settings and the delivery of care to difficult-to-reach populations (Botinelli, 1975).

Community Hospitals

Because most community hospitals do not have the numbers of faculty physicians and house staff that are characteristic of larger medical centers, in some respects they may be more manageable settings. Community hospitals are highly individual cultures that are shaped by the practicing physicians in these settings. In addition, it is not uncommon for psychologists who work in such settings to be the only representative of their discipline and to feel somewhat isolated. Because community

hospitals often do not have access to the same level of resources for referral as other settings, psychologists in community medical centers must function very independently as organizers of programs (Linton, 1981).

Rehabilitation Hospitals

In keeping with the goal of restoration of psychological
and physical functioning to individuals who have suffered dis-
abling illnesses or injuries, psychological consultation in
rehabilitation hospitals has a highly specialized flavor
(Grzesiak, 1979). In these settings, patient populations are
very complex and require the efforts of many professional
disciplines. Given their unique expertise, psychological consultants in rehabilitation hospitals may also assume leadership
roles in organization and implementation of treatment plans.

THE PROCESS OF PSYCHOLOGICAL CONSULTATION

The consultation process usually begins with a request for
"help" from a physician or other health care professional to
the psychologist. This request may reflect issues such as
confusion about the overall diagnosis and management of a
case, an interest in specific information, and concerns of
family members or other staff. In addition, a number of other
pressures, which may not be stated, may influence the request.
For example, a psychological consultation request may be an
unstated way to obtain help with the uncertainties and frustrations of emotionally demanding patients (Groves, 1978). In
view of the fact that many psychological problems are perceived by physicians as inherently difficult and unsatisfying
(Duff, Rowe, & Anderson, 1972), psychological consultation
provides an avenue to have someone else manage these problems. Psychological consultation requests may also be triggered
by highly stressed and angered patients who present with confusing physical symptoms. The multifaceted nature of consultation requests requires psychologists to become familiar with
the nature of the physician's relationship with patient, family,
or staff, ideally in a close, day-to-day working collaboration.
The psychologist's appreciation of the physician's work context
will often facilitate his or her understanding of consultation
requests that initially may seem poorly articulated.

Consultation Etiquette

Requests for a psychological consultation should be sanc-
tioned by the physician who is in charge of the patient's
medical care. Even though many referrals for psychological

consultation are stimulated by other professionals, especially nursing staff, it is important that these requests be cleared with the physician of record lest the psychologist be seen as encroaching on the patient. Another important issue concerns preparation of the patient for the psychological consultation. More often than not, the physician requests a referral in situations where problems have not been identified by the patient or family as psychological in character. Since many people understandably resist labeling of their problems as psychologically based, physicians sometimes shy away from discussion of psychological consultation with their patients. Unfortunately, unless the patient is prepared, the consultation may not be as productive as it otherwise might be. For this reason, the physician and psychologist should discuss what to tell the patient concerning the reason for the consultation and what to expect. However, given the demands of medical care and the difficulties some physicians have in explaining psychological issues to patients, the consulting psychologist should also be prepared for the fact that the patient may not have been told very much about the consultation.

What are the responsibilities of the psychological consultant? As in medical consultation, the psychological consultant is expected to respond rapidly and provide useful information to the physician. We have found that feedback to the referring physician is often most helpful when repeated in several modes, such as a note in the medical chart followed by face-to-face verbal communication and a psychological report (Drotar, Benjamin, Chwast, Litt, & Vajner, 1981). In addition to information about the patient's psychological status, many physicians are interested in direct help with case management. For example, a psychologist is asked to consult with a 22-year-old patient with chronic abdominal pain to determine to what extent stress may be playing a role in the expression of the symptoms. The interview and psychological testing (MMPI) suggest that the patient's symptoms reflect a maladaptive response to family stresses, including severe marital discord, and the psychologist recommends marital therapy. The physician who is given the results of this consultation is likely to ask: "What do I do now?" Many physicians are quite appreciative if they receive help with the patient's disposition, especially with such things as information concerning referral sources or direct help with intervention and follow-up. In my experience, conjoint psychological and medical intervention offers an especially productive opportunity for psychologists and physicians to learn to work together.

Recurrent Tensions in Consultation

Experienced psychological consultants eventually learn that the course of consultation to physicians is not always smooth

and that it is useful to anticipate interdisciplinary tensions
that can arise. Psychological consultation requires communication among at least three parties: the patient, the physician,
and the psychologist. In addition, the psychological consultant
has two distinct consumers of his product: the physician and
the patient, whose satisfaction with the product of a given
consultation may not be comparable. Given differing professional perspectives and the complexity of clinical problems,
disagreements between psychologists and physicians concerning
the nature of a patient's problem and course of treatment are
inevitable. Consider the following case: a physician consults
a psychologist concerning a cancer patient's symptoms of
anxiety, requesting behavioral intervention to reduce them.
The psychologist sees the patient and family and discovers
that the patient's distress is related to the realities of her
medical condition, which is terminal. Moreover, the patient and
family are upset by what they perceive as the physician's withdrawal from them at a critical time. They say they can never
find the physician, whom they feel never gives them a straight
answer about what to expect, and report that they are angered
and insulted by the psychological consultation. Given the
stated referral problem, should the psychologist go ahead and
do behavioral modification? Would this be in the patient's best
interest? If one doesn't fulfill the consultation as stated in the
request and instead communicates the nature of the family's
feelings to the physician, would this alienate the physician?
The "answer" to this difficult consultation request is a very
ambitious one: that is, to listen to physician, patient, and
family to make a determination about what is in the patient's
best interest, and strive to reconcile conflicting interprofessional perspectives in the patient's interests.

WORKING WITHIN THE HOSPITAL CULTURE

In view of the fact that functioning in a medical system
depends upon knowledge of the hospital culture, the psychological consultant should take the initiative in learning about
the hospital or clinic and its staff. Attendance at formal conferences and medical rounds, as well as informal presence in
hospital wards and clinics are useful ways to facilitate this
learning. Physical presence communicates visibility, availability,
and interest in the medical and nursing staff's activities. In
addition, the informal exchanges facilitated by an active physical presence helps medical staff become familiar with the
psychologist's individual style, values, and interests (Geist,
1977). Even more important, such contacts give the psychologist an opportunity to discover those physicians who have a
special interest in psychological issues and are congenial collaborators in patient care or research (Drotar, Benjamin, et al.,
1981).

Beyond visibility, psychological consultants in medical settings gain credibility through demonstration of effective actions in clinical assessments, interventions, and research that prove helpful to patients and to medical and nursing staff. In the action-dominated medical setting, the psychologist's willingness to become involved with difficult patients and facilitate effective case dispositions is highly prized by medical staff. In fact, individual physicians' initial requests for psychological consultation often include an unstated "test" of the psychologist's competence or ability to work with their patients. Thus it is not uncommon for initial referrals for psychological consultation to be among the physician's most vexing, or "hateful," patients (Groves, 1978). In the interests of fostering relationships with the medical staff, it is helpful to respond to such initial consultation requests even if they seem poorly framed, ambiguous, unreasonably emergent, or downright impossible. In such situations, at the very least, one can acknowledge and commiserate with the physician's frustrations. As the consultant becomes established in the setting and gains credibility, referrals for psychological consultation can be screened with greater consistency (Drotar, Benjamin, et al., 1981).

THE IMPACT OF HOSPITAL CULTURE
ON PSYCHOLOGICAL CONSULTATION

With few exceptions (Ack, 1974), most hospital environments are not designed to address patients' emotional needs. In most hospitals, physical space is limited, and patients and their families spend time on crowded wards or in congested, noisy clinics. The close proximity of rooms, lack of sound-proofing, and frequent interruptions constrain patient-professional transactions (Drotar, Benjamin, et al., 1981).

Medical diagnosis and treatment take place within a compressed time span relative to psychological services. Physicians see large numbers of patients each day and are mandated to solve each clinical problem quickly. Physicians who are accustomed to working with many patients in a brief time tend to underestimate the time involved in psychological services and may not recognize that meaningful psychological intervention often takes place in a series of extended contacts rather than in one encounter. Although the enterprising psychologist will accommodate to the time pressures inherent in hospital culture by working more quickly than is necessary in other settings, working as rapidly as physicians might wish may not always be realistic or in a patient's best interests.

Physicians' expectations concerning the psychologist's functioning are heavily influenced by their prior experiences with medical consultations. For example, many physicians perceive psychologists as diagnostic experts similar to medical consultants and may expect that a psychological evaluation will inevitably generate quantifiable information in the same way that other medical consultations involve quantifiable laboratory test results. It should be noted that in some instances, specific requests for psychological testing reflect broader problems in the delivery of psychological services to difficult patient populations. For example, we were asked to screen the psychological adjustment of patients with severe renal disease to determine who would be a "good" candidate for transplantation. Such requests could not be answered accurately and did not address the compelling needs of each and every patient. In the interests of furthering collaboration, we initially complied with these requests as best we could. Over time, our clinical experiences with patients and families eventually helped develop services that facilitated the provision of psychosocial support to all patients with renal failure and their families so that psychological screening was no longer judged as necessary (Drotar, Ganofsky, et al., 1981).

The Impact of Work-Related Stresses

Professionals in hospital settings work under a high level of stress (Cartwright, 1979). Physicians and nurses witness great suffering that they cannot assuage, and most function within the limitations and uncertainties of medical knowledge (Fox, 1979). Because their volume of work cannot be easily controlled, medical staff can feel overwhelmed and, hence, not in control of their work. Moreover, in medical school settings, faculty members face the added demands of teaching, research, and writing, which can pull them in a variety of directions. Such work-related stresses can influence the staff's appraisal of psychological functioning of their patients such that understandable patient reactions to stress may be misconstrued as psychopathology. To be most effective, the psychologist must recognize when requests for psychological consultation are influenced by the staff's feelings of helplessness or anxiety, such as in the following case: The parents of a very sick premature infant, who had been on a respirator for two months, troubled the staff and triggered a request of psychological consultation. The family wanted a new doctor and "their own" nurse who would care for their child. The family's response was characterized not only by anger but also by attachment, especially to the nursing staff. The parents had brought gifts for the nurses and made positive relationships with a number of staff members. The staff was helped to see that there was a realistic basis to the parents' anxiety and anger concerning their infant's life-threatening condition. In addition, with support, the staff began to deal more completely with the parents' difficult but realistic questions concerning the child's condition.

The Acute Illness Model

In medical hospitals, patient care is conducted according to an acute infectious disease model, which involves rapid diagnosis, institution of treatment, and anticipated remission of symptoms. In this model, attention is given to present rather than past problems and directed toward physical diagnosis rather than consideration of the patient's psychosocial functioning in life contexts. Clinical problems that clash with this model of care are not easily accommodated in medical settings. For example, chronic illnesses or psychosocial problems that require more prolonged assessment and intervention are especially frustrating to physicians because they do not fit an acute disease model (Engel, 1977) and cannot be treated rapidly or easily (Duff et al., 1972). In other situations, application of the acute disease model to conditions that do not fit this model, such as functionally based pain, can lead to simplistic clinical dispositions. The focus on acute care also can influence expectations for psychological consultation. For example, some physicians expect that a psychological consultation will fit within the framework of an acute infectious disease and lead inevitably to a rapid and effective intervention.

The infectious disease medical model also has significant implications for the structuring of patient-physician interaction. For many medical conditions, treatments are prescribed for and applied to a patient who is directed to take them. When a patient or family is unwilling or unable to follow medical advice, they may be labeled as uncooperative, or as having a serious emotional problem. It is often very difficult for physicians to recognize the transactional nature of the patient-physician relationship and that patients' expectations can legitimately clash with their own views.

The Hospital as an Interdisciplinary Organization

To facilitate patient care, medical facilities require cooperative interaction among a large number of professional disciplines. Because lines of authority and communication in most hospitals are structured along disciplinary lines rather than with regard to patient care functions, coordination of patient care is inevitably disputed (Friedman, 1985; Mechanic, 1972). The sheer numbers of professional disciplines, each with its own responsibilities, language, perspective, and physical location cannot easily be molded into a cohesive unit with a unifying purpose. Moreover, the array of professional disciplines is often quite confusing to families, who may receive discrepant information from different people (Mechanic, 1972). Since sound psychological assessment usually involves an understanding of the patient's adjustment in the context of his or her transactions with other professional disciplines, psychologists in medical settings face a formidable task in gathering relevant information concerning the staff's observations of the patient as well as in integrating their interventions with that of other professional disciplines.

INTERDISCIPLINARY COLLABORATION

In the interdisciplinary world of the medical setting, it is very important that psychologists recognize and value the potential contributions of other disciplines. Concerted and effective planning among psychologists and those professions who share expertise in the psychosocial aspects of medical care is critical to effective patient care and consultation. Psychiatrists and social workers provide valuable consultation-liaison services that potentially complement psychological consultation. However, given the fact that there are few structures for interdisciplinary collaboration in medical settings, competition and fragmentation of effort often characterize the relationships among psychologists and other psychosocial disciplines. In addition, because more than one profession can perform consultation services such as interviewing patient and family, case formulation, and recommendations for management, the medical staff is not always certain whom they should call concerning a given clinical problem. This is a special problem if guidelines have not been worked out and articulated to the medical staff. For example, a medical intern who was quite concerned about the psychological status of a depressed and suicidal young man requested consultations from three separate disciplines: psychology, psychiatry, and social work. This was not only very confusing to the patient and his family but to the nursing staff. After a number of meetings, the three consultants organized a plan that involved one person taking major responsibility for evaluation of the patient's emotional status and another for the family.

Given the wide individual differences in expertise within professions and differences in level of program development in different settings, it is difficult to set policies concerning optimal deployment of psychosocial services. In my experience, physician utilization of psychosocial services from various professional disciplines relates more to such factors as availability and visibility, perceived helpfulness, and experiences with individuals than it does to professional affiliation per se. Some settings have strong departments of liaison psychiatry that perform a great many functions including assessment, treatment, and research that are accomplished by psychologists or social workers in other settings (Naylor & Mattson, 1973). Social workers may also have a predominant role as consultants on hospital wards and may be leaders of specialized areas of program development such as child abuse and neglect services.

Despite considerable overlap in roles, psychosocial consultants from different disciplines can contribute unique expertise. For example, psychologists are generally experienced in assessment and research and can respond very effectively to requests concerning information about intellectual functioning, academic achievement, or behavioral interventions. Many psychiatrists are especially well versed in the use of medication and in interventions with individuals on medical wards who present with serious psychopathology or psychosomatic disorders. In some settings (although this is by no means universal), psychiatrists may handle the majority of consultations concerning emergencies such as suicide attempts. Many social workers have special expertise in family dynamics and knowledge of community agencies and are heavily utilized as front-line consultants in some hospitals.

ADAPTING CLINICAL AND CONSULTATION METHODS TO MEDICAL SETTINGS

Effective styles of psychological consultation should fit the problems of the patient, the needs of the medical consultee, and the setting demands. In many settings, the curbside or hallway consultation is a valuable strategy. Standing in a busy clinic intersection to give advice or clarify a case may appear superficial or vague but has very real value in building relationships and providing effective clinical services. In addition, conjoint psychologist-physician assessment and follow-up can be particularly helpful in psychosomatic disorders and chronic physical conditions, in which judicious diagnosis and treatment requires close interdisciplinary collaboration. In such cases, conjoint conduct of patient and family interviews is a productive collaborative approach.

Successful psychological consultants often develop a range of roles and strategies in their work with physicians and nursing staff, which may include group-oriented approaches to consultation, skills in teaching physicians, and specialized clinical interventions (Stabler & Mesibov, 1984).

Group-Oriented Consultation

Given the scarcity of contexts for different professional disciplines to discuss their work as a group in medical settings, psychologists may be very helpful to staff by facilitating joint meetings for staff to address patient care problems. Such groups may take very different forms, depending on the work environment and the nature of the clinical problems that are encountered. For example, a group case conference may begin with a brief history by the physician or nurse who requested that a case be discussed. After a presentation of the history,

input can be obtained from other staff concerning their observations. If the psychology staff has seen the patient or family,
these impressions are useful to present. As the staff share
their concerns and provide further information, management
approaches and alternatives for working with patients and their
families can be discussed.

The free-ranging discussions that can take place in interdisciplinary group meetings can sometimes involve role conflicts
with nursing and house staff (Bates, 1970), diagreements between house staff and senior staff, and generalized frustrations
about the work environment. For example, in a discussion of a
patient with sickle cell anemia who presented in a pain crisis
and was described as psychologically distrubed, the medical
staff reported that they felt especially helpless because they
could neither make a diagnosis nor solve the presenting complaint. They did not have objective evidence to know how much
was "real" pain and how much was due to other factors. A
related concern included the staff's fears that they might "hurt"
the patient through their efforts by addicting him to pain
medications if he did not have "real" pain. As these sources
of stress were clarified, the staff's anxieties diminished and
they were able to relate more productively to the patient and
his family.

Teaching Physicians

Using psychological consultation to teach physicians about
the psychological aspects of care has a number of advantages.
There is a need for physicians to learn about the psychological
aspects of patient care, diagnosis and intervention with psychosocial problems, and communication with patients and their families. To the extent that physicians learn more effective ways
of interacting with patients, they may make earlier diagnoses
of psychological problems, more effective referrals, and conduct more effective preventive intervention (Caplan, 1959).
In addition, to the extent that physicians can learn about the
contributions of psychology to patient care, they may begin
to construe psychological services as integral to their efforts.

Unfortunately, there are many obstacles to the education
of physicians concerning the psychological aspects of patient
care. Such teaching must compete with demands to learn specialized medical knowledge. However, the interested psychological consultant can develop teaching methods such as
informal teaching via consultation, formal conferences, and
elective experiences, which are suited to the setting (Drotar,
1974).

In many hospitals, psychological consultations provide the
main vehicle for teaching psychological principles to physicians.
Discussion of the physicians' conceptualizations of the referral
problem can improve their formulation of future referral ques-

tions. The psychologist may facilitate additional learning by inviting the physician to observe psychological testing or interviewing of the patient or family. Finally, discussions of the implications of the psychological evaluation, followed by collaborative communication of recommendations to the patient, is another means of providing teaching.

Formal conferences are another effective means of teaching. Conferences can be integrated into the medical training program and function most effectively if staff-level physicians participate in their respective areas of interest and expertise. In addition, conferences are most effective if case material is brought in to illustrate principles of management and if abstract, theoretical discussions of psychological data are minimized. Video and audio tape recordings of interviews and evaluations are useful teaching aids.

One of the most effective means of teaching physicians includes elective experiences for residents in the psychological aspects of practice. An elective can involve a one- or two-month rotation in the senior resident's program. Since the resident is freed of most other obligations during this elective time, he or she is able to have a more intensive training experience in a particular area of interest. A major advantage of this means of teaching is that it allows the psychologist to organize the content and structure of the resident's teaching experience and still plan a flexible teaching experience that addresses the interests of the individual resident. In the course of an elective the physicians see a variety of patients with psychological disorders, some of which respond positively to relatively brief interventions and provide an opportunity for prevention (Caplan, 1959).

PSYCHOLOGICAL INTERVENTIONS

The psychological consultant should be familiar with the range of intervention modalities that are appropriate to medical-psychological problems. In view of the heavy service demands of medical settings, expertise in brief interventions and behavioral approaches are particularly valuable. In addition, familiarity with family-centered intervention approaches are especially useful with chronic illness populations and psychosomatic disorders (Drotar, Crawford, & Bush, 1984). Clinical problems commonly referred to psychologists in the medical setting often involve a complex interplay between organic and environmental influences. Psychologists may be asked to evaluate the relative contributions of psychological influences to psychosomatic problems such as asthma or diabetes, to help differentiate between psychological and organic influences in somatic symptoms such as pain or seizures, or to evaluate the factors involved in chronically ill patients' psychological adaptation to their diseases. Since each and every physical disease has a unique natural history, set of treatment regimens, and psychological demands that must be understood in order to appraise maladaptive versus adaptive adjustment, psychological consultants need to understand physical diseases, their treatment regimens, and the impact of physical disease and treatment on patient and family functioning (Johnson, 1979; Pless & Pinkerton, 1975). Prospective experience with patients of different ages and a lifespan developmental perspective are quite valuable to the psychological consultant who works with chronically ill patients and their families (Eisenberg, Sutkin, & Jansen, 1984). In addition, clinicians in medical settings often find it useful to construe clinical problems in ways that depart from psychopathology-based concepts. For example, a coping and adaptational framework that emphasizes the functional relationship of a patient's behavior to the unique circumstances associated with a chronic illness is especially well suited to medical populations (Lazarus, 1966).

Crisis Intervention and Brief Therapy

Crisis intervention techniques characterized by immediate clarification and specification of a course of action are often effective with highly stressed patients or family members. For example, a young mother presented in the ambulatory practice with her infant son who was "crying all day and night" and keeping everyone in the family awake. She was angered by an alleged insulting remark by the receptionist, became defensive and hostile, and demanded to have the infant hospitalized. In collaboration with the nurse and physician, the psychologist's clarifications and supportive crisis work with this distraught mother allowed amelioration of this problem. When this mother was able to receive reassurance that her baby would not be taken away from her, she behaved more rationally and responded to supportive follow-up (Drotar, Benjamin, et al., 1981).

One of the appeals of brief therapy stems from its promise to provide economical, explicit, and specific treatment analogous to the prescriptive treatment of the physician. In medical settings, time-limited brief therapy can be used with great advantage to facilitate the adjustment of patients who present with a range of psychological problems. For example, a 25-year-old young woman with cystic fibrosis, a chronic, life-threatening condition, presented with depression during a hospitalization. This was her first hospital admission in a long time and she experienced it as catastrophic. During her two-week hospitalization, psychological intervention helped her to recognize that her depression was related to a number of factors such as a recent transition from home to college and a break-up with her boyfriend, and was not a direct consequence of her illness. With the help of her physician, she was helped to understand her physical status, which was much better than she had feared, and she eventually returned to her life activities.

Behavioral Approaches

Many physicians are quite interested in behavior modification and biofeedback interventions for their patients. Although requests for behavioral approaches may not always be realistic, they can reflect a physician's appropriate interest in an action-oriented solution to a difficult patient care problem as well as familiarity with the impressive application of learning principles to an increasing range of clinical problems (Degood, 1979; Keefe, 1982; Russo & Varni, 1982). For example, the application of biofeedback and relaxation training in clinical practice was demonstrated in the case of a young man with multiple symptoms including anxiety, abdominal pain, and headaches who had received multiple psychiatric diagnoses during multiple hospital admissions. However, he did not comply with prior recommendations for psychotherapy. The psychologist's use of a systematic program of desensitization for his anxiety and biofeedback for his headaches and abdominal pain proved to be an effective way for him to obtain mastery over his symptoms. Conjoint psychological and medical follow-up helped to maintain his symptom-free status when he returned home.

RESEARCH

Research in Consultation-Liaison Programs

Although psychological consultation is often thought of as a strictly clinical activity, our experience suggests that there are many advantages in establishing psychological research within a consultation-liaison program. Research can generate new knowledge concerning biopsychosocial conditions, the interrelationship between health and behavior, and the efficacy of consultation-liaison. Such research is critical to the development of the emerging field of psychological applications to medical settings (Christopherson & Rapoff, 1980; Routh, 1985). The incorporation of research activities into consultation-liaison programs is also quite attractive to physicians and can facilitate program development. Physicians are generally interested in psychological research that is potentially applicable to clinical practice. In addition, because research grants and publications are important to the career advancement of physicians in academic settings, collaborative medical and psychological research is seen as personally advantageous as well as helpful to patients.

Perhaps the major obstacle to the development of psychological research activity in medical settings is one that is all too familiar to clinician-researchers: the demands of time and energy required by the conjoint conduct of clinical and research activities. This dilemma is especially acute in medical settings where service demands are so high. Applied research in medical settings also involves special demands such as development of collaborative arrangements and time spent in subject recruitment. Despite these constraints, the setting provides a unique opportunity to conduct research on exciting, clinically relevant topics. In this regard, one of the most useful consultation-liaison strategies is to develop research projects with interested physician-collaborators. The trust that can emerge from initial clinical consultations concerning individual patients often provides a foundation for the kind of working relationship necessary to conduct collaborative research. For example, in our setting, clinical consultations concerning children, adolescents, and young adults with cystic fibrosis who were referred for a variety of adjustment problems (such as depression and school and family problems) stimulated interest in a number of research questions, including: (1) are the problems that were manifested by patients referred for psychological consultation the same as or different from those experienced by the majority of cystic fibrosis patients?; and (2) what are the individual and familial factors that differentiate patients who show age-adequate adjustment from those who show psychological difficulty? Aided by the interests and talents of student researchers, a number of research projects were completed that described the psychosocial adjustment of this interesting population (Kucia, Drotar, Doershuk, Stern, Boat, & Matthews, 1979; Drotar, Doershuk, Stern, Boat, Boyer, & Matthews, 1981).

Evaluation of Consultation

Research directly pertaining to psychological consultation-liaison is a much-needed but complex endeavor. Psychological consultation can be evaluated from the standpoint of impact on patient care, including psychological and health outcomes, as well as impact on physician education or behavior. Although controlled evaluations of consultation programs are difficult to accomplish, descriptive evaluations are important for both practical and scientific reasons. In a cost-conscious era, it may be increasingly difficult to justify hospital expenditures for psychological consultation-liaison services, especially without data concerning their nature and potential efficacy. Documentation of consultation services can also serve an important purpose in educating hospital administrators and physicians concerning the potential contributions of psychological services to their programs. In addition to such pragmatic considerations, empirical studies of consultation services can be useful in helping psychologists to develop the most effective ways of providing services to medical patients and physicians and of reporting service innovations to colleagues in psychology and medicine.

Evaluation of consultation-liaison activities can occur at a number of different levels. At the first level, description, one can document the nature and type of psychological services provided to patients, especially increases or decreases over the course of time, special problems encountered in the course of delivering services, and solutions that were tried. Such basic information, which can be readily computerized, is extremely useful to administrators. A second kind of descriptive information concerns consultation to and education of physicians and hospital staff including the time spent in educational activities and the nature of educational approaches. Another kind of documentation concerns description of processes that occur in team meetings or group-oriented consultation. Description of the consultation process can be a helpful means of understanding the medical culture and its impact on physicians and nurses as well as in developing consultation techniques (Drotar, 1976a,b, 1977b).

A second level of evaluation concerns efficacy of consultation. Efficacy can be considered from the standpoint of consumer (patient and physician) satisfaction or, more formally, from an objective evaluation of intervention efficacy. Objective empirical studies are best accomplished in a limited area of focus such as the effects of psychological education on physicians' behavior and communication with patients or the efficacy of psychological consultation on staff perceptions of their work environment. Another relevant area of research concerns evaluation of the effects of psychological service innovations on patient care and symptoms. For example, evaluations of the impact of psychological services on medical utilization are quite relevant to the planning of consultation services. Follette and Cummings (1967) found significant reductions in medical usage after psychological treatment for a treated group with no reductions for an untreated comparison group. These differences were apparent on a five-year follow-up. Similar findings have been noted by Rosen and Wiens (1979) and Graves and Hastrup (1981) for children and adolescents in low-income families. Although these demonstrations were restricted to ambulatory services in prepaid health care plans, they provide a model for how one may look at outcomes in psychological consultation services that are provided to populations at risk.

TRAINING OF PSYCHOLOGICAL CONSULTANTS

Despite an increasing number of graduate programs that offer specialized training in health psychology, behavioral medicine, and pediatric psychology (Drotar 1978; Matarazzo, 1980; Olbrisch & Sechrest, 1979; Tuma, 1977, 1981), many psychologists begin their work in medical settings with traditional training backgrounds in clinical psychology that are supplemented by practicum, internship, or postdoctoral training experiences in medical settings. The psychologist who wishes to pursue a career in a medical setting should certainly not assume that traditional clinical or research training provides sufficient preparation to function effectively in a medical hospital. Clinical work and research in medical settings require special perspectives that can be acquired only by an intensive exposure to the workings of medical hospitals (Gabinet & Friedson, 1980; Stabler & Whitt, 1980; Tefft & Simeonsson, 1979) and the full range of clinical and consultation skills that are applicable to patient populations in these settings. Fortunately, there is an increasing number of training opportunities for psychological consultants in medical settings at graduate, internship, and postdoctoral levels (Drotar, 1978; Gabinet & Schubert, 1981). Although useful training experiences can be offered productively at all levels, postdoctoral training has special advantages for training psychologists to work in medical settings because such trainees can assume a high level of independence.

The development of training opportunities for psychologists in consultation-liaison in individual medical settings depends on a number of factors. First, a program of psychological consultation-liaison needs to be sufficiently well established to allow students to be supervised successfully. Given the patient care and collaborative demands of medical settings, it is asking too much of students, including those at an advanced level, to function without strong support of a supervisor. Another key ingredient of such training is access to an academic training program in psychology or a sufficient number of students who are interested in training in psychological consultation. Perhaps the most critical ingredient in a successful training program is the commitment and expertise of the clinical supervisor. An effective consultation training program needs to have an experienced supervisor who is interested in developing the talents of psychologist-clinicians to enable them to pursue careers in medical settings.

The heart of psychological training in consultation is the clinical consultation, which is a vehicle to learn skills in assessment, communication with physicians, intervention, and case management. Case consultations expose students to a range of medical and psychological problems in which they are expected to make rapid assessments and assume a high level of responsibility. It should be noted that the high level of clinical responsibility assumed by students is a double-edged sword. Although clinical students generally enjoy their active role in patient care, they also can feel stressed by the multiple demands and clinical problems they encounter (Drotar, 1978).

Beyond experiences in individual consultation, students can make effective use of observational experiences and development of independent consultation relationships with individual physicians and subspecialty groups. To participate in such programs, it is necessary for students to have both an in-depth and a prolonged exposure to the setting.

ACADEMIC DEPARTMENTS OF PSYCHOLOGY AND MEDICAL SETTINGS: PROSPECTS FOR COLLABORATION

The relationship among academic departments of psychology and medical settings has received very little attention in writings on consultation-liaison. The nature of this collaboration depends on the physical proximity of the settings and upon the degree to which mutual faculty interests can be identified and cultivated. Although the differing institutional aims of academic psychology versus medical settings generally limit the prospects for collaboration, there are potential advantages for each institution. For example, the training of psychologist-researchers and clinicians is very much enhanced by their exposure to medical settings. In addition, access to knowledge-able physicians and to research populations can facilitate the development of psychological knowledge concerning the biological basis of behavior and provide career opportunities for psychologists to conduct research with special populations such as chronic physical conditions, neurological disorders, and psychosomatic conditions. In light of a relatively limited job market for academic psychology, the opportunities for psychologists in medical settings to collaborate with physicians, nurse practitioners, and other professional disciplines assume special importance.

There are also a number of advantages for hospital and medical school settings to develop collaborations with psychology and academic departments. Psychology departments can provide expertise and resources that can be utilized in collaborative research that will advance knowledge. Medical clinicians are faced with many problems that can be productively handled by a psychologist's specialized clinical methods. Psychologists can establish unique programs of clinical assessment and intervention that can address the considerable clinical needs of patients in medical settings (Schraa & Jones, 1983; Wright, 1979).

Although collaboration between medical settings and psychology departments offers clear advantages, it is difficult to carve out space and time for such collaborations amidst other activities. In addition, unfamiliarity with the other discipline's culture and methods can breed interprofessional mistrust and contribute to isolation. Finally, there is generally little administrative precedent for interdisciplinary collaboration in medical settings.

PROGRAM DEVELOPMENT: PROFESSIONAL SURVIVAL AND GROWTH IN A MEDICAL SETTING

Given the demanding nature of work in medical settings, it is desirable for psychologists to reshape the direction of their professional roles and responsibilities in line with their interests to avoid diffusion of effort. Setting research or clinical priorities in accord with mutually productive and satisfying professional partnerships with physicians is a promising strategy. For example, one can choose to focus clinical energies on patient groups of special interest and consultative efforts toward physicians who have an interest in sharing decisionmaking. We have found that development of independent areas of interest is a singularly important means of reducing "burnout," which is increasingly recognized as a potential problem in high-stress pediatric or general medical settings (Koocher, 1980; Kushner & Asken, 1980). Group support is another aid to professional growth among psychologists in medical settings, who often work in highly specialized environments and need a chance to get together to discuss common professional concerns and directions for their work. Developing new initiatives as a group and participation in departmental-level planning is another useful goal. Planning new programs of research and intervention that are primarily directed by psychologists not only facilitates professional autonomy but also provides useful alternatives to strictly medical models of care (Drotar, Benjamin, et al., 1981).

In addition, active negotiation concerning the direction of psychology positions is critical to maintain professional integrity. One of the most troubling features of medical settings is that they have little administrative precedent to encompass the functioning of psychologists. One aspect of this problem concerns the administrative lines of authority for the functioning of psychologists. Should psychologists be responsible to hospital administrators, physicians, or members of their own discipline? A related issue, and one that is especially critical given the financial pressures on hospitals in a competitive marketplace, concerns responsibility for funding of psychological consultation services. There is no ideal administrative arrangement for psychological consultants in medical settings. In fact, a certain degree of administrative confusion may be the norm for such settings. Administrative arrangements under hospital or medical departments have various costs and benefits. Regardless of their specific administrative arrangement, one can anticipate that psychologists in medical settings will experience increasing pressure to generate funds for their activities through patient fees and grants. The programs that expand and develop their psychological services will be those that somehow manage to maintain a high-quality service with attention to fiscal responsibility. In addition, to achieve maximum autonomy within a medical setting, psychologists must become active in developing and maintaining control over sources of funding through patient fees and grants.

The fate of interprofessional relationships between physicians and psychologists may depend on the extent to which obstacles to collaboration can be addressed in the administrative and fiscal structures that are the basis of psychological consultation programs. Unfortunately, programmatic models of collaborative psychological service, training, or research in medical settings that have resulted in a long history of accomplishments, are relatively rare. Successful programs often depend upon a unique mix of local resources, especially the talents and interests of individual psychologists and physicians who have a special commitment to collaboration. The critical ingredients of successful long-term collaboration between physicians and psychologists in individual settings need to be defined, studied, and replicated (Wright, 1979).

TOWARD PRODUCTIVE COLLABORATION
WITH PHYSICIANS

Productive collaboration may be defined as an interdisciplinary relationship that is mutually beneficial to each profession, enhances the health of consumers, and yields a demonstrable product that advances knowledge in medical psychology (Drotar, 1985). Although it is tempting to assume that mutually beneficial professional interchanges will always result in demonstrable benefits to patients, the potential for competing claims between professional and family needs, particularly in an era of rapidly expanding medical technology (Friedson, 1970; Illich, 1975; McNett, 1981), is a reality that also must be considered. Obstacles that limit the quality of collaborations between psychology and medicine include intraprofessional divisiveness, interprofessional conflicts, and external constraints. Although the fact that psychologists differ greatly in their interests and ideas can be considered a strength of the profession, significant differences of opinion among psychologists concerning professional priorities are very confusing to physicians and disrupt collaboration.

Potential sources of conflict between psychologists and physicians include disagreements over method and practice (for example, which approach to take with patient populations), conflicts over role (for example, which discipline should perform a certain function), and conflicts over administrative control (for example, who has the authority to conduct programs).

In addition, interprofessional competition for patients and grant monies within a changing marketplace will continue to pose difficult challenges for collaboration. On the one hand, the survival and progress of medicine and psychology will depend upon the capacity of each discipline to secure resources for the conduct of practice, science, and training. However, these professions will have to choose between resource-securing strategies that promote one profession at the expense of (or in isolation from) the other versus those that occur in respectful concert with mutual aims. A reciprocal strategy is not only in the best interest of patients and their families but would appear to be the most productive way to generate new scientific knowledge (Drotar, 1983).

General institutional constraints can also have profound effects on the quality and productivity of interdisciplinary collaboration and delivery of services. As Friedman (1985) has well described, administrative structures in medical settings tend to encourage competition, isolation, and fragmentation of effort among professions. In addition, patterns of insurance reimburseability that channel hospital care toward acute, catastrophic diseases and specialized technological procedures rather than prevention (Gallagher, 1972; Iscoe, 1981) pose formidable constraints that profoundly shape the nature of patient care and professional functioning.

CONCLUSION

From the standpoint of public health, the most important consequence of the rapid expansion of medical health and psychology is the access afforded our profession to the health care of large numbers of patients and their families. Such access provides not only a viable professional alternative to traditional clinical settings (Schofield, 1969), but also a unique opportunity to contribute to the improvement of psychological health in ways that cannot be accomplished by physicians alone.

Psychologists have made significant strides in the practice of psychology in medical settings, which is characterized by pluralistic methods tailored to the patients' presenting problems and the exigencies of specific settings. Productive forms of psychological consultation include patient-centered, consultee- or physician-centered, and systems-oriented consultation. Psychological consultation takes place in a complex social system that must be thoroughly understood in order to provide effective psychological consultation. The course of psychological consultation is heavily influenced by aspects of hospital culture such as differing professional perspectives, the time pressures of patient care, work-related stresses, the interdisciplinary organization of the hospital, and the acute illness model. Effective implementation of psychological consultation depends upon the psychologist's ability to tailor clinical methods to individual settings. Techniques of consultation and clinical practice that are particularly suited to medical settings include conjoint physician and psychologist collaborative management, group-oriented consultation, crisis intervention, and behavior modification. Specialized aspects of program development in psychological consultation include research that is directly related to consultation activities, training physicians in the psychosocial aspects of care, training psychologists to function as consultants in medical settings, and developing collaborative links between academic departments of psychology and medical settings.

To best facilitate their professional functioning, psychologists in medical settings need to develop mechanisms of group planning, mutual support, and funding for their programs. The fate of interprofessional relationships between physicians and psychologists may well depend upon the extent to which obstacles to collaboration can be addressed in administrative structures that form the basis of psychological consultation programs. The profession of psychology has a primary responsibility to develop approaches to clinical care and research that change existing patterns of medical care to facilitate the psychological well-being of patients and families.

REFERENCES

Ack, M. (1974). The psychological environment of a children's hospital. *Pediatric Psychology, 2,* 3-5.

Bates, B. (1970). Doctor and nurse: Changing roles and relations. *New England Journal of Medicine, 283,* 129-134.

Blanchard, E. B., & Andrasik, F. (1982). Psychological assessment and treatment of headache: Recent developments and emerging issues. *Journal of Consulting and Clinical Psychology, 50,* 859-879.

Bloom, L. J. (1979). Psychology and cardiology: Collaboration in coronary treatment and prevention. *Professional Psychology, 10,* 485-490.

Botinelli, S. B. (1975). Establishment of an outpatient psychology screening clinic: Preliminary considerations. *Pediatric Psychology, 3,* 10-11.

Brownell, K. D. (1982). Obesity: Understanding and treating a serious, prevalent, and refractory disorder. *Journal of Consulting and Clinical Psychology, 50,* 820-840.

Caplan, G. (1959). Practical steps for the family physician in the prevention of emotional disorder. *Journal of the American Medical Association, 77,* 1497-1506.

——. (1970). *The theory and practice of mental health consultation.* New York: Basic Books.

Cartwright, L. K. (1979). Sources and effects of stress in health careers. In G. C. Stone, F. Cohen, & N. E. Adler (Eds.), *Health psychology* (pp. 419-446). San Francisco: Jossey-Bass.

Christopherson, E. R., & Rapoff, M. A. (1980). Pediatric psychology: An appraisal. In B. B. Lahey & A. E. Kazdin (Eds.), *Advances in clinical child psychology* (Vol. 3, pp. 311-332). New York: Plenum Press.

Creer, T. L. (1982). Asthma. *Journal of Consulting and Clinical Psychology, 50,* 912-921.

Davidson, P. O., & Davidson, S. (1980). *Behavioral medicine: Changing health lifestyles.* New York: Brunner/Mazel.

Degood, D. E. (1979). A behavioral pain management program: Expanding the psychologist's role in a medical setting. *Professional Psychology, 10,* 491-502.

Drotar, D. (1974). The role of the pediatric psychologist in the training of physicians. *Clinical Psychologist, 29,* 20-21.

——. (1975). Death in the pediatric hospital: Psychological consultation with medical and nursing staff. *Journal of Clinical Child Psychology, 4*(1), 33-35.

——. (1976a). Mental health consultation in the pediatric intensive care nursery. *International Journal of Psychiatry in Medicine, 7,* 69-81.

——. (1976b). Psychological consultation in a pediatric hospital. *Professional Psychology, 7,* 77-83.

——. (1977a). Clinical psychological practice in the pediatric hospital. *Professional Psychology, 8,* 72-80.

——. (1977b). Family oriented intervention with the dying adolescent. *Journal of Pediatric Psychology, 2,* 68-71.

——. (1978). Training psychologists to consult with pediatricians: Problems and prospects. *Journal of Clinical Child Psychology, 7,* 57-60.

——. (1982). The child psychologist in the medical system. In P. Karoly, J. J. Steffen, & D. J. Grady (Eds.), *Child health psychology: Concepts and issues* (pp. 1-28). New York: Pergamon Press.

——. (1983). Transacting with physicians: Fact and fiction. *Journal of Pediatric Psychology, 8,* 117-127.

——. (1985). Psychology and behavioral pediatrics. *Journal of Developmental and Behavioral Pediatrics, 6,* 207-208.

Drotar, D., Benjamin, P., Chwast, R., Litt, C. L., & Vajner, P. (1981). The role of the psychologist in pediatric inpatient and outpatient facilities. In J. Tuma (Ed.), *Hand-*

book for the practice of pediatric psychology (pp. 228–250). New York: John Wiley.

Drotar, D., Crawford, P., & Bush, M. (1984). The family context of childhood chronic illness: Implications for psychosocial intervention. In M. G. Eisenberg, L. Sutkin, & M. A. Jansen (Eds.), *Chronic illness and disability through the life span: Effects on self and family* (pp. 103–132). New York: Springer.

Drotar, D., Doershuk, C. F., Stern, R. C., Boat, T. F., Boyer, W., & Matthews, L. (1981). Psychosocial functioning of children with cystic fibrosis. *Pediatrics, 67,* 338–343.

Drotar, D., Ganofsky, M. A., Makker, S., & DeMaio, D. (1981). A family oriented supportive approach to renal transplantation in children. In N. Levy (Ed.), *Psychonephrology I: Psychological factors in hemodialysis and transplantation* (pp. 79–92). New York: Plenum Press.

Duff, R. S., Rowe, D. S., & Anderson, F. P. (1972). Patient care and student learning in a pediatric clinic. *Pediatrics, 50,* 839–846.

Eisenberg, M. G., Sutkin, L., & Jansen, M. A. (Eds.). (1984). *Chronic illness and disability through the life span: Effects on self and family.* New York: Springer.

Engel, G. L. (1977). The need for a new medical model: A challenge for biomedicine. *Science, 196,* 127–136.

Epstein, L. H., & Cluss, P. A. (1982). A behavioral medicine perspective on adherence to long-term medical regimens. *Journal of Consulting and Clinical Psychology, 50,* 950–971.

Follette, W., & Cummings, N. A. (1967). Psychiatric services and medical utilization in a prepaid health plan setting. *Medical Care, 5,* 25–35.

Fox, R. (1979). *Essays in medical sociology.* New York: John Wiley.

Friedman, S. B. (1985). Behavioral pediatrics: Interaction with other disciplines. *Journal of Developmental and Behavioral Pediatrics, 6,* 202–206.

Friedson, E. (1970). *Profession of medicine.* New York: Harper and Row.

Gabinet, L., & Friedson, W. (1980). The psychologist as front line mental health consultant in a general hospital. *Professional Psychology, 11,* 939–945.

Gabinet, L., & Schubert, D. S. P. (1981). Teaching hospital inpatient consultation-liaison to psychology trainees and interns. *Teaching of Psychology, 8,* 85–88.

Gallagher, E. B. (1972). The health enterprise in modern society. *Social Science and Medicine, 6,* 619-623.

Gallesich, J. (1982). *The profession and practice of consultation.* San Francisco: Jossey-Bass.

Geist, R. (1977). Consultation on a pediatric surgical ward: Creating an empathic climate. *American Journal of Orthopsychiatry, 47,* 432-444.

Graves, R. L., & Hastrup, J. L. (1981). Psychological intervention and medical utilization in children and adolescents of low income families. *Professional Psychology, 12,* 426-433.

Griswold, P. M. (1980). A family practice model for clinical psychology. *Professional Psychology, 11,* 628-636.

Groves, J. E. (1978). Taking care of the hateful patient. *New England Journal of Medicine, 298,* 883-887.

Grzesiak, R. C. (1979). Psychological services in rehabilitation medicine: Clinical aspects of rehabilitation psychology. *Professional Psychology, 10,* 511-520.

Harper, R. G., Wiens, A. N., & Hammerstad, J. (1981). Psychologist-physician partnership in a medical specialty screening clinic. *Professional Psychology, 12,* 341-348.

Illich, I. (1975). *Medical nemesis.* New York: Random House.

Iscoe, I. (1981). Conceptual barriers to training for the primary prevention of psychopathology. In J. M. Joffee & G. W. Albee (Eds.), *Prevention through political action and social change* (pp. 110-134). Hanover, N.H.: University Press of New England.

Johnson, M. R. (1979). Mental health interventions with medically ill children: A review of the literature 1970-77. *Journal of Pediatric Psychology, 4,* 147-164.

Keefe, F. J. (1982). Behavioral assessment of chronic pain: Current status and future directions. *Journal of Consulting and Clinical Psychology, 50,* 890-911.

Koocher, G. P. (1980). Pediatric cancer: Psychosocial problems and the high costs of helping. *Journal of Child Clinical Psychology, 9,* 2-5.

Koocher, G. P., Sourkes, B. M., & Keane, W. M. (1979). Pediatric oncology consultations: A generalizable model for medical settings. *Professional Psychology, 10,* 467-474.

Kucia, C., Drotar, D., Doershuk, C. F., Stern, R. C., Boat, T. F., & Matthews, L. (1979). Home observation of family interaction and childhood adjustment to cystic fibrosis. *Journal of Pediatric Psychology, 4,* 189-195.

Kushner, K., & Asken, M. (1980). *Burnout among psychologists working in primary health care settings: Potential origins and recognition of the problem.* Paper presented at the meeting of the American Psychological Association, September, Montreal.

Lazarus, R. S. (1966). *Psychological stress and the coping process.* New York: McGraw-Hill.

LeBaron, S., & Zeltzer, L. (1985). Pediatrics and psychology: A collaboration that works. *Journal of Developmental and Behavioral Pediatrics, 6,* 157-161.

Linton, J. C. (1981). The psychologist on a spinal cord injury team in a community medical center. *Professional Psychology, 12,* 229-236.

Lipowski, Z. J. (1967a). Review of consultation psychiatry and psychosomatic medicine I: General principles. *Psychosomatic Medicine, 29,* 153-171.

——. (1967b). Review of consultation psychiatry and psychosomatic medicine II: Clinical aspects. *Psychosomatic Medicine, 29,* 201-224.

Magrab, P. R. (Ed.). (1978). *Psychological management of pediatric problems: Vol. 1. Early life conditions and chronic disease.* Baltimore: University Park Press.

Magrab, P. R., & Davitt, M. K. (1975). The pediatric psychologist and the developmental follow-up of intensive care nursery infants. *Journal of Clinical Child Psychology, 4(3),* 16-18.

Matarazzo, J. D. (1980). Behavioral health and behavioral medicine: Frontiers for a new health psychology. *American Psychologist, 35,* 807-817.

Matarazzo, J. D., Weiss, S. M., Herd, A. J., Miller, N. E., & Weiss, S. M. (Eds.). (1984). *Behavioral health: A handbook of health enhancement and disease prevention.* New York: John Wiley.

McNamara, J. R. (1981). Some unresolved challenges facing psychologists' entrance into the health care field. *Professional Psychology, 12,* 391-399.

McNett, I. (1981). Psychologists in medical settings. *APA Monitor,* December, pp. 12-13.

Mechanic, D. (1972). *Public expectations and health care.* New York: John Wiley.

Miller, W. B. (1973). Psychiatric consultation: Part I. A general systems approach. *Psychiatry in Medicine, 4,* 135-145.

Nathan, R. G., Lubin, B., Matarazzo, J. D., & Persely, G. W. (1979). Psychologists in schools of medicine—1955, 1964, and 1977. *American Psychologist, 34,* 622-627.

Naylor, K. A., & Mattson, A. (1973). "For the sake of the children": Trials and tribulations of child psychiatry-liaison service. *Psychiatry in Medicine, 4,* 389-402.

Olbrisch, M. E., & Sechrest, L. (1979). Educating health psychologists in traditional graduate training programs. *Professional Psychology, 10,* 589-595.

Pavlou, M., Johnson, P., Davis, F. A., & Lefebvre, K. (1979). A program of psychologic service delivery in a multiple sclerosis center. *Professional Psychology, 10,* 503-510.

Pless, B., & Pinkerton, P. (1975). *Chronic illness and childhood adjustment.* Chicago: Year Book Medical Publishers.

Rosen, J. C., & Wiens, A. N. (1979). Changes in medical problems and use of medical services following psychological intervention. *American Psychologist, 34,* 420-431.

Routh, D. K. (1985). Child health and human development. In A. R. Zeiner, D. Bendell, & E. Walker (Eds.), *Health psychology: Treatment and research issues* (pp. 99-111). New York: Plenum Press.

Routh, D. K., Schroeder, C. S., & Koocher, G. P. (1983). Psychology and primary health care for children. *American Psychologist, 38,* 95-98.

Russo, D. C., & Varni, J. W. (1982). *Behavioral pediatrics: Research and practice.* New York: Plenum Press.

Schofield, W. (1969). The role of psychology in the delivery of health services. *American Psychologist, 24,* 565-584.

Schraa, J. C., & Jones, N. F. (1983). A model psychometrically based medical psychology program. *Professional Psychology: Research and Practice, 14,* 78-89.

Schroeder, C. S. (1979). Psychologists in a private pediatric practice. *Journal of Pediatric Psychology, 4,* 5-18.

Schroeder, C., Goolsby, E., & Strangler, S. (1975). Preventive services in a private pediatric practice. *Journal of Clinical Child Psychology, 4*(3), 32-33.

Schubert, D. S., & Friedson, W. S. (1980). Compliance with psychiatric consultation advice. *Journal of Psychiatric Treatment and Evaluation, 2,* 275-280.

Schwartz, G. E. (1982). Testing the biopsychosocial model: The ultimate challenge facing behavioral medicine. *Journal of Consulting and Clinical Psychology, 50,* 1040-1053.

Smith, E. E., Rome, L. P., & Freedheim, D. K. (1967). The clinical psychologist in the pediatric office. *Journal of Pediatrics, 71*, 48-51.

Stabler, B. (1979). Emerging models of psychologist-pediatrician liaison. *Journal of Pediatric Psychology, 4*, 307-313.

Stabler, B., & Mesibov, G. B. (1984). Role functions of pediatric and health psychologists in health care settings. *Professional Psychology: Research and Practice, 15*, 142-151.

Stabler, B., & Whitt, J. K. (1980). Pediatric psychology: Perspectives and training implications. *Journal of Pediatric Psychology, 5*, 245-251.

Starr, P. (1982). *The social transformation of American medicine.* New York: Basic Books.

Tefft, B. M., & Simeonsson, R. J. (1979). Psychology and the creation of health care settings. *Professional Psychology, 10*, 558-570.

Tuma, J. (1977). Practicum, internship and post-doctoral training in pediatric psychology. *Journal of Pediatric Psychology, 2*, 9-12.

—— (Ed.). (1981). *Handbook for the practice of pediatric psychology.* New York: John Wiley.

Wertlieb, D. (1979). A preventive health paradigm for health care psychologists. *Professional Psychology, 10*, 548-557.

Whitehead, W. E., & Bosmajian, L. S. (1982). Behavioral medicine approaches to gastrointestinal disorders. *Journal of Consulting and Clinical Psychology, 50*, 972-983.

Wright, L. (1979). A comprehensive program for mental health and behavioral medicine in a large children's hospital. *Professional Psychology, 10*, 458-466.

5

ROLE PLAYING:
CLINICAL ASSESSMENT
AND THERAPY CONSIDERATIONS

Craig A. Blumer
J. Regis McNamara

Roles and role playing have many meanings. The term has theatrical, sociological, and dissimulation connotations (Shaw, Corsini, Blake, & Mouton, 1980). In this chapter, role playing will refer to the enactment of a nonpresent situation for therapeutic reasons. Role plays have many uses in education, industry, and research, but the unique aspects of role plays in those settings will not be addressed.

Role plays seek to simulate interactions and, by definition, have contrived elements, which is their greatest weakness. Yet that weakness becomes the greatest asset of role plays. Without the binds of "reality," the situation can be altered, modified, recreated, and replayed as needed to aid the client. Further, these enactments take place in the relative safety of therapy, where inadequacy and emotion are less consequential.

Role playing has been most strongly advocated by two divergent schools of thought. Behavioral clinicians have encouraged the growth of role play assessment and treatment, particularly in the areas of social skill, assertiveness, dating skill, and marital therapy. Behaviorists sought to assess social competence and its components by role playing social interactions and rating the resulting behavior. Treatments have often relied heavily on training and practicing new, more competent behaviors through role plays (Hersen, 1979).

Moreno (1923), the originator of modern, therapeutic role playing, took a very different approach in his development of psychodrama. Psychodrama is generally performed in groups in which the clients enact or reenact situations of emotional significance. Clients may enact their own public behavior, private thoughts and feelings, or the personalities of others. Through role playing, clients gain insight and strong emotions are released (Kahn, 1964).

Despite role play's close connection to some behaviorists and to psychodramatists, role playing is not a technique restricted to a few therapeutic schools. Role plays have been used by many other theoretical orientations including psychoanalytic, Adlerian, Rogerian, and eclectic (Kahn, 1964). In this chapter the major techniques and uses of role playing will be explicated without regard to theoretical orientation. The chapter looks at general issues in role playing, role play assessment, and role play treatments.

GENERAL ISSUES IN ROLE PLAYING

Role Playing Theory

Role playing is a unique approach to assessment and treatment. Several features of role playing make it useful as a clinical procedure; the first is simultaneity. As in an actual response, role playing requires clients to react as a whole. Perception, processing (thinking and feeling), and performance, which are the basic components of a reaction, are necessary to produce a role play response. Other techniques often assess only one mode, generally verbal processing, without simultaneous assessment of other elements of behavioral production (Corsini & Cardone, 1966).

Second, role plays have some veridicality. The relationship between samples of naturally occurring behavior and role plays appears less than was hoped (McNamara & Blumer, 1982). However, role plays are sufficiently realistic and evocative to yield significant insight, understanding, and behavior change (Heimberg, Montgomery, Madsen, & Heimberg, 1977; Starr, 1977).

A final advantage is the flexibility and personalization role playing allows. With no materials required, almost any situation can be developed and tailored to the needs of the client. These aspects of role plays—simultaneity, veridicality, and flexibility—seem to be significant elements of role play's clinical utility.

Role playing can be used in five basic therapeutic ways (Corsini & Cardone, 1966).

1. It has been used extensively for assessment and diagnostic purposes. Problematic situations can be sampled to evaluate clients' reactions to those situations. For instance, a dating scene can be role played to determine when and how problems arise for an infrequently dating client.

2. Insight and understanding can be increased through role playing. Role plays can allow clients to see how they behave. Clients may also see how others perceive them. The problematic elements of situations can be highlighted to increase clients' understanding of the components of more

effective behavior. A client may deny using an angry tone of voice with her husband, but when her husband role plays her sarcastic tone of voice, the anger becomes immediately apparent.

3. Catharsis or emotional release is another therapeutic use of role playing. An adult client can role play a traumatic interaction he had as an adolescent, expressing powerful emotions, heretofore unexpressed.

4. Role playing also can be a useful teaching aid. First, the desired behavior or reaction can be demonstrated or modeled. For example, appropriate levels of voice volume can be demonstrated with a very impaired client. Second, new behaviors can be practiced. If an adolescent client is troubled by confronting her parents with independence issues, assertion skills can be rehearsed before attempting the actual confrontation at home.

5. Finally, role playing provides a means to reduce anxiety and inhibition. Experiencing and practicing behaviors, thoughts, and feelings increases the client's comfort and acceptance of these new reactions. Therefore, a client experiencing and expressing anger in a role play can decrease his anxiety and avoidance of anger and increase his confidence in being able to express it.

Role playing techniques can assist in all phases of therapy: assessment, understanding, emotional release, anxiety reduction, and skill training. Thus role plays have significant potential applications with many theoretical orientations in many therapeutic situations.

Common Role Play Procedures and Issues

Regardless of the basis for the role play or the technique used, a number of common problems confront the clinician. Role playing requires preparation of the client. Clinicians must decide when to use it, what scenes are appropriate, how to structure the situation, and who will assist. Role playing also presents the therapy and therapist with some unique problems that must be addressed and monitored.

Preparation

Role play procedures are generally preceded by a discussion of the nature of role plays and a rationale for their use. Most people are reluctant, initially, to participate in role plays. Comments such as, "I'm not a good actor," "This is so unreal," or "I can't do that!" are common. Frequently helpful is some brief reassurance before role playing that clients will not be acting, but expressing themselves naturally; that this method provides information that cannot be obtained in any other way; and that client and therapist will be working

together on the role play. After having verbally prepared the
client, it is best to begin quickly as delay does not diminish
the inevitable anxiety of a new experience.

Psychodramas are typically preceded by a warm-up, which
is any task that prepares the client for role playing. This
type of experience helps deal with the problem of getting clients more receptive to role play techniques. There are many
warm-ups and most psychodrama texts list some that may be
very helpful (see Shaw et al., 1980; Starr, 1977). Three
are discussed here because of their wide applicability (Starr,
1977).

The first procedure consists of talking through a role
play scene. The scene to be role played is described, then
the client and partner talk through the interaction without
acting it out. In scene elaboration, both role players attempt
to elaborate on the details of the scene as extensively as
possible, even becoming somewhat fanciful to encourage the
client's involvement. Second, setting the stage involves having
both role players rearrange the room to fit with the role play
scene as well as determine the placement of important elements
of the setting. These and other warm-ups help prepare clients
for role playing. The third element in preparing subjects is
scene description. The context of role plays has been shown
to have significant impact on the behavior portrayed (Eisler,
Hersen, & Miller, 1974), so scenes must be described carefully
to elicit the desired reactions.

Thorough, accurate, and detailed scene descriptions are
important, if not essential, for client involvement in the role
play (Bellack, 1985). Features to consider are the physical
surroundings, the people present, the relationships and
experiences with these people, and the emotional climate.
Further, sufficient time and detail must be allowed for the
clients to at least visualize the scene and their role in it
(Bellack, 1985).

Recreating past events can be enhanced through role
reversal. The client displays someone else's behavior to increase scene elaboration and accurate portrayal of characters
(Leveton, 1977). For example, the client may demonstrate a
ward attendant's behavior to improve the therapist's understanding and portrayal of the attendant.

In sum, role playing requires some explanation and discussion to educate the client in the uses and goals of role
play approaches. Role playing should be preceded by some
warm-up and by detailed elaboration and description of the
scene.

General Issues in Therapeutic Role Playing

Contraindications for role playing are few. Acutely psy-
chotic patients are unable to manage the changes in time and
person required in role playing; therefore, role playing with

this type of patient population is not recommended. Role playing may also be contraindicated in individual therapy with clients who have severe problems establishing a personal relationship and with whom a primary goal of therapy is such a relationship. It seems that the changes in roles required in a role play both allow the client to avoid relating in a real manner and increase the difficulty of seeing the therapist in a realistic way.

Having chosen to role play, the therapist must decide what scene to use. The primary guide for choosing a scene is its relevance and salience to the client. Listening carefully to clients about problem situations provides the best source of scenes to role play. The more invested clients are in a scene, the more likely they are to role play it adequately.

The selection of the role-model is an important part of the role playing process. Groups are well suited for role playing, in part, because of the many available role-models. Generally, the client should choose the group member with whom to role play. In individual therapy, the use of an assistant can be very helpful as it allows the therapist some emotional and physical distance to observe the entire situation. However, practicality often necessitates the therapist to act as the role-model.

Role playing presents the therapist with a variety of unique problems. Therapists are more directly confronted with their limits and limitations. This is particularly true if the therapist is also the role-model. Some client problems may present dilemmas for the therapist. Problems in sexuality, intimacy, violence, and psychoticism potentially can be dealt with through role playing. Yet each of these areas could lead to awkward, inappropriate, even unethical situations. It is one thing to discuss homosexuality intellectually; it is quite another for a heterosexual therapist to role play a homosexual partner. Therapists must be aware of their own anxieties and limitations. In cases of mild discomfort, it may be best to be aware but to continue. In situations of greater anxiety or potential inappropriateness, role playing is best not used. An honest expression of the therapist's discomfort may be necessary to diminish any negative repercussions from the therapist's behavior.

A related, but potentially more serious, problem concerns the concept of countertransference, which may be thought of as therapists' thoughts, feelings, and actions toward a client that do not benefit the client and are therefore inappropriate (Greenson, 1967). These inappropriate reactions are almost invariably antitherapeutic. The active and interactive nature of role playing presents many potent opportunities to act on countertransference reactions. For example, a client shows little progress and the therapist feels considerable frustration. It would be all too easy, even unavoidable, for this frustration to be ventilated to the client in a role play in an unplanned and untherapeutic manner.

Countertransference problems should be considered if the therapist's role playing is frequently inaccurate or inadequate or leads to decreased involvement or increased distress in the client without clear benefit. Insight into one's own reactions can lead to modifications of inappropriate reactions.

However, the ultimate control of countertransference is in the structure of the technique. Psychodrama manages countertransference by placing the therapist outside of the role-played interaction and its accompanying arousal (Keller-mann, 1979). In general, therapists should use role-models when strong positive or negative feelings are held for a client. Further, in long-term individual therapy, role playing techniques should include an assistant as role-model if at all possible.

Issues of countertransference have not been well re-searched and investigation of these hypotheses and suggest-tions is needed. Yet it is clear that psychotherapy, and role playing in particular, relies greatly on the behavior and per-sonage of the therapist. Therefore, all therapeutic approaches must attempt to safeguard clients from therapists' limitations.

ROLE PLAY ASSESSMENT

Behavioral Approaches

Behavioral therapies have made extensive use of role play assessment techniques and thereby have made significant re-finements in them. Role play tests and extended interactions are the two primary types of behavioral assessment procedures.

Overview

Role Play Tests. In a role play test, clients enact a series of situations as if they were real. For example, the Behav-ioral Assertiveness Test—Revised (BAT-R) consists of 20 interpersonal situations requiring positive and negative asser-tion (Eisler, Hersen, Miller, & Blanchard, 1975). The thera-pist presents a brief scene description, such as, "You go to a party where everyone pairs off, and you are left with a girl you have just met." The role-model then gives a prompt line, "Could you pass the ashtray?" The client then responds. The responses are recorded and rated on a variety of spe-cific dimensions.

Role play tests attempt to assess a client's behavior over a range of situations within a skill area such as assertiveness. The tests seek to provide a simple measure of clients' defi-cits and strengths within the skill area. Further, the limited format of role play tests allows for some standardization both of the situation and its rating.

Extended Interactions. Many researchers have utilized extended interactions lasting from one to ten minutes. This assessment technique has the client role play with a role-model a relevant past or hypothetical situation. By extending the role play, this approach seeks to elicit more naturalistic affect and behavior and to assess interaction skills necessary in social situations.

Two kinds of role play scenes have been used, prototypical and replication. With prototypical scenes, clients are asked to role play hypothetical situations. Curran, Gilbert, and Little (1976) described a date in a pizza parlor following a movie. Replication scenes involve role plays that seek to reproduce the client's actual past events—for example, role playing an argument the client had with a friend the night before.

Administration

The recommendations regarding client preparation made in the introductory section are applicable for role play assessment, particularly warm-ups and careful scene description. However, severe problems with role play tests limit their utility. Bellack (1985), who has worked extensively with role play tests, believes the limited, single-response format of the role play test can no longer be considered adequate to assess social functioning. Role play tests have sought to assess clients' abilities in complex social situations that are fundamentally interactive. Problems can occur anywhere in the interaction: initiation, maintenance, or termination. A brief, single response to a prompt does not tap these qualities of social relations.

Multiple-response formats have also been used with role play tests (Van Hasselt, Hersen, & Bellack, 1981). Such formats follow the subject's response with counterresponses. For example, if the role play is about an overcharge for a small sale item, the "clerk" may follow the client, pointing out the overcharge with, "But the tag here says 79 cents." The clerk may then answer the client's response with, "Well, if you insist, I will have to check with my manager." However, the multiple-response format did not yield improved validity correlations over the single-response format. Without further work in this area, multiple-response role play tests cannot be recommended.

The limitations of format noted for role play tests are not present with extended interactions. Wessberg, Mariotto, Conger, Farrell, and Conger (1979) typify administration of extended interactions. They told subjects to imagine they were seated in the student union with a girl from one of their classes. They were to get to know her better. Interactions were then role played and allowed to proceed for three minutes.

The length of role play interactions has varied greatly, but no research exists on the necessary and sufficient lengths of role plays. Interactions probably should be no less than two to three minutes, but the additional value of extending longer than five minutes, in most cases, is probably minimal.

Client preparation has often been quite brief in the research on role plays, probably too brief. Careful preparation of clients for role playing is probably the single most important factor for adequate and informative role plays. Explaining and practicing role plays, assisting clients in visualizing the scene, and detailed scene descriptions can greatly enhance role play performances (Bellack, 1985).

A related issue concerns the choice of scenes for role playing. Clients' suggestions of problematic areas is an obvious and prime source of scenes. Role play research is another important resource. The clinician must evaluate scenes on at least two dimensions: relevance to the client's problems and difficulty level (Bellack, 1985). The role play scenes must be of events reasonably likely to occur in the client's life. Scenes must also be relevant to the problem area. It is essential to confirm with clients the significance and relevance of each role play scene prior to its enactment.

The difficulty of the scene must also be evaluated. Scenes should be of intermediate difficulty to gather the most information. For example, simulating a telephone call asking a woman, whom the client knows from class, for a date to a movie would be a more appropriate role play than one involving a total stranger or a close friend. Scenes that are so difficult that few clients perform them adequately or so easy that most clients do very well provide little assistance in understanding the client.

Ratings

Having administered a role play, the assessment is only half completed—a means of evaluating the enactment is necessary. Role play ratings are important in clinical practice as well as research; they support and enhance clinical impressions by providing greater consistency and permanence. Rating procedures assist both therapist and client in focusing on the targets of change. Also, comparisons across time can more easily be made and changes delineated for clients who are unable to perceive their progress.

The range of possible ratings is enormous. However, the emphasis has been on small discrete behaviors or more inferred global concepts. The molecular ratings have included gazing, response time, response latency, voice volume, posture, and spatial proximity. These behaviors are scored with an occurrence/nonoccurrence rating or chronological measurement. Molar ratings generally are made by rating, on a scale of 1 to 7, such concepts as skill, anxiety, and effectiveness.

Molecular behaviors have been used because of their reliability in scoring and an assumption that they are the building blocks of social interactions (Bellack, 1979). However, the relationship of individual, discrete behaviors to the overall gestalt of a social event is complex and not well understood (Curran, 1978). Further, considerable effort is required to train raters and score a sufficient number of behaviors to evaluate a situation adequately. Some use of molecular ratings is still needed in research on role plays. In most clinical practice, however, precisely measured molecular ratings are not of sufficient benefit or practicality for regular use. The one exception is if a behavior is the specific target of change. For example, if a client makes extremely little eye contact, targeting and rating eye contact appear warranted.

Part of the inadequacy of discrete behavioral ratings to evaluate social interactions is the use of simple frequency or duration measures without accounting for the sequence or timing of responses (Fischetti, Curran, & Wessberg, 1977). Trower and his associates (Trower, Bryant, & Argyle, 1978) suggest a means to overcome some of the difficulties of molecular ratings. They use a 0 to 4, bidimensional scale. For example, gaze is rated as follows: (0) Normal gaze frequency and pattern; (1,a) Tends to avoid looking, but no negative impression, (1,b) Tends to look too much, but no negative impression; (2,a) Looks too little, negative impression; (2,b) Looks too much, negative impression; (3,a) Abnormally infrequent looking, unrewarding; (3,b) Abnormally frequent looking, unpleasant; (4,a) Completely avoids looking, very unrewarding; (4,b) Stares continually, very unpleasant. Such a system could be integrated into a therapy session without significant problems and provide specific feedback.

The other main approach to evaluating role plays has been global ratings on dimensions such as anxiety. The ratings vary from 4- to 11-point scales, although 7-point scales are most common. The points on the continuum are anchored in a general manner. For example, Wessberg et al. (1979) rated skillfulness as (1) not at all skillful, (2) very slightly skillful, (3) mildly skillful, (4) moderately skillful, (5) quite a bit skillful, (6) markedly skillful, and (7) extremely skillful.

The strongest argument for global ratings is the greater correspondence of the rating and criterion measures (Wessberg et al., 1979). However, a major limitation with global ratings is that reliability is difficult to establish and maintain. This problem obscures the meaning of the ratings. The nonspecific nature of global ratings is an additional limitation. The rating "very slightly skillful" provides no direct feedback to clients on the strengths and weaknesses of their performances. Thus, global ratings can point out relative adequacy or inadequacy, but it remains for the clinician to describe the specific problems and to develop alternatives.

Ratings should be completed by all involved: therapist, client, observer. However, the various ratings may be quite discrepant (Farrell, Mariotto, Conger, Curran, & Wallander, 1979). Such differences can provide important information on the perceptual, cognitive, and behavioral components of the problem and its relationship to a real-time enactment.

The number of ratings must be limited. It has been repeatedly shown that the reliability of ratings drops radically when judges are asked to rate more than two or three behaviors at the same time. Furthermore, the ratings made can adversely affect each other. Taping sessions can be quite helpful, even mandatory, for the rating process. It allows the session to be reviewed and rated later, thereby minimizing the work load of rating during or immediately after the role play.

Therefore, there are a number of methodological issues with ratings. When choosing ratings the following factors should be considered (Bellack, 1985). The rating should have a documented relationship to the criterion. Further, the rating should be of behavior elicited by the role play. A role play of a date may reveal conversational skills, but not reactions to anger. Also, the scoring procedure should tap relevant aspects of the behavior. For instance, the cumulative duration of gazing provides information that is difficult to use whereas the bidimensional rating may be very helpful. Finally, the therapeutic goals should be considered. A more broadly focused or emotion-oriented therapy may seek to assess the emotional tone of a relationship through a role play. A behavior-oriented or more concretely targeted therapy may choose to evaluate posture and voice volume in an interaction with a stranger.

In summary, several recommendations can be made about rating procedures in role play assessment. Ratings should be used with role plays to allow better tracking of change in therapy. The ratings should be completed by the client, therapist/role-model, and, if possible, therapist/observer. The number and type of ratings made at one time should be limited to avoid overloading the rater. Taping allows a greater number of ratings without the possible interference of the presence of judges in the session.

Of most relevance and practicality in a clinical setting are ratings of intermediate to molar levels of behavior. Molar ratings allow adequate measurement of overall competence. Intermediate ratings provide information on more specific features of a client's performance while still attending to the interactive qualities of social events. Choosing the specific ratings depends on the problem, client, and therapeutic goals. Although problems have been noted in rating role plays, the field seems to be displaying increasing concern about these issues. This trend is seen in the growing work on the psychometric qualities of role play assessment.

Psychometrics of Role Play Assessment

The psychometric properties of role plays have been investigated for less than ten years. Interrater reliabilities are most frequently reported. In the assertiveness literature, most interrater reliabilities were in the range of .90 (Heimberg et al., 1977). Overall, the behavioral literature has produced interrater reliabilities in the .75 to .99 range with occasional lows in the .50s. Global ratings tend to be lower than ratings of specific behaviors, but they are adequate (McNamara & Blumer, 1982).

Test-retest reliability has been assessed by a few studies. Kern and MacDonald (1980) compared a total assertiveness score obtained from their role play test and found the one-week retest correlation was .85, four-week was .84, and ten-week was .57. Van Hasselt et al. (1981) did a one-week retest reliability check with their role plays of social competence for children. For the role play test, six of the seven behaviors yielded significant correlations, which ranged from .06 to .91. The extended interaction had nine significant correlations, ranging from .54 to .94. Based on these two studies, test-retest reliability seems adequate for short intervals of one week.

Although some reliability characteristics have been explored, it is the validity of role play assessment that has received the most investigation. Of greatest interest is ecological validity, that is, whether behavior seen in a role play accurately reflects behavior in a similar naturalistic setting.

Early evaluations of role play validity were supportive. Role play assessment revealed behavioral change and differences when used as an outcome measure in treatment studies. Role plays were moderately successful in discriminating groups known to differ on some behavioral dimension (McNamara & Blumer, 1982). Likewise some of the first investigators of role play's validity found moderately high levels of correspondence between ratings of role play behavior and estimates of friends, spouses, or ward staff of how the subject would behave (Kreitler & Kreitler, 1968; Stanton & Litwak, 1955; Warren & Gilner, 1978).

The laboratory of Bellack and Hersen has made a number of attempts to assess the validity of their role play test, the BAT-R. The correlations between individual behaviors in the role play test and a criterion situation have been modest to low (Bellack, Hersen, & Lamparski, 1979; Bellack, Hersen, & Turner, 1978; Van Hasselt et al., 1981). In the best of the BAT-R validity studies, Bellack et al. (1979) found that three of six behaviors significantly correlated between the role play test and similar naturalistic samples. The significant correlations ranged from .33 to .49.

Another group of studies compared an extended role play of a hypothetical event to an unobtrusively observed waiting room interaction. The global ratings of the role play and the waiting room were significantly correlated. The anxiety ratings correlated from .33 to .77 and skill ratings from .22 to .58 (Cole, Howard, & Maxwell, 1981; Conger & Farrell, 1981; Wessberg et al, 1979). Thus, global ratings performed at a level equal to or superior to specific behaviors.

A third set of research has investigated replication role plays, the role playing of an actual, previous event. The studies have shown significant correlations more consistently using the replication format than other role play techniques. Further, the correlations have tended to be higher, ranging from .28 to .89 (Blumer & McNamara, 1982; Kern, 1982; Kern, Miller, & Eggers, 1983). However, Blumer and McNamara (1983), in a therapy analogue using replication role plays, found only sporadic significant correlations.

To examine further the effects of role playing, several studies have compared subjects' behavior in a role play setting that was enacted as if the scene were real to subjects uninformed and responding to the situation naturally. In each study, role playing behavior was found superior to "actual behavior" (Gorecki, Dickson, Anderson, & Jones, 1981; Higgins, Alonso, & Pendleton, 1979; Higgins, Frisch, & Smith, 1983). The differences seem to become most evident when the situation requires risk-taking—role play subjects are more willing to take risks. For example, role-play subjects are more assertive and willing to refuse demands than actual-behavior subjects. These findings are consistent with the research that has shown that role play demands for assertiveness or skill result in improved or superior role play behavior (Nietzel & Bernstein, 1976).

Instructions to be effective or even to act like another, "successful" person may be a helpful assessment technique. The ability to role play a behavior does not prove competence to enact the behavior in an actual situation. However, such an approach may aid in distinguishing a deficiency of knowhow from an inhibition of ability. Further investigation of alternative instructions on role play assessment is needed.

Efforts to improve the predictiveness of role play assessment have led investigators to examine the effect of increasing the number of observations or measures. Cole et al. (1981), Conger and Farrell (1981), and Farrell et al. (1979) found that multiple measures or multiple observations improved the validity of the role play assessment. Using simple linear composites such as adding subject talk time, confederate talk time, and gaze time, Conger and Farrell (1981) were able to improve the predictiveness of role play measures.

These findings are consistent with Epstein's (1979) research on the stability of personality. He found in reviewing the literature and his own research that single samples of behavior correlated in the .20 to .50 range. However, with sufficient samples, generally 4 to 12, the intercorrelation of all the measures jumped to the .70 to .90 range. He argues that a single measure of behavior, like a single test item, has too much error variance. Only with a sufficient number of observations is any behavioral stability evident.

At this time, tentative conclusions can be reached about role play assessment. It seems the role play test as originally developed and rated on specific behaviors is the least ecologically valid means of role play assessment. Extended role plays when rated globally can be modestly correlated to more naturalistic samples of behavior. These procedures are probably adequate to allow general screening of social competence or assess pre- or posttest change. However, role play assessments are clearly inadequate for accurate prediction of performance in an extratherapy situation. Where possible, replication role plays may allow some enhancement of role plays' predictiveness. Regardless of format, role play behavior tends to be superior to "actual" behavior.

The ecological validity of role plays may be improved if based on a sufficient number of observations. This can be achieved in a combination of ways. The number of behaviors rated, the number of raters, or the number of role plays can be increased. Taken in total, increased sampling may significantly improve the ecological validity of role play assessments.

Insight-Oriented Approaches

Overview

Relatively little has been written about assessment by the proponents of role playing techniques to increase insight. This is in part due to an antidiagnostic stance of many of these approaches. Furthermore, evaluation is seen as an ongoing therapy process without a separate assessment phase.

Psychodrama does recommend assessment of its groups through the use of sociometry (Starr, 1977). Sociometry consists of charting the relationships within a group including their valence (positive or negative) and relative strength. Sociometric assessment can be done "live" as well. Action sociometry has the group members portray their relationships to increase understanding and to change behavior (Leveton, 1977).

Role plays have been used in a variety of settings to assist in clinical decisionmaking. The goal of decision-oriented role plays is to increase the appropriateness of decisions. The role plays are usually very specific to the question at hand, such as role playing a job interview to assess readiness to seek work.

Finally, projective role plays will be discussed briefly. As with other projectives, the procedure is to place clients in an ambiguous situation wherein they will project or portray their basic anxieties and primary means of defending against those anxieties.

Administration

Psychodrama. A sociogram diagrams information on group relationships. This is usually displayed graphically using circles
to represent individuals and arrows to show the direction and
valence of relationships. A variation of the graphic display is
to enact a client's sociogram and is known as a "sculpture" or
a "tableau" (Starr, 1977).

The task is explained briefly as an attempt to get a true-
to-life picture of how the client sees the group, family, and
so on. The client next, if needed, chooses group members for
each of the roles. Along with the therapist, the client then is
asked to construct one of several kinds of tableaus.

The client may be asked to arrange family or group members as they commonly are at home or as the client expects
them to be at some event. The client should describe characters' posture and looks, what they are doing, where they
are, and a line of dialogue to speak (Starr, 1977). Another
approach is to arrange the characters such that the physical
distance represents the emotional closeness of the character
and the protagonist. Each character is given a line of dialogue
to say to the client (Leveton, 1977).

The line of dialogue is sometimes difficult for clients to
choose. They should be reassured that they simply need to
select something the person being portrayed would say. It is
not necessary to choose the most representative comment.

After constructing the tableau, the client is led through
it. Each character interacts with the client in turn, using the
given dialogue. The client may need to demonstrate characters'
roles to enhance their characterization.

The therapist, throughout, carefully observes the client
and his relationships. All of this provides much information on
the client's perceptions and relationships. Further, the tableau
is a means to warm up the group for other psychodramatic
interactions and a valuable source of future events to portray.

Decision-Oriented Role Plays. Role plays have been used in
many settings to address clinical judgments. The administration
of these role plays is as described in the "Behavioral Approaches" section. The client receives a clear explanation of
the rationale, purpose, and format of the role play with a
complete description of the scene. Whereas practice and warm-
ups are helpful, the scene should relate directly and clearly
to the question at hand. The role play is then conducted while
the clinician observes. The evaluation is concluded with some
discussion and feedback about the client's performance. This
type of role play assessment is different from role play tests
or extended interactions in its focus on understanding and evaluating the client's performance regarding a specific question.

A variety of studies dealing with decision-oriented role
plays have been published. Hudson (1973) had clients role
play the situation of returning home from the hospital to

assess discharge readiness. Similarly, job readiness has been assessed by role playing job interviews and interactions with receptionists (Shaw et al., 1980). Finally, therapeutic interactions have been role played and evaluated for therapists' level of empathy (Rose, Cayner, & Edleson, 1977).

Thus, a variety of clinical issues related to clients' competence in interpersonal situations have been assessed through role playing problematic scenes. Competence was usually assessed by relying on clinicians' evaluations of the role play. However, rating devices have been used and may be helpful in making judgments about the role play.

Projective Role Plays. Perhaps most unique to insight-oriented approaches is projective role playing (Corsini & Cardone, 1966). The administration consists of instructing the clients and then noting their behavior in the role play. The instructions are that this is a test, they must listen closely to follow the instructions, and ask no further questions. A brief scene is described after which the client is to respond however he or she chooses. For example, the client is told to say or do whatever he or she wants for three minutes with an invisible book, candle, and pencil that are lying on a table (Corsini & Cardone, 1966). The clinician observes to make hypotheses about the client's style and areas of conflict.

Issues in Insight-Oriented Role Play Assessment

The brief discussion on insight-oriented role play assessment evidences the primary problem in this area. Assessment has received extremely limited attention from most of the writers and investigators in the field.

Psychodrama has advocated sociometric techniques. Written sociograms plot the network of interrelationships of groups. From this plot, one can check the reciprocity of interactions and consistency of perceptions among the clients. Action sociograms focus on one client so comparisons between clients are not possible. It appears that the type of information and the individual focus makes the tableau primarily a therapeutic instrument. The tableau seems best as a means to explore perceptions, physically portray relationships, and as a warm-up for other psychodramatic techniques.

Role play assessment to aid clinical decisionmaking is likewise an approach with many positive features. The relationship between assessment and outcome is direct and logical. Thereby, decisionmaking and outcomes become more easily tolerated by clients. Decisions such as discharge or appropriateness for therapy are often based on value impressions such as "attitude." This provides the client with little feedback, opportunity to change, or participation in the decisionmaking. However, role plays are understandable and provide for clients' active involvement in the process. Further, problems indicated by the assessment lead directly to issues for treatment. For these reasons, greater use of role plays in decision-making processes seems warranted (Shaw et al., 1980).

However, much work is needed in the area. Virtually no research exists on the psychometrics of role playing in a decisionmaking context. Further, this procedure is probably differentially valid among the many possible questions; the predictive and external validity of these role plays needs to be addressed. Finally, rating procedures should be developed to assist the clinician. Behavioral ratings may be of some assistance. Perhaps better would be more specialized ratings such as the empathy scores used by Rose et al. (1977). In this system, therapist responses were broken down into six categories. These were then scored from 0 to 4 points depending on specific criteria as to their adequacy, and the points were totaled for an empathy score. From this procedure, both the adequacy and areas of difficulty could be assessed and decisions made about therapist competence and need for remediation.

In regard to projective role plays, it is difficult to understand their role in the assessment process. Other projective procedures exist with much greater clinical experience to guide interpretations, including the Rorschach and the Thematic Apperception Test.

The validity of what may be called projective role plays has been evaluated only by Borgatta (1955). He found that the role plays were correlated from .32 to .74 with a more naturalistic sample of behavior in 10 of 12 ratings. Untested is the validity of inferential interpretations often used with projectives. Even if carefully rated, projectives have questionable advantages over more explicitly defined role play scenes. Thus, projective role plays seem to have limited utility until further research and experience can explicate the situations for their use.

In sum, insight-oriented approaches have proposed a number of role play assessment procedures. These represent an interesting variety of adjunctive techniques. Yet much is needed in accumulated clinical experience and research to enhance and refine the use of techniques such as tableau and decision-oriented role plays.

ROLE PLAY TREATMENTS

Role play provides a potentially effective treatment for diverse clinical populations. Behavioral approaches have used role plays as the principal component of a "package" of interventions to train interpersonal skills. Behavior change has been sought in a distinctly different manner by insight-oriented approaches, psychodrama in particular. Role play techniques have been used to intensify emotional expression, increase insight, and assist change regarding significant events and relationships.

This section explains how each approach has used role playing and briefly discusses the outcome research. Many of the issues described in previous sections such as behavioral targets, ratings, role play partners, and therapist involvement are highly pertinent to role play treatments.

Behavioral Approaches

Administration

Role playing techniques have been the core component of a number of treatment packages that emphasized skill development, anxiety reduction, and behavior modification. Role playing, in the context of practicing skillful behavior, has been of particular importance, although other approaches such as modeling, feedback, contingent reinforcement, behavioral contracts, social activities, homework, and lectures have been used in conjunction with role playing.

Three treatment packages will be presented as examples. First is a package developed to treat males who dated with a very low frequency (MacDonald, Lindquist, Kramer, McGrath, & Rhyne, 1975). The subjects met for six weekly two-hour group meetings. They were presented with a treatment rationale that all behavior is learned and can be changed with practice. The primary intervention was a series of behavioral rehearsals. Therapist-constructed situations were role played and ranged from smiling at a woman in class to discussing personal topics when alone with a woman. The difficulty of the role plays and the performance expectations increased with time. All group members role played at least one scene each session. The subjects received modeling and feedback from peers, female role-models, and group leaders. Leader-initiated group discussions were held on starting conversation, communicating interest, assessing another person's interest, where to date, and when to initiate physical contact. Finally, subjects were given extratherapy assignments involving increasingly demanding contacts with women.

Hersen (1979) described a treatment program for depressed women of 12 one-hour weekly sessions. Through videotaped role plays and an interview, the therapist identified specific verbal and nonverbal deficiencies in each of four areas: family, work, friends, and strangers. Four to eight problematic situations were developed for each content area—for example, asking for a day off at work or correcting a child's misbehavior.

Training began by the therapist instructing the patient in how to handle the problem situation, and, if necessary, modeling. "We are going to begin with the situation in which you tell a salesperson at a crowded counter you are next. It is important that you speak in a loud voice if you are to make your point. Try to speak loudly." The therapist then prompted the patient and the interaction was role played. Following the role play, feedback and suggestions were given and the role play was repeated until the patient performed adequately.

At the same time, perceptions were trained by having the patient interpret and evaluate the therapist's role-played responses. The therapist occasionally modeled a poor response as well as competent ones. Homework assignments were made as well, designating a number of responses to be performed during the week. The treatment was followed by a six-month maintenance phase in which the patient attended occasionally for "booster" sessions.

Liberman, Wheeler, and Sanders (1976) describe a multi-faceted program for distressed marital couples. At intake, each member of the couple was seen separately and allowed to ventilate. Couples recorded pleasing actions of the spouse and were encouraged to develop mutually rewarding shared activities. The couples were involved in couples group therapy for eight to ten sessions, in which role plays were used to improve communication. Liberman et al. (1976) believed this was the most important component. Therapist-provided structured exercises and behaviors were rehearsed. These were aided by therapist modeling and feedback, when necessary. Couples were assigned homework to practice the behaviors outside of therapy. The sessions focused on expressing positive and negative emotions, assertiveness, and communicating about sex and affection.

These three packages are fairly representative of behavioral approaches to building skills in three diverse populations. Similar approaches have been used with chronic psychiatric patients, alcoholics, physically aggressive men, and obsessive-compulsives (Heimberg et al., 1977).

One additional treatment format warrants mention, Fixed Role Therapy (Kelly, 1955). In this approach the client is first administered several questionnaires, which explicate the primary constructs or dimensions of his or her behavior. The therapist then develops a role characterization whose central constructs are very dissimilar to the client's. This role is given to the client to enact. The client practices several scenes in the role of the character with assistance from the therapist. The client then assumes the role of that character for two weeks. Two to five therapy sessions a week are held, during which time the client and therapist discuss the client's reactions to the role and improve the enactment of it through role playing. Finally, after two weeks, the client ends the characterization and the therapist and client discuss the changes in the client. Therapy is then ended (Bonarius, 1970).

This approach is similar to other skill building therapies in its focus on expanding clients' repertoires through behavioral rehearsal and practice outside of therapy. However, Fixed Role Therapy differs in its theory with strong emphasis on cognitive mechanisms. Further, it takes role playing to the ultimate by attempting to have the client role play a whole new person 24 hours a day for two weeks.

From a behavioral perspective these packages can be seen as dealing with five elements of behavior change: acquisition, response practice, shaping, cognitions, and generalization (Rich & Schroeder, 1976). Response acquisition concerns training new responses or the appropriate timing and use of existing responses. To aid response acquisition, modeling and instructions have been the primary procedures used. No research has explicated the best means by which to instruct and model in treatment.

However, related research suggests that direct, clear, and specific instructions are generally desirable, such as, "Talk loud," or "Ask the man to change his behavior" (Hersen, 1979). Modeling is most effective when the display is vivid and novel and presented by several models of the same age and sex. Furthermore, modeling is most useful when accompanied by instructions pointing out the most important elements (Bandura, 1971). Multiple models can be difficult to provide, but can be used advantageously in group therapy.

The necessity for modeling and instructions should be evaluated for each client. Social skills training with college students has shown little enhancement with modeling, whereas in psychiatric populations modeling appears to be important in assisting change (Heimberg et al., 1977). Presumably, most college students have knowledge of the requisite skills, but this knowledge is deficient in most psychiatric patients.

Once the client has the necessary skills, it becomes important to practice, refine, and strengthen their display. Response practice is seen by most behavioral approaches as the key element in skill-building packages. This is done through many role plays of situations calling for the adequate performance of a target behavior.

Response practice can be done overtly or covertly. An overt response has the possible advantages of motivating disinterested subjects, being more effective in response generalization, and being more effective with nonverbal behaviors (Rich & Schroeder, 1976). Further, since overt practice is observable, feedback and assistance are possible.

Covert response practice has been used in a few studies. It may be less threatening to anxious subjects, more flexible, and easier to implement (Rich & Schroeder, 1976). Of course the two processes are not mutually exclusive. Covert rehearsal may function as a warm-up and means of beginning the rehearsal process. Subsequently, overt rehearsal and feedback

may be employed, finally fading to covert rehearsal for naturalistic settings when overt practice is not feasible.

The response to be practiced may be clearly and completely specified or the response may be improvised following
general performance rules. The clinical bromide of doing
nothing for clients that they can do for themselves seems to
apply. More impaired clients may require precise description
of the behavior. Less impaired clients can provide their own
response alternatives. Further, competent individuals tend to
avoid copying others' behavior (Rachman, 1972), so over-
specifying the behavior may cause the client to resist treatment.

The third element of role play treatments, response shaping, refers to techniques that seek to refine and improve
responses. Shaping techniques include feedback, coaching,
video or audiotape feedback, and self-evaluation. Shaping
in severely impaired populations requires the therapist's
assistance. Such clients appear to improve little from relying
solely on self-observation. Likewise, it appears that in most
cases videotape feedback alone is not effective and potentially
can be undesirable. However, videotapes combined with verbal
instructions and discussion can be a powerful tool to improve
responses (Birchler, 1979).

Cognitive operations, the fourth category, are those tasks
designed to alter thinking and expectations. This element of
skill development packages has not been widely used but a
number of techniques are available. Doom-saying, self-punitive
comments, and exaggeration of potential negative outcomes all
can adversely affect performance. Rehearsal of coping statements deals with these negative ideas by presenting reasonable
alternatives and creating more psychological balance in the
self-commentary of the individual. Although research does not
suggest the best comments to use, it seems likely that positively toned, realistic statements would be most desirable.
Overly negative social perceptions can also be addressed.
Role plays in Hersen's treatment with depressed women had
clients interpret therapists' behavior and discuss those interpretations (Hersen, 1979). The use of multiple raters, discussed in the "General Issues in Role Playing" section, is
another means of analyzing social perceptions.

Finally, exaggerated role playing (Lazarus, 1971) or
enactment of radically different behaviors (Kelly, 1955) can
have dramatic effects on perceptions. Lazarus has clients act
out their fears exaggerated as much as possible. This often
serves to decrease fears and anxieties since, at its ridiculous
worst, things are not as bad as the client feared.

The fifth element of skill packages is response transfer
or generalization. However, role play elements frequently have
not been included in such packages. The techniques most
commonly used to aid transfer of training are self-assessment
in naturalistic settings or homework assignments. Also, it

seems likely, the greater control the client has over selecting, evaluating, and modifying behavior within therapy, the greater the likelihood of transfer (Rich & Schroeder, 1976). Thus, to the extent that client abilities allow, the structure of the therapy should promote client responsibility.

In sum, behavioral approaches have used role playing toward a number of goals to aid the development of social and communication skills. These skill development packages have been applied to many different treatment populations. The effectiveness of these packages is the next focus.

Outcome Evaluations

Many studies have looked at the effectiveness of role play treatments within skill development packages for a number of problem areas. Skill-training programs have used a number of components. However, behavioral rehearsal is considered the primary element.

Heterosocial Competence. Heterosocial competence can be defined as abilities relevant to initiating, maintaining, and terminating a social or sexual relationship with a member of the opposite sex (Barlow, Abel, Blanchard, Bristow, & Young, 1977).

A number of flaws and limitations characterize the outcome research in heterosocial competence. Heterosocial research has, with rare exceptions, been applied only to men—an obvious and serious shortcoming. Second, the treatment approaches used in the studies have varied greatly. This limits the generalizability of the results and often means that treatment packages have not been cross-validated. Much of the research has made brief interventions with populations of questionable clinical significance. Finally, limited use has been made of generalization measures or extensive follow-up (Galassi & Galassi, 1979).

Thus it is difficult to draw firm conclusions. The treatment packages have been superior to alternative treatments, attention placebos, and no-treatment control groups. However, the results were modest and often did not lead to increased dating frequency (Galassi & Galassi, 1979).

Social Competence. Social competence is similar to heterosocial competence and refers to a group of abilities to initiate, maintain, and terminate social relationships effectively (Rich & Schroeder, 1976; Rimm & Masters, 1974). This area has been referred to as social anxiety, social skill, or assertiveness.

Social competence research does not suffer some of the limitations of heterosocial competence research. Social competence treatment packages have been applied to a wide variety of populations, including clinical populations. However, variations in the packages limit generalizations and cross-validation.

The outcome research has not adequately assessed extratherapy generalization or long-term effectiveness of the treatments.

With college students, social competence skill training has produced results superior to placebo or no-treatment controls, although not clearly superior to other therapy techniques (Heimberg et al., 1977). Both overt and covert modeling have significantly affected assertiveness. Behavioral rehearsal, modeling, and coaching have been found singly or in combination to improve social competence. However, a "ceiling effect" seems to be present; after one or two components, more elements yield minimal additional benefit (McFall & Twentyman, 1973).

Similarly, in psychiatric populations, skill-training packages have been superior to placebo and no-treatment comparisons (Hersen, 1979). Response rehearsal alone appears insufficient for psychiatric groups, but, when supplemented with instructions and modeling, the combination is usually better than alternative treatments (Heimberg et al., 1977).

Skill training within groups shows promise as an effective treatment approach. However, the lack of adequate controls and well-designed studies limits conclusions at this time. In sum, social competence appears to be improved through interventions on a skill-training basis using role play techniques. However, further research is needed to clarify the strength and continuity of the changes outside of treatment.

Aggression. Skill-training approaches have attempted to modify the behavior of individuals who are frequently and inappropriately verbally and physically aggressive. The research in this area has been characterized by single-subject or small group designs. Thus there is a great need for group research to evaluate the preliminary findings of these case studies.

Of the studies reviewed, aggressive clients decreased or eliminated their inappropriate aggression following skills-training packages to teach alternative, prosocial responses to violence. These were often supplemented with education, contracts, and token economies to decrease violence (Hersen, 1979).

Marital Communication Skills. Marital communication training uses similar techniques as the above social skills-training programs, but focuses on communications, negotiating, and problem-solving. This research area has evaluated treatment effectiveness and the unique contribution of the elements of marital treatment programs. Further, this area, more than other social skill-training approaches, has utilized extended follow-ups and some of the most sophisticated behavioral assessment procedures in interpersonal research. However, several problems remain in these outcome evaluations. There has been a lack of studies with treatment-seeking or more seriously impaired couples. Most of the studies to date have relied on fairly small numbers of subjects limiting the adequacy of the evaluations.

The studies have shown that skills-training approaches with recruited, distressed married couples were superior to placebo, no-treatment, and "traditional therapy" comparisons. The behavioral treatments showed pre- to posttest improvement and between-group superiority on measures of marital communication and marital satisfaction (Birchler, 1979).

Fixed Role Therapy. The therapeutic approach of Fixed Role Therapy described by Kelly (1955) is a unique role play approach to behavior change. However, controlled research has not examined the effectiveness of this approach. A number of case studies have been made and are promising (Bonarius, 1970). However, until controlled research can adequately evaluate Fixed Role Therapy, the approach must be assumed experimental.

Summary

Role playing has been applied from a skill-training perspective to a wide range of clinical populations. A number of well-articulated treatment packages have been developed for increasing social competence, improving marital communication, and decreasing aggression. The training may be thought of as dealing with five response elements: acquisition, response practice, shaping, cognitions, and generalization. These treatment packages generally have been found to be effective in improving the targeted skill. However, the outcome research has often been limited by inadequate follow-up and lack of testing on relevant clinical populations.

Insight-Oriented Approaches

Insight-oriented approaches to psychotherapy and behavior change have also used role play techniques. Foremost has been the development of psychodrama (Moreno, 1923). The psychodramatic construction of therapy and many of its common techniques will be reviewed. Psychodrama was designed and typically is used for groups. However, many of its principles can be applied in individual therapy, and such use is discussed.

Format

The format of traditional psychodrama is a threefold process of warm-up, drama, and group therapy. The warm-up phase seeks to orient the clients to the task and encourage maximum participation. Further, this process often provides material or candidates for additional work (Leveton, 1977).

The director (the psychodramatic term for therapist) uses warm-ups, including explanations, discussions, introductions of new members, brief exercises, or other processes to aid clients' transition from workaday roles to active role playing. Role playing can be a difficult task, and to attempt role playing without adequate preparation and acclimation almost insures that clients will have difficulty and resist. Warm-up exercises and resources were discussed in the "General Issues in Role Playing" section.

An additional important process of the warm-up is to aid clients and the therapist in selecting potential treatment targets for the session. By observing and talking with the group members, the therapist assesses who is ready for role playing and who is not. Possible problem areas are also likely to be revealed. The therapist then can choose with whom and in what area to lead the group.

The second phase is the drama or role play. A patient may volunteer a problem to work on, but often the director must choose a client to begin the interaction. The choice should be based on some problem displayed by the client that appears amenable to role playing. This client is, typically, asked to sit next to the director and in front of the whole group. The director then interviews the client, eliciting further information and a scene to be role played. The director and client then begin setting the stage for the drama. Any additional actors needed are chosen by the client to enact the auxiliary roles of the drama. Generally, the director is not an actor in the drama. The director aids in controlling the drama, highlighting important points, intensifying or redirecting the actor through psychodrama techniques, and observing and involving the audience.

An example may be helpful (Starr, 1977). In the first session of a psychodrama group in a state hospital, a group of male patients, staff, and student nurses met with the director. In the warm-up, the director asked the group a number of questions about the ward. The topic of student nurses came up. In the back a patient, Warren, was attempting to kiss a student nurse and she was wrestling with him to avoid the kiss. The director chose to go with the event, noting to Warren that he treated the nurse like a girlfriend. Warren was initially resistant, but in the interview he answered a number of questions. This led to some discussion of sex. Warren felt all masturbation, adultery, and fornication were wrong.

The director asked which student nurses had been approached for a kiss by the patient. All of the students raised their hands. The director had each student choose a patient and they all simultaneously acted out how Warren behaved. These actions and interviews warmed-up the group and prepared Warren and the group for the psychodrama. The patients and student nurses then met in small groups to come up with theories of why Warren behaved as he did. One theory was that he did not get enough love. Warren and his physician were asked to come forward to role play Warren's childhood interactions with his mother. Warren played the role of his mother and the physician played the role of Warren. This brought out the high expectations made of Warren and his mother's prediction that women would lead to his downfall.

The final phase of therapy is group therapy. The group processes and discusses the events of the psychodrama. This is a time to integrate and make sense of the actions and feelings elicited by the drama. Further, it is an opportunity to make generalizations applicable to many people from the particulars of a single patient's situation. This is conducted much as any group therapy session with the primary focus being the preceding events in the psychodramas.

If psychodrama is used in individual therapy, strict use of the three phases may be less apparent. However, it is important to prepare the client through warm-up. Further, it is essential to follow the psychodrama with discussion. This maximizes the learning from the drama, allows the client and therapist to reestablish their roles, and aids in dissipating some of the strong feelings aroused in the drama to gain perspective and interpret the meaning of the events (Stein & Callahan, 1982). This flow of events is assisted by a number of techniques.

Techniques

Clients can be more or less involved, have preconceived judgments, and display affinities and avoidances to certain feelings and thoughts about the dramas. A variety of techniques have been developed to intensify clients' involvement or redirect the focus or feelings enacted in the situation.

Straight Role Playing. Straight role playing is the most basic approach. This is simply enacting a scene as it was. The primary character, the protagonist, plays him- or herself and additional roles are played by other clients. This has been discussed throughout the chapter and requires no further elaboration.

Role Reversal. The protagonist is asked to play a role other than him- or herself and another client plays the role of the protagonist. This technique is useful to clarify for the actors how to play a role. Reversal also aids in increasing spontaneity by requiring the clients to think and behave in a novel manner. Reversal can be very helpful in increasing understanding and empathy for another person's position. Finally, role reversal allows exploration of alternative means of reacting to a situation (Shaw et al., 1980).

Some clients may have difficulty with this intervention if they are unable to perceive and portray adequately the roles of others separate from themselves. Extreme resistance by a client can at times be approached by the protagonist reversing roles with the director (Kellermann, 1983). Role reversal can easily be applied to individual therapy sessions.

Doubling. Doubling is used to express the hidden content of a protagonist's communication (Kellermann, 1983). The protagonist plays the role as usual; however, closely behind the protagonist is the double who speaks the unexpressed feelings of the protagonist. So while the protagonist may be apologizing for bumping into someone, the double is muttering angrily about the clumsy oaf. This technique may require extensive assistance by the director, but it can be very helpful in intensifying the protagonist's involvement and increasing awareness of unexpressed feelings. Further, by concretizing the unexpressed, these reactions become more amenable to intervention. This technique can be very helpful for increasing involvement for shy, withdrawn, and reticent clients. It is also applicable to individual therapy.

Mirroring. Similar to role reversal and doubling, mirroring involves the protagonist watching the portrayal of himself by another client. Mirroring is useful in showing how the protagonist is perceived by or presents to others (Stein & Callahan, 1982). Mirroring may also be used to involve a client who resists acting. Appointing someone else to play the resistant client's part often leads to the client's direct participation. The mirror may be exaggerated in the portrayal of the protagonist to further highlight and involve the participants. Mirroring must be used with some care in individual therapy. The client may interpret the therapist's mirror as an insult and the unavailability of confirmation by others allows easy discounting of the mirrored portrayal.

Soliloquy. The soliloquy is a momentary stop in the action to comment, clarify, or investigate (Shaw et al., 1980), and thereby allows a number of interventions within a drama. The director can explore a client's reactions, make a theoretical point, aid the client in developing alternatives, or involve the audience in the drama.

Monodrama. As the name implies, the protagonist plays all of the roles of a situation in a monodrama. The monodrama displays the client's unique interpretation of entire events. This approach may be helpful with clients too distrustful or anxious to allow others to portray characters in the scene. The monodrama asks a great deal of the protagonist and may require assistance and coaching. It is best to use changes in seating or position to differentiate the roles. The monodrama allows the classic psychodrama format within individual therapy by allowing the therapist to remain the director and the client the actor (Stein & Callahan, 1982).

The "empty chair technique" is perhaps the most famous modification of the monodrama (Perls, 1969). The client directly expresses feelings to an empty chair as if the relevant person or thing were in the chair.

Other Techniques. Maximizing or exaggerating behavior or scenes has been discussed as a beneficial approach to role playing some situations. Concretizing abstractions similarly can enhance a role play. For example, if a client says she cannot role play because the director does not understand her, a human wall may be set up between the client and director to symbolize the division (Kellermann, 1983). Concretizing may also take the form of exaggerated physical positioning. A client who has trouble listening to criticism may be placed with his hands over his ears and his back to the group (Shaw et al., 1980). These techniques all serve to enhance and clarify clients' reactions, often intensifying the feelings and making the reactions more accessible for intervention.

The techniques can, of course, be used in conjunction. The director could choose to use role reversal and doubling or monodrama and concretization. While much has been written on the technique and practice of psychodrama, relatively little research exists to confirm these impressions.

Outcome Evaluations

The research on psychodrama is quite limited, both in quantity and quality. Less than 20 studies have evaluated experimentally the effectiveness of psychodramatic therapy or its specific techniques (Kipper, 1978). Further, these studies are often seriously flawed by small numbers of subjects, questionable outcome measures, and a lack of careful control.

In the studies completed, most found that psychodrama groups have been marginally or clearly superior to a no-treatment control or equal to that of another active treatment group (Kipper, 1978). A few, better-controlled studies have looked at psychodrama techniques. Doubling appears helpful in withdrawn hospitalized patients (Goldstein, 1971) and positive effects on negotiations have occurred following role reversal by the opposing negotiators (Johnson, 1971).

In sum, the research is encouraging that psychodrama and its techniques may be helpful. But, until further research is conducted, psychodrama's effectiveness remains unproven scientifically.

CONCLUSION

As has become apparent in this chapter, role playing is a technique with many facets. However, two principal therapeutic orientations have consistently utilized and refined role playing. Behaviorally oriented therapies have taken a skill-building approach. First, they have used role plays to identify the strengths and weaknesses of clients' behavior within certain contexts. Next, role plays are used, in conjunction with other techniques, to develop, shape, and practice new or more effective behaviors.

Insight-oriented therapies, particularly psychodrama, have used role plays in a different manner. Role plays are used to understand clients' phenomenology of situations with emphasis on emotional release around critical events (Kellermann, 1984). Thus a dichotomy has developed between a scientific, standardized, and logically constructed approach with one using greater spontaneity, emotion, and personal involvement.

The behaviorally oriented approaches have made a serious attempt to develop a comprehensive and coherent program of skill development. Emphasis has been put on assessment, which leads directly to treatment. Treatment has usually involved a range of interventions to aid behavior change. Finally, the large amount of research in behavioral, skill-building approaches to improving interpersonal skills has resulted in a noticeable progression in the literature. There seems to be a refinement in the questions addressed by the behavioral research and an improvement in the methodology of the studies, especially the research on the validity of role play assessment. For years, role plays were merely assumed to be valid, then a number of studies looked at "validity," and, in turn, the research began focusing on particular types of validity using a variety of methodologies and statistics. Yet to come are individual validities for specific questions with specific populations.

Although behaviorally oriented approaches have noteworthy strengths in their use of role plays, role playing remains underutilized in many ways. The emphasis on methodological issues has led to a lack of attention to the importance of involvement and emotionality in role playing. Bellack (1985) believes that clients' visualization of a scene is critical, whereas this approach would surely be insufficient for a psychodramatist.

One source of the problem of emotion and involvement in behavioral role playing is related to the frequent use of brief standardized scenes, which often have limited relevance and salience for clients. There has been also an overemphasis on the measurement and treatment of the simple frequency of specific behaviors, for example, duration of eye contact. While such a primary level of analysis may be necessary for ultimately understanding social behavior, at present an intermediate level of focus is likely to be more fruitful (Curran, 1979). For example, dealing with problematic situations such as accepting compliments, asserting onself with strangers, or making requests of superiors have greater social and clinical relevance than simple micro-behaviors.

Finally, there appear to have been few systematic efforts to encourage and support emotional expression among behavioral role playing treatments and assessments. Consequently, behavioral approaches have underutilized affect and motivation in understanding and treating interpersonal problems.

Psychodrama is in many ways the reverse of behaviorally oriented approaches. The strengths of psychodrama have been its powerfulness and ability to elicit strong emotion. Psychodrama has sought and gotten active involvement from clients. This has been true with diverse populations, including severely impaired groups frequently believed inappropriate for insight-oriented treatments (Starr, 1977).

Yet psychodrama seems stymied, perhaps due to its failure to make use of scientific methodologies. Psychodrama appears to have remained in much the same place for a long time, and Moreno remains the primary source on psychodramatic therapy. Psychodramatic writings are generally descriptive and case-oriented. The literature has not shown a refinement or focusing of its issues and research remains sporadic and unsystematic. There appears to be an emphasis on the dramatic and the cathartic, which attenuates the importance of cognitive understanding and behavioral skill building (Kellermann, 1984). Consistent with the lack of a scientific perspective is the limited nature of psychodramatic theory. It is primarily metaphoric, with repeated links made between therapy and the stage. Many useful insights have come from understanding human behavior as a staged event, yet all metaphors are limited, inadequate, and, at times, incorrect. More situationally relevant theories are needed to guide treatment and research.

Therefore, role playing appears in need of cross-pollenization. A learning and sharing of information and procedures among different approaches to role playing should be attempted. Behavioral role playing could benefit from psychodramatic techniques that encourage and deepen emotional involvement and expression. These would enhance the treatment process. Further, psychodramatic techniques could aid in eliciting the emotions of a situation, thereby increasing the similarity and congruity of the role play to naturalistic situations.

Likewise, psychodrama needs to utilize research methodologies to focus and direct its energies. Research could aid in defining and clarifying how best to use techniques with certain problems. A research perspective may also serve as a counterbalance to the emphasis on emotions and catharsis. Finally, behavioral theories would serve as models for teaching cognitive and intellectual understanding to clients.

Cross-pollenization would not and should not attempt to seek a single "best" role playing therapy. Instead, strengthening of different approaches should be the goal. In sum, role playing has shown itself to be a versatile technique for many problems. With appropriate refinement and change, it is likely to play an important part in clinical assessment and intervention.

REFERENCES

Bandura, A. (1971). Psychotherapy based on modeling principles. In A. Bergin & S. Garfield (Eds.), *Handbook of psychotherapy and behavior change*. New York: John Wiley.

Barlow, D. H., Abel, G. G., Blanchard, E. B., Bristow, A. R., & Young, L. D. (1977). A heterosocial skills behavior checklist for males. *Behavior Therapy, 8,* 229-239.

Bellack, A. S. (1979). Behavioral assessment of social skills. In A. S. Bellack and M. Hersen (Eds.), *Research and practice in social skills training*. New York: Plenum Press.

———. (1985). Recurrent problems in the behavioral assessment of social skill. *Behaviour Research and Therapy, 21,* 29-41.

Bellack, A. S., Hersen, M., & Lamparski, D. (1979). Role-play tests for social skills: Are they valid? *Journal of Consulting and Clinical Psychology, 47,* 335-342.

Bellack, A. S., Hersen, M., & Turner, S. (1978). Role play tests for assessing social skills: Are they valid? *Behavior Therapy, 9,* 448-461.

Birchler, G. (1979). Communication skills in married couples. In A. Bellack and M. Hersen (Eds.), *Research and practice in social skills training*. New York: Plenum Press.

Blumer, C. A., & McNamara, J. R. (1982). The adequacy of a role play of a previous event as affected by high and low anxiety and rehearsal. *Journal of Behavioral Assessment, 4,* 21-37.

———. (1983). Therapist effects in role play validity. Paper presented at the meeting of the Southeastern Psychological Association, March, Atlanta.

Bonarius, J. C. (1970). Fixed role therapy: A double paradox. *British Journal of Psychology, 43,* 213-219.

Borgatta, E. F. (1955). An analysis of social interaction: Actual, role playing, and projective. *Journal of Abnormal and Social Psychology, 51,* 394-405.

Cole, D. A., Howard, G. S., & Maxwell, S. E. (1981). Effects of mono- versus multiple-operationalization in construct validation efforts. *Journal of Consulting and Clinical Psychology, 49,* 395-405.

Conger, A. J., & Farrell, A. D. (1981). Behavioral components of heterosexual skills. *Behavior Therapy*, *12*, 41-55.

Corsini, R. J., & Cardone, S. (1966). *Role playing in psychotherapy: A manual.* Chicago: Aldine.

Curran, J. P. (1978). Comments on Bellack, Hersen, and Turner's paper on the validity of role play tests. *Behavior Therapy*, *9*, 462-468.

——. (1979). Social skills: Methodological issues and future directions. In A. S. Bellack & M. Hersen (Eds.), *Research and practice in social skills training.* New York: Plenum Press.

Curran, J. P., Gilbert, F. S., & Little, L. M. (1976). A comparison between behavioral replication training and sensitivity training approaches to heterosexual dating anxiety. *Journal of Counseling Psychology*, *23*, 190-196.

Eisler, R. M., Hersen, M., & Miller, P. M. (1974). Shaping components of assertiveness with instructions and feedback. *American Journal of Psychiatry*, *131*, 1344-1347.

Eisler, R. M., Hersen, M., Miller, P. M., & Blanchard, E. B. (1975). Situational determinants of assertive behaviors. *Journal of Consulting and Clinical Psychology*, *43*, 330-340.

Epstein, S. (1979). The stability of behavior: I. On predicting most of the people much of the time. *Journal of Personality and Social Psychology*, *37*, 1097-1126.

Farrell, A. D., Mariotto, M. J., Conger, A. J., Curran, J. P., & Wallander, J. L. (1979). Self-ratings and judges' ratings of heterosexual social anxiety and skill: A generalizability study. *Journal of Consulting and Clinical Psychology*, *47*, 164-175.

Fischetti, M., Curran, J. P., & Wessberg, H. W. (1977). Sense of timing: A skill deficit in heterosexually-socially anxious males. *Behavior Modification*, *1*, 179-194.

Galassi, J. P., & Galassi, M. D. (1979). Modification of heterosocial skills deficients. In A. S. Bellack & M. Hersen (Eds.), *Research and practice in social skills training.* New York: Plenum Press.

Goldstein, J. A. (1971). Investigation of doubling as a technique for involving severely withdrawn patients in group psychotherapy. *Journal of Consulting and Clinical Psychology*, *37*, 155-162.

Gorecki, P. R., Dickson, A. L., Anderson, N. N., & Jones, G. E. (1981). Relationship between contrived in vivo and role-play assertive behavior. *Journal of Clinical Psychology*, *31*, 104-107.

Greenson, R. (1967). *The techniques and practice of psycho-analysis.* New York: International Universities Press.

Heimberg, R. G., Montgomery, D., Madsen, C., & Heimberg, J. (1977). Assertion training: A review of the literature. *Behavior Therapy, 8,* 953-971.

Hersen, M. (1979). Modification of skill deficits in psychiatric patients. In A. S. Bellack & M. Hersen (Eds.), *Research and practice in social skills training.* New York: Plenum Press.

Higgins, R. L., Alonso, R. R., & Pendleton, M. G. (1979). The validity of role-play assessments on assertiveness. *Behavior Therapy, 10,* 655-662.

Higgins, R. L., Frisch, M. R., & Smith, D. (1983). Comparison of role-played and natural responses to identical circumstances. *Behavior Therapy, 14,* 158-169.

Hudson, W. (1973). Pre-discharge conference psychodrama. *Journal of Group Psychotherapy, Psychodrama, and Sociometry, 26,* 101-103.

Johnson, D. W. (1971). Role reversal: A summary and review of the research. *International Journal of Group Tensions, 1,* 318-334.

Kahn, S. (1964). *Psychodrama explained.* New York: Philosophical Library.

Kellermann, P. F. (1979). Transference, countertransference, and tele. *Journal of Group Psychotherapy, Psychodrama, and Sociometry, 32,* 38-55.

——. (1983). Resistance in psychodrama. *Journal of Group Psychotherapy, Psychodrama, and Sociometry, 36,* 30-43.

——. (1984). The place of catharsis in psychodrama. *Journal of Group Psychotherapy, Psychodrama, and Sociometry, 37,* 1-13.

Kelly, G. A. (1955). *The psychology of personal constructs* (Vol. 1). New York: John Wiley.

Kern, J. M. (1982). The comparative external and concurrent validity of three role-plays for assessing heterosexual performance. *Behavior Therapy, 13,* 666-680.

Kern, J. M., & MacDonald, M. L. (1980). Assessing assertion: An investigation of construct validity and reliability. *Journal of Consulting and Clinical Psychology, 53,* 532-534.

Kern, J. M., Miller, C., & Eggers, J. (1983). Enhancing the validity of role-play tests: A comparison of three role-play methodologies. *Behavior Therapy, 14,* 482-492.

Kipper, D. A. (1978). Trends in the research on the effectiveness of psychodrama: Retrospect and prospect. *Journal of Group Psychotherapy, Psychodrama, and Sociometry, 31*, 5-18.

Kreitler, H., & Kreitler, S. (1968). Validation of psychodramatic behaviour against behaviour in real life. *British Journal of Medical Psychology, 41*, 185-192.

Lazarus, A. A. (1971). *Behavior therapy and beyond.* New York: McGraw-Hill.

Leveton, E. (1977). *Psychodrama for the timid clinician.* New York: Springer.

Liberman, R. P., Wheeler, E., & Sanders, N. (1976). Behavioral therapy for marital disharmony: An educational approach. *Journal of Marriage and Family Counseling, 2*, 383-396.

MacDonald, M. L., Lindquist, C. U., Kramer, J. A., McGrath, R. A., & Rhyne, L. (1975). Social skills training: Behavior rehearsal in groups and dating skills. *Journal of Counseling Psychology, 22*, 224-230.

McFall, R. M. D., & Twentyman, C. T. (1973). Four experiments on the relative contribution of rehearsal, modeling, and coaching in assertion training. *Journal of Abnormal Psychology, 81*, 199-218.

McNamara, J. R., & Blumer, C. A. (1982). Role playing to assess social competence: Ecological validity considerations. *Behavior Modification, 6*, 519-549.

Moreno, J. L. (1923). *Das stegreif theater.* Potsdam: Kiepenhever.

Nietzel, M. T., & Bernstein, D. A. (1976). Effects of instructionally mediated demand on the behavioral assessment of assertiveness. *Journal of Consulting and Clinical Psychology, 44*, 500.

Perls, F. S. (1969). *Gestalt therapy verbatim.* Moab, Utah: Real People Press.

Rachman, S. (1972). Clinical applications of observational learning, imitation, and modeling. *Behavior Therapy, 3*, 379-397.

Rich, A. R., & Schroeder, H. E. (1976). Research issues in assertiveness training. *Psychological Bulletin, 83*, 1081-1096.

Rimm, D. C., & Masters, J. C. (1974). *Behavior therapy: Techniques and empirical findings.* New York: Academic Press.

Rose, S. D., Cayner, J. J., & Edleson, J. L. (1977). Measuring interpersonal competence. *Social Work, 22*, 125-129.

Shaw, M. E., Corsini, R. J., Blake, R. R., & Mouton, J. S. (1980). *Role playing: A practical manual for group facilitators.* San Diego: University Associates.

Stanton, H. R., & Litwak, E. (1955). Toward the development of a short form test of interpersonal competence. *American Sociological Review, 20,* 668-674.

Starr, A. (1977). *Psychodrama: Rehearsal for living.* Chicago: Nelson-Hall.

Stein, M. B., & Callahan, M. L. (1982). The use of psychodrama in individual psychotherapy. *Journal of Group Psychotherapy, Psychodrama, and Sociometry, 35,* 118-129.

Trower, P., Bryant, B., & Argyle, M. (1978). *Social skills and mental health.* Pittsburgh: University of Pittsburgh.

Van Hasselt, V. B., Hersen, M., & Bellack, A. S. (1981). The validity of role play tests for assessing social skills in children. *Behavior Therapy, 12,* 202-216.

Warren, N. J., & Gilner, F. H. (1978). Measurement of positive assertive behavior: The behavioral test of tenderness expression. *Behavior Therapy, 9,* 178-184.

Wessberg, H. W., Mariotto, M. J., Conger, A. J., Farrell, A. D., & Conger, J. C. (1979). Ecological validity of role plays for assessing heterosexual anxiety and skill of male college students. *Journal of Consulting and Clinical Psychology, 44,* 525-535.

6

PSYCHOLOGICAL INTERVENTION FOR DISTURBED ADOLESCENTS

Irving B. Weiner

Mental health professionals commonly divide themselves into those who work primarily with children and those who work primarily with adults. Unfortunately, child therapists tend to regard disturbed adolescents as the province of clinicians who work with adults, especially after they are out of early adolescence, while adult therapists regard them as the responsibility of child clinicians, at least until they reach late adolescence. In between fall young people roughly of high school age who are in middle adolescence, the developmental period that Blos (1962) aptly terms "adolescence proper." Although these middle adolescents are more likely than children and almost as likely as adults to become psychologically disturbed (see Weiner, 1982, Chap. 1), the supply of practitioners, clinics, and residential facilities able and willing to accept referrals of disturbed high school students is scarce in most communities.

This gap in available mental health services reflects at least in part the fact that disturbed adolescents can be difficult to understand and treat. Even clincians who have led the way in promoting psychotherapeutic work with troubled teenagers have consistently sounded this alarm. Anna Freud (1958) cautioned that "the analytic treatment of adolescents is a hazardous venture from beginning to end" (p. 261). According to Josselyn (1971), "therapy with the adolescent is probably, in general, the most challenging of all therapies" (p. 172). Meeks (1980) is even more specific in this regard: "Adolescent patients can be very frustrating. . . . At times it even appears that the young patient is more intent on making the therapist miserable than in using his help" (p. 4). Laufer and Laufer (1984) summarize the problem in this way:

> A large part of the professional community remains
> hesitant to treat [psychologically disturbed] adoles-
> cents. To some extent, this reluctance . . . can be
> understood as part of the historical caution or
> uncertainty in applying psychoanalytic and psychi-
> atric views to a period of psychological development
> that is characterized by changes of body and mind
> of such a magnitude that they might make our work
> unpredictable at best and dangerous at worst (p. xi).

On the other hand, the developmental characteristics of
adolescence make young people remarkably accessible to psychological interventions. Adolescents have matured sufficiently
to think about themselves, express their feelings, understand
other people, and take responsibility for their actions in a
much more sophisticated and effective manner than children.
At the same time, they have usually not developed the kinds
of crystallized psychopathology or chronic personality warps
often seen in disturbed adults, nor have they become as bur-
dened by past failures or current obligations that will restrict
them in taking their lives in new directions.

Hence, whatever challenges and hazards it entails, working
with adolescents to help them overcome psychological disturbances can be a fruitful and rewarding endeavor. Professionals
who understand adolescents and are skillful in involving
young people in a constructive psychotherapy relationship can
frequently make a big difference in their lives. In turn, adolescents who need professional help are generally able to
derive considerable benefit from it. Tramontana (1980) found
in a review of research on psychotherapy outcome with adolescents that about 75 percent of all adolescents receiving
psychotherapy (including individual, group, and family therapy) showed a positive outcome.

To maximize the likelihood of a positive outcome in working
with adolescents, psychotherapists need to tailor their approach
to fit the developmental needs of this age group. They need
in addition to be knowledgeable about the kinds of psychological disturbances that are most likely to occur during the
adolescent years and about specific kinds of interventions that
help to alleviate these disturbances.

Accordingly, the first section of this chapter addresses
general guidelines of conducting psychotherapy with adolescents. These guidelines are applicable for the most part
whether adolescents are being seen individually, in a group,
or with their families. In addition, the guidelines obtain
whether treatment is being conducted on an inpatient or outpatient basis. Subsequent sections of the chapter then consider specific interventions for (1) the two behavior problems
most commonly manifest in adolescents referred for professional help—misconduct or delinquency and academic underachievement; (2) two major varieties of psychopathology that

frequently first begin in adolescence—schizophrenic disorders and depressive disorder; and (3) two serious public health problems that often threaten the physical as well as psychological well-being of disturbed adolescents—suicidal behavior and drug abuse.

GENERAL GUIDELINES FOR CONDUCTING PSYCHO-THERAPY WITH ADOLESCENTS

In conducting psychotherapy, some younger adolescents can be treated like children and some older adolescents can be treated like adults. For most of the "middle adolescents" with whom this chapter is concerned, however, successful treatment requires a different frame of reference. As stressed by Kimmel and Weiner (1985, Chap. 1), the typical adolescent is "no longer a child; not yet an adult." This means that many of the strategies that clinicians customarily employ in treating adults or children must be replaced by an orientation and style of interaction that is distinctively geared to adolescent ways of thinking, feeling, and acting.

The manner in which patients of different ages enter psychotherapy demonstrates the need for a distinctive approach to adolescents. Adults typically come voluntarily and with some sense of what seeing a mental health professional signifies. Even those "involuntary" patients whose treatment is being mandated by someone else have made their own decision to appear for sessions rather than face whatever sanction is being held over their head—such as imprisonment being threatened by a judge, or divorce being threatened by a spouse, or dismissal from a job being threatened by an employer—unless therapy is undertaken. No matter how little they know about the procedures of psychotherapy, adults recognize that being in treatment identifies them as a person with mental or emotional problems for which professional help is needed.

Children, by contrast, are brought to psychotherapy by their parents, without having made any voluntary decision to pursue this course of action, and they comprehend very little of the professional identity and role of the therapist or of the purposes of their coming for regular visits. To be sure, child therapists may indicate that "This is a place where we try to help children who are having problems in school" or "Your parents wanted me to see you because they're worried that you don't get along with your friends very well." However, the next step is not to begin talking directly about such problems, but instead to direct the child to the playroom or indicate that "We'll be working together in the school part of the hospital."

Adolescents fall in between children and adults in these respects. Because they are not yet adults, they are typically brought to psychotherapy by their parents, and only in rare

instances have they had either the opportunity or the inclination to make a decision on their own to seek psychological
help. Yet being no longer children, they usually recognize
the implications of being taken to see a "shrink"—implications
they regard with varying degrees of anger, anxiety, and
embarrassment. The therapist cannot sugar-coat this pill by
techniques of the playroom or by acting as if the sessions
were intended for any purpose other than dealing with the
adolescent's psychological problems. Few things offend or
humiliate adolescents more than being treated like a child. On
the other hand, beginning to talk directly with adolescents
about their problems ordinarily does not cut the mustard either.
Not having sought professional help voluntarily, and often not
feeling any need for it, adolescents rarely come prepared to
talk about themselves with a total stranger. Typically their
first inclination is to resent and resist efforts by the therapist to initiate their participation in the kind of working alliance that usually characterizes psychotherapy with adults (for
example, "Why don't you begin by telling me something about
the problems you've been having").

Several strategies can help overcome these obstacles to
getting adolescents involved in a productive treatment relationship. Especially important in this regard are techniques for
promoting comfort, establishing motivation, and maintaining
the flow of communication in treatment sessions.

Promoting Comfort

Therapists should anticipate that their adolescent patients
will begin seeing them in a state of apprehension and aversion.
In almost every case, they will enter the therapist's office
worrying about what will be said and done to them and wish-
ing they were somewhere else. To avoid compounding such
concern and reluctance to no good purpose, the therapist
needs from the first moment of the initial contact to promote
an adolescent's feeling comfortable in the treatment situation.

An effective way of helping adolescent patients feel
comfortable is for the therapist to guide the treatment sessions
with easily answered questions. Consider, for example, opening
a first session with, "I understand you've been having some
problems in school; what's it like?" This gets the conversation
underway without demanding any particular kind of response.
Adolescents can answer by saying something about the problem, if they feel ready to do so, or they can make an appropriate response merely by saying something about what the
school is like. Generally speaking, open-ended questions that
allow optional ways of responding give adolescents a welcome
opportunity to proceed at their own pace without feeling particularly threatened. Similarly, asking an adolescent boy,
"What is your father like?" allows him to express his attitudes

toward his father, if he is prepared to be this forthcoming, or merely to describe his father in some objective terms—"Oh, he's about 40, and he has a business and he works pretty hard at it."

If even such nondemanding questions prove, because of their open-endedness, to be too difficult for a frightened or resistive adolescent to handle, the therapist should follow them up with even easier, more specific questions. For example, if "What is your school like?" is answered with "I don't know" or "What do you mean?", then the situation calls for "How many students are there?", "How far is it from where you live?", "What subjects are you taking?", or any other question that requests only a simple, factual bit of information.

For most adolescents the kinds of questions that should be avoided initially are those that require self-disclosure or speculation. "Why do you think you did that?" and "How do you feel about your parents?" are examples of two kinds of subjective probes that convince already apprehensive adolescents that they are indeed under an unfriendly gun. The clinical significance of such inquiries makes them very tempting for the therapist to employ; by avoiding them, however, and sticking instead with uncomplicated, unchallenging requests for seemingly mundane information, the therapist can turn a quick therapeutic profit. In the first place, the responses to simple questions are often surprisingly revealing (for example, the patient's father is described as working hard at his business) and provide background information the therapist will want to have sooner or later anyway (such as, what is the patient's school like?). Second, and of even greater import, a directive, nonchallenging approach in the initial interviews gives the adolescent the experience of having been engaged in a pleasant mutual conversation, albeit with a "shrink," and not in any kind of awkward, embarrassing, or painful interaction.

Allowing an adolescent to feel comfortable in psychotherapy sessions is of course not the key to providing effective treatment. For therapy to make a difference in the young person's life, attention will sooner or later have to focus on problems that are distressing to think about and feelings that are difficult to express, even at the expense of confrontations that disrupt the adolescent's sense of well-being. However, treatment is unlikely ever to reach a point where such confrontation can be endured and turned to constructive advantage unless the therapist can first promote comfort in the treatment situation.

Establishing Motivation

To counteract the initially involuntary status of adolescents as psychotherapy patients, the therapist needs to elicit some expression of their own wish or at least willingness to participate in treatment sessions. There are two obstacles to be overcome in this regard. First, adolescents typically experience a strong need to feel and to convey to others a sense of competence and self-assurance, which makes them reluctant to lay their faults and foibles on the table, especially in front of a stranger. Second, adolescents are also typically intent on asserting their self-reliance and individuation, which deters them from turning to adults for help, especially with respect to concerns about their family, peer, and heterosocial relationships (see Kimmel & Weiner, 1985).

Hence the therapist cannot sit back and expect adolescent patients to demonstrate their "motivation" for therapy by taking the initiative in talking about their problems or by expressing appreciation for having an opportunity to receive professional assistance. The therapist begins to surmount these obstacles by promoting comfort in the manner already discussed, which at least eases the patient's initial uneasiness and spares him or her from having to take the initiative. However, therapists who work hard to help their new adolescent patients feel comfortable and then wait for them in turn to say how glad they are to be in therapy and how eagerly they are looking forward to the treatment process will have a very long wait indeed—perhaps one lasting for their entire professional career.

The therapist needs to resist the temptation to sidestep this issue. The easy road taken (which involves going along with the likelihood that the adolescent will be brought for therapy and bypassing any struggle to get him or her to construe it as voluntary) usually turns out to be a road to nowhere. Adolescents who are allowed to cast themselves as involuntary participants will persist in seeing the therapist as someone else's agent, and not much will happen in the treatment. Research findings confirm that the more adolescents perceive themselves as having chosen voluntarily to enter and remain in psychotherapy, the more progress they are likely to make in the treatment (Bastien & Adelman, 1984); in a similar vein, the more strongly young people feel committed to their therapy, the better they adjust to it initially and the more they profit from it eventually (Adelman, Kaser-Boyd, & Taylor, 1984). Hence prospects for an effective treatment interaction are much better when the therapist invites discussion of the adolescent's feelings about discussing personal matters in a professional context and conveys sincerely that these feelings will play an important role in determining whether and how treatment will proceed.

To implement this strategy, the therapist should ask as an initial interview draws to a close, "What's it been like talking with me today?" If the interview has been conducted adequately with an eye to promoting comfort, the response is likely to be something on the order of "Okay, I guess" or

"Not as bad as I thought it would be." Instead of disappointing the therapist by falling short of unbridled enthusiasm ("This has been a marvelous experience"), such muted or even grudging allowances that the session has been something other than terribly painful or totally worthless provide some assurance that a good start has been made in building a constructive working relationship.

To capitalize on such indications of the adolescent's amenability to going further, the next question should be, "How would you feel about coming in again?" What the therapist is looking for in response is once more not a ringing endorsement, but only some at least fleeting indication of a self-determined willingness to continue, as in "I don't mind" or "It's all right with me."

When matters proceed in this way, the therapist has expressed respect for the adolescent's autonomy and the adolescent has come to his or her own decision about continuing. In pursuing this objective, the therapist should studiously disallow any response in which the adolescent avoids speaking in the first person. To the adolescent who answers, "I'd be willing to come back if *you* want me to," the therapist needs to say, "*I* think it would be worthwhile for us to talk some more, but it's what *you* want to do that's most important." To the adolescent who answers, "It doesn't matter how I feel about it, because *my parents* are going to bring me anyway if *you* say so," the therapist needs to say, "It may be true that your parents would bring you if I say so, but what I want to find out is how *you* feel about it, because that will be important in *you* and *I* deciding what *we* should do." With this kind of emphasis, the therapist keeps the focus where it belongs in establishing motivation, namely, on respect for the adolescent's dignity and for his or her own role in making a commitment to a treatment relationship.

The therapist's efforts to promote comfort and establish motivation in adolescent patients are especially important in the initial phase of the treatment. Although these strategies may continue to foster progress later on as well, adolescents who have become engaged in a trusting relationship with their therapist become increasingly able to tolerate discomfort during treatment sessions—so long as they can see being uncomfortable as a worthwhile price to pay for working meaningfully on difficult issues. They also become increasingly self-motivated over time—so long as they can see their discussions with the therapist as yielding some changes for the better in themselves or their situation. To sustain a good start in therapy that has been facilitated by allowing comfort and establishing motivation, the therapist subsequently needs to implement ways of maintaining a steady flow of communication.

Maintaining the Flow of Communication

Even after having committed themselves to a course of psychotherapy during some initial sessions, adolescents are still not as prepared as most adults to be spontaneous and forthcoming, especially in talking with a relatively unfamiliar adult. Moreover, young people are more likely than adults to worry about sessions that seem to go awkwardly ("If I weren't such a nerd there would be more to talk about") or involve long silences ("I wonder what will happen next?" "What is he thinking about me?" "Why can't I think of anything to say?"). As the treatment proceeds, the therapist needs to minimize awkwardnesses and silences by taking responsibility for maintaining the flow of communication during sessions. Two useful ways of implementing this strategy involve being *active* and being *direct*.

Activity

Therapists can help adolescent patients communicate by continuing to guide them during treatment sessions and responding promptly to what they have to say. This involves being more active than is customary in psychotherapy with adults and avoiding the usual practice of waiting for the patient to take the initiative in starting the conversation and choosing the topics for discussion. Such an unstructured approach often creates an unproductive uncertainty in working with adolescents, as does opening sessions with such questions as "Where would you like to begin?" or "What would you like to talk about today?" A preferable approach is to start the session off with some guidance as in "What's been happening since last week?" Similarly, as a session proceeds the therapist should be prepared to bring up topics for discussion, as in "How did that party you were talking about turn out?" or "I think we should spend a little time today talking about what's been going on in school."

As for responding promptly, the pregnant pauses that often stimulate significant verbalizations in therapy with adults suggest to adolescents that the thereapist is inattentive, disinterested, or at a loss for words. Hence the therapist is well-advised to opt for short response latencies that sustain a constant back-and-forth exchange. This rapid-cadence technique does not allow therapists much time to contemplate what the adolescent is saying or to formulate precisely phrased replies; indeed, therapists whose preferred treatment style involves reflecting leisurely on what is transpiring during a session and couching their observations in carefully chosen words often do not work as effectively with adolescent as with adult patients. What adolescents typically need to continue communicating in therapy is a forthcoming, up-front, nonmys-

terious style that gives them little occasion to wonder what is
going through the therapist's mind.

For most adolescents some of the time, and for some adolescents most of the time, having the therapist initiate the
session and keep up a running commentary may not be necessary and may even be experienced as patronizing or intrusive.
The therapist needs to recognize when the adolescent has a
story to tell or some feelings to express and would prefer not
to be interrupted or given any guidance concerning what to
talk about. On these occasions, therapy sessions with adolescents may proceed very similarly to those with adults. Ordinarily, provided the therapist is alert to them, these are
not the occasions that challenge his or her skills. The challenge comes when young people are having difficulty communicating, and that is when a high level of therapist activity
can make the difference between having a profitable or a
fruitless session.

Directness

Therapists can promote a steady flow of communication
with their adolescent patients by taking pains to be explicit
and concrete in their remarks and to explain themselves in
a forthright manner when asked to do so. The types of metaphorical activities that help children express themselves in
therapy, as in Gardner's (1971) story-telling technique, do
not sit well with most adolescents, nor do the types of
unstructured inquiry or elliptical allusion that often helps
adults increase their self-awareness (for example, "What comes
to your mind about that?" or "It's as if something is making
you afraid"). From a developmental perspective, adolescents
already have more than enough questions to which they are
trying to find answers, and they do not need or want their
therapist to add to this burden. The more ambiguous the
therapist is, and the more difficult it is for adolescents to
understand what their therapist means or intends by a particular comment, the harder they will find it to continue
responding.

For this reason, the best way for therapists to phrase
their observations on what the adolescent is saying is with
as little ambiguity or conjecture as possible. Hence, "I think
you're afraid of something" is better than, "It's as if something is making you afraid," because it is more explicit; it
places the matter directly on the table as something to be
discussed, without asking the adolescent to meditate on its
possible existence and without leaving the therapists's impression uncertain. Even better would be, "I think you get a
little frightened whenever you get in a situation where you
might fail," because, in addition to being explicit, it identifies in concrete terms the nature of the apparent problem.

Even in response to such explicit, concrete comments,
adolescents may feel unsure about whether to disclose them-

selves or exactly what the therapist has in mind. Then they
are likely to ask in turn, "Where did you get that idea?" or
"What do you mean by that?" or "Why did you bring that up?"
With adolescents, such questions usually do not call for the
therapist to remain silent or noncommittal or to turn them
back on the patient (for example, "What do you think I had
in mind?"). Once more this illustrates a tactic that can work
effectively with a reflective, voluntary adult patient who has
made a commitment to participate in exploratory psychotherapy,
but that will be viewed by adolescents as an insincere, non-
genuine way of playing games. Instead, therapists working
with adolescents need to be prepared to explain themselves.
Questions about what the therapist means or why he or she
has said something should be answered, promptly and directly
("Where I got that idea is that this is the third time this
month you've talked about getting ready to do something
where others would be judging how well you were doing, and
each time, although it was something you felt you really
wanted to do, you found some reason for backing out at the
last minute").

However, there are limits to how far the therapist should
go in providing such explanations. On some occasions what
the therapist has meant will be perfectly obvious, or the circumstances to which a statement refers will have already been
discussed several times, and yet the adolescent asks "What do
you mean" or "What are you talking about?" On these occasions the therapist needs to recognize that the adolescent is
not perplexed, but only stalling or perhaps trying to avoid
doing his or her share of the work in the treatment. Then,
consistently with the strategy of directness, the therapist
needs to say as much ("I mean just what I said" or "You know
what I'm talking about"). Used at the proper time and expressed without rancor, such seemingly testy statements serve
the useful purpose of conveying to the adolescent that the
therapist, in return for his or her being direct, expects the
adolescent not to play any games either.

INTERVENTION FOR MISCONDUCT
OR DELINQUENCY

A large percentage of adolescents seen by mental health
professionals have been referred because of some kind of
misconduct or delinquent behavior. The appropriate psychological intervention with these young people depends on
whether their misbehavior represents a pattern of socialized,
characterological, or neurotic delinquency.

Socialized delinquency is associated with membership in a
subculture that endorses antisocial standards of conduct and
in which breaking the law is a customary expression of a
way of life; socialized delinquents typically misbehave in

collaboration with peers among whom they are psychologically well-adjusted and socially accepted group members. Characterological delinquency reflects an essentially asocial orientation in which disregard for the rights and feelings of others and an inability or unwillingness to exercise self-control create a high likelihood of engaging in aggressive, inconsiderate, lawbreaking behavior; characterological delinquents are basically undersocialized individuals who become involved in solitary rather than group delinquency and meet standard diagnostic criteria for having a psychopathic or antisocial personality disorder. In neurotic delinquency, young people commit illegal acts neither as well-integrated members of a delinquent subculture nor as a reflection of personality disorder, but instead as a way of communicating some unmet psychological needs; like many other neurotic behaviors, neurotic delinquency is thus symptomatic of underlying concerns that it serves indirectly to express or "act out" (see Quay, 1965; Shaw, 1983; Weiner, 1975a, 1982, Chap. 11).

Treating Socialized Delinquency

When adolescent misconduct represents a pattern of socialized delinquency, there is usually little to be gained by employing traditional forms of psychotherapy. As relatively comfortable and well-integrated members of their peer group, and as people who tend to see any problems they have as residing in society and not in their own psychological makeup, socialized delinquents are rarely interested in or responsive to the ministrations of mental health professions. To date the best prospects for fostering change in these young people have been found in social or educational programs designed to attract subcultural delinquents to different value systems and different ways of living.

For example, some success has been achieved by neighborhood-based programs intended to acquaint socialized delinquents with opportunities for making money and enjoying themselves while remaining on the right side of the law. Such programs promote the Police Athletic League, provide job training and vocational counseling, instruct parents in ways of reinforcing socially acceptable behavior, and identify for socialized delinquents how their talents and energies could be profitably redirected into nondelinquent means of getting ahead in school and work situations. Other promising programs have been developed for training delinquent adolescents in specific academic, social, and vocational skills that can help them achieve success and deal with problem situations effectively (Coates, 1981; Collingwood & Genthner, 1980; Safer, 1982; Sarason & Sarason, 1981; Shore & Massimo, 1973; Ulrici, 1983).

Treating Characterological Delinquency

Because of its relationship to psychopathic or antisocial personality disorder, characterological delinquency is also difficult to treat. Adolescents whose misconduct represents this pattern of delinquency rarely trust or identify with other people, and they seldom feel inclined to consider changing their attitudes or outlook. This makes characterological delinquents difficult for even the ablest therapists to treat successfully. Some way must be found to break into the asocial orientation of these young people and foster feelings of closeness to and concern for others. As a barrier to such efforts, the characterological disorder of these delinquents leads them to shun personal intimacy and to distrust demonstrations of kindness and affection. They regard people who are nice to them as stupid or insincere and people who tolerate them as weak or indifferent. Hence their personality style blunts the expressions of caring and warmth on which therapists customarily rely to foster a good treatment relationship with disturbed adolescents (see Berman, 1964; Noshpitz, 1957).

In working with these young people, the therapist should strive to adopt a firm, controlling stance without being overbearing, punitive, or rejecting; to show interest and a willingness to listen while not appearing easy to impress or manipulate; to demonstrate determination to persist in trying to be helpful without seeming to offer or ask for a great deal of personal involvement; and to come across to the adolescent as someone who knows the ways of the world, has been successful in managing his or her own affairs, and can be depended on to talk good sense. In this kind of atmosphere, the therapist should talk with characterological delinquents about events in their lives and offer his or her perspectives on how these events might be viewed or responded to differently. If in this way therapists can help these young people function more effectively and experience more fun with less trouble, they have a shot at establishing some minimal trust and grudging respect on the part of the adolescent. This then gives the therapist some leverage for promoting better judgment, improved self-control, and the beginnings of a positive identification with others (see Awad, 1983; Chwast, 1977; Gibbs, Arnold, Ahlborn, & Cheesman, 1984).

Most clinicians experienced in working with characterological delinquents concur that successful implementation of this kind of treatment approach almost always requires residential care over an extended period of time. The defective interpersonal capacities of these young people make it extremely difficult to establish an engaged relationship with them in short-term therapy or on the basis of office visits alone. In addition, a milieu setting provides valuable opportunities for around-the-clock observation, which reduces obstacles to progress associated with the fact that characterological delinquents often cannot be relied on to give accurate reports about themselves in therapy sessions. Residential care also offers the salutary impact of a controlled external environment, which contributes to these young people building better internal controls (see Marohn, 1981; McCaughan, 1985; Sutker, Archer, & Kilpatrick, 1981).

Treating Neurotic Delinquency

As a symptomatic expression of unmet psychological needs, neurotic delinquency is in most cases more accessible to psychological intervention than socialized or characterological delinquency.

The most commonly felt needs of neurotic delinquents are for more attention and recognition than they have been getting from their parents and peers and for some help in resolving problems that are being ignored or misunderstood by others. This means that the inception of a treatment relationship can by itself minimize considerably the motivation to neurotic delinquency. The therapist provides a measure of attention that the young person has felt was lacking in his or her life and also stands able and willing to help address problems for which the adolescent has not been finding a responsive or empathic ear. For this reason, therapists often find that the misbehavior of neurotic delinquents begins to diminish shortly after regularly scheduled treatment sessions have started to occur.

In addition to drawing on the general effects of the treatment relationship to reduce the misbehavior of neurotic delinquents, therapists need to help these young people understand their motivations. The positive effects of being in treatment are unlikely to outlast the relationship with the therapist unless neurotic delinquents come to recognize exactly how and why their needs for attention or assistance led to their misbehavior. The persisting preventive effects of therapy with neurotic delinquents can be strengthened even further if the therapist can find occasions for guiding them in gaining the notice and support of other people in constructive ways that do not involve acting up or acting out.

INTERVENTION FOR ACADEMIC UNDERACHIEVEMENT

Among adolescents who demonstrate adequate intelligence and no specific learning disabilities but are nevertheless doing poorly in school, the gap between their capacity and their performance reflects either a *socioculturally determined* or a *psychologically determined* pattern of academic underachievement. Socioculturally determined underachievement involves a

disinterest in school learning fostered by some combination of
a family environment that discourages intellectual pursuits, a
peer-group context that devalues academic achievement, or a
set of sex-role attitudes that inhibits educational ambition.
Psychologically determined underachievement arises in connection with a constellation of (1) anger or resentment that young
people feel toward their parents but cannot express directly;
(2) concerns about competition and rivalry that are generating
fears of failure or success; and (3) a passive-aggressive
style of dealing with stressful situations. This constellation of
feelings and attitudes does not inevitably produce school
learning difficulties. However, in families that value education,
it disposes young people to a reluctance or refusal to do well
in school that can be termed *passive-aggressive underachievement* (see Baker, 1979; Canavan-Gumpert, Garner, & Gumpert,
1978; Weiner, 1982, Chap. 10; White, 1982).

Treating Socioculturally Determined Underachievement

Like socialized delinquency, and for many of the same
reasons, socioculturally determined underachievement can be
difficult to treat. Underachievers who are conforming to parental or peer-group values that denigrate school learning typically do not regard themselves as having a problem. They
see little to gain by improving their grades, and they are
seldom inclined to consider different ways of thinking or acting in relation to school. The therapist's task is to impress
upon socioculturally unmotivated students the distinct advantages of becoming as well-educated as they can. Typically
this involves fostering mutual confidence, trust, and respect
in the treatment relationship, despite the sociocultural underachiever's usual disinterest in being treated at all, and then
using the relationship as a basis for broadening the young
person's perspectives on the potential rewards of becoming
generally knowledgeable and occupationally well-qualified.
When this approach works successfully, unmotivated students
are likely to end up identifying and aspiring to goals that are
not shared by their parents and peers.

The school performance of unmotivated adolescents can
also be improved at times through direct efforts to modify or
circumvent the negative academic influences to which they
have been responding. For example, special instructional programs in the school aimed at improving basic language, reading, or math skills have been found to enhance the performance and personal satisfaction of underachieving students to
good effect, especially among adolescents from disadvantaged
backgrounds (Becker & Carnine, 1980). Promising results
have also been achieved through parent counseling aimed at
fostering more positive attitudes toward education and encouraging a more supportive home environment, such as by having

parents discuss homework assignments with their child and praise good school work (Adelman & Taylor, 1983; Rodick & Henggeler, 1980).

Treating Psychologically Determined Underachievement

Passive-aggressive underachievement, like neurotic delinquency, is relatively responsive to psychotherapy. The treatment should focus on helping adolescents with this problem recognize and express their anger toward their parents, work through their concerns about failure or success, and appreciate the ways in which they have been using passivity as a way of earning poor grades in school and thereby making their parents unhappy (see McIntyre, 1964; Weiner, 1971). Along with seeking to eliminate the symptom of underachievement by thus unraveling its motivations, the therapist should also look for opportunities to attack the problem in two more direct ways.

First, psychological underachievers should be helped to realize that their avoidance of good grades is self-defeating. That is, their method of making an impact on their parents is damaging their own prospects to achieve an education and a career commensurate with their abilities—they are cutting off their noses to spite their faces. If psychological underachievers can gain this recognition and be encouraged to look out more sensibly for their own best interests, their motivation to do well in school (in order to make themselves happy) may be increased sufficiently to inhibit their motivation to do poorly (in order to make their parents unhappy).

Second, the therapist may be able to use parent counseling to good effect. If the passive-aggressive underachiever's parents can be encouraged to relax whatever pressures they are placing on their child for academic excellence, the adolescent's motivation to bring home mediocre or failing grades will be lessened. Of particular significance in this regard, parents who no longer express as much concern or become as visibly upset about their youngster's bad grades make poor school performance no longer such an effective way for their son or daughter to act aggressively toward them.

The differing approaches recommended for working with parents of adolescents who are underachieving for different reasons illustrate the importance of an accurate differential diagnostic assessment in planning effective intervention. Whereas a useful strategy with parents of sociocultural underachievers is to increase their involvement in their child's school work, the indicated strategy with parents of psychological underachievers is often to get them to become less involved.

INTERVENTION FOR SCHIZOPHRENIC DISORDERS

Schizophrenic disorders involve multiple impairments of personality functioning, some of which may reflect inborn dispositions or vulnerabilities that are not remediable (Nuechterlein & Dawson, 1984; Wallace, 1984). However, two features of these disorders that are usually accessible to psychotherapy, especially in young people, consist of a limited capacity for interpersonal relatedness, and a diminished ability to perceive reality accurately. Accordingly, *relationship building* and *reality testing* can be considered the two Rs of treating schizophrenia, most particularly in conducting therapy with schizophrenic adolescents (see Arieti, 1974, Part 7; Karon & Vandenbos, 1981; Rinsley, 1980; Weiner, 1982, Chap. 6). The therapist should strive above all else to create an engaged, trusting, mutual relationship that gives schizophrenic adolescents a positive experience of interpersonal relatedness and then to use this relationship to help them recognize and revise their distorted impressions of themselves, their environment, and the consequences of their actions.

Relationship Building

Successful psychotherapy with schizophrenic adolescents hinges on how well the therapist can impress them as a warm, genuine, and understanding person who is interested in their welfare, who can be relied on to nurture without exploiting them, and who, as a professional, can bring special psychological skills to bear on their behalf. Most schizophrenic adolescents have suffered repeated experiences of frustration, humiliation, and rejection in social situations, as a consequence of which they have become physically or emotionally withdrawn from other people. To begin reversing this chain of circumstance, the therapist needs to demonstrate that he or she is at least one person who can comprehend the young person's thoughts and feelings and will respond to them without scorn or ridicule. Once a positive experience of interpersonal relatedness begins to become established with the therapist, it creates possibilities for adaptive generalization to the adolescents' interactions with other people in their lives, and it also provides a basis for working on the schizophrenic adolescent's defective reality testing.

Building a positive relationship with schizophrenic adolescents does not always entail being accepting and agreeable, however. A tolerant approach fosters engagement when adolescents are frightened or depressed, but it has little constructive impact when they are angry or rebellious. Some schizophrenic adolescents manifest antisocial attitudes or behavior along with their interpersonal and cognitive impairments. For these youngsters, as in working with characterological delinquents, relationship building requires actively challenging their views and setting strict limits on their behavior. When properly employed, without anger or punitiveness, criticism and firmness convey that the therapist cares enough and is strong enough to persist, even in the face of belligerence, with efforts to help the adolescent get along better.

Whatever balance seems best to strike between tolerance and firmness in order to make contact with a schizophrenic adolescent, the therapist needs to recognize that many of these young people will enter therapy heavily insulated against forming any emotional ties. The more fearful they are of intimacy, the more intently they will fend off the therapist's overtures, whatever form they take, and the more necessary it may be to interpret these fears in order to initiate an engaged treatment relationship. In framing such interpretations, the therapist must be attuned to the frequently metaphorical quality of the schizophrenic youngster's speech (see Parker, 1962). Thus to an adolescent who says, "I'm a machine," an effective response may be, "If you were a machine, you wouldn't have any feelings and you wouldn't have to worry about anyone hurting you."

Reality Testing

Therapists need to provide schizophrenic adolescents with continual and direct corrections of their distorted perceptions (see Gibson, 1974; Holmes, 1964, Chap. 10). Severely disturbed young people who are having delusions or hallucinations must be helped to recognize that these impressions grow out of their fears and expectations and have no firm basis in reality. This involves neither pretending to accept delusions and hallucinations as real, which would be dishonest, nor disparaging them as not worth talking about, which would be rejecting. Instead, the therapist needs first to indicate to schizophrenic adolescents that, although such experiences are real to them, they are not real to the therapist or to most other people. The next step is to identify from the content of such unreal experiences and from the circumstances in which they occur what kinds of underlying concerns they reflect. Gaining some understanding of why and when unreal experiences have been occurring typically reduces the frequency of their recurrence and achieves two other purposes as well: It lessens the anxiety that is felt when these experiences do recur, and it increases the schizophrenic person's ability to prevent them from influencing what he or she says or does.

In less severely disturbed schizophrenic adolescents, impaired reality testing tends to be manifest primarily in poor social judgment. Because these adolescents misperceive the

impact of their behavior on others and misinterpret the significance of others' actions toward them, they are often awkward,
inept, or even offensive in interpersonal situations, without
intending to be. An effective way of dealing with this problem
consists of working directly on improving the adolescent's
social skills. In discussing unpleasant interpersonal experiences, for example, the therapist can initiate consideration
of how these situations could have been seen more accurately,
how the consequences of what was said or done could have
been anticipated more correctly, and what alternative ways
of behaving might have produced a more desirable outcome.

Forthcoming situations also provide opportunities for
direct attention to sharpening social judgment. Often, for
example, techniques of role-playing and role-rehearsal can be
used to good effect in helping schizophrenic adolescents prepare for and handle social interactions more effectively than
they would have otherwise. Like the elements of a positive
relationship with the therapist, bits and pieces of improved
reality testing achieved through such strategies elicit positive
reinforcements from the environment that contribute to their
generalizing to increasing numbers of situations. Once fostered,
then, improved reality testing has good prospects for sustaining itself through the enhanced satisfaction it provides
the schizophrenic person.

As in balancing tolerance and firmness to build a good
treatment relationship with schizophrenic adolescents, however,
efforts to sharpen their reality testing must be undertaken
judiciously. Pointing out errors in how people view their world
without seeming derogatory or hostile is not easy to do, and
schizophrenic adolescents are quick to take criticism as meaning "You don't like me" or "You don't think much of me."
Therapists cannot afford to be apostles of reality at the expense of undermining their relationship with a schizophrenic
young person. This means that they must keep their efforts
to improve the young person's reality testing within the limits
of his or her ability to see them as well-intended and not as
dislike or rejection.

INTERVENTION FOR DEPRESSIVE DISORDER

Depressive disorder is commonly characterized by an experienced sense of loss that has precipitated the onset of the
disorder and is serving to perpetuate it. A depressing sense
of loss may be experienced on either a *real* or a *fantasied*
basis. Real loss involves actual events that deprive people of
something that is important to them. Among adolescents, for
example, being spurned by a boyfriend or girlfriend, failing
a test or finishing last in a race, and having to wear braces
on their teeth deprive a young person, respectively, of a
valued personal relationship, a desired success, and a grati-

fying sense of bodily integrity. Fantasied loss involves unrealistic concerns that cause people to feel deprived in the absence of any apparently depriving circumstances. Feelings of
having been rejected, of having performed poorly, or of
having become unattractive, arising without solid basis in
fact, are among the fantasied losses that frequently contribute
to people becoming depressed (see Malmquist, 1976; Toolan,
1978; Weiner, 1975b). The key element in successful psychotherapy of depressive disorder consists of relieving the depressed person's sense of loss. In addition, recovery from
the disorder can be hastened by a variety of strategies aimed
at minimizing its manifest symptomatology.

Relieving the Sense of Loss

Therapists usually begin to relieve a depressed person's
sense of loss as soon as they enter into his or her life as
someone genuinely interested, concerned, and wanting to be
of help. By becoming a new object for the adolescent and increasing by at least one the number of dependable relationships he or she has with other people, they can lessen from
the first session on the feelings of loneliness that a depressed
adolescent typically feels. In addition to drawing on the salutary effects of the relationship they are providing, therapists
can hasten recovery from depression by helping depressed
young people effectively come to grips with the particular circumstances that are generating their sense of loss (see Arieti
& Bemporad, 1978, Chap. 15; Feinstein, 1975).

When loss has been experienced in relation to a real
event, such as a broken friendship or a failure in school, the
resulting depression often responds to relatively superficial
discussions that assist young people in seeing the loss as
less tragic, less permanent, and less irreparable than they
had thought it to be. If the sense of loss stems from fantasied
or unrealistic concerns, especially if the young person is not
fully aware of the nature of these concerns, then more extensive exploration may be necessary to identify and arrive at
a less troubling perspective on the problem.

Minimizing Manifest Symptomatology

Although tracing and resolving a sense of loss holds the
key to psychological treatment of depression, therapy also
needs to address the manifest symptoms of the disorder. In
adolescents as in adults, these typically comprise some combination of (1) a dejected mood state that is undermining the
depressed individual's capacity to experience pleasure and
diminishing his or her interest in people and previously enjoyed pursuits; (2) negative attitudes toward themselves, the

world, and the future that are causing depressed persons to suffer from low self-esteem, a gloomy and pessimistic outlook, and feelings of helplessness and hopelessness; and (3) a depleted energy level that is being manifest in pervasive lethargy and apathy (see Kazdin & Petti, 1982; Strober, 1983; Weiner, 1982, Chap. 7). Over time such symptoms can become so habitual that they persist even after the depressive concerns that prompted them have been dispelled. Hence it is important for therapists to treat these symptoms directly along with making efforts to help depressed adolescents understand and overcome their sense of loss.

Dejected Mood

Depressed people cannot easily be cheered up; if they could, the efforts of well-meaning friends and relatives would be sufficient to relieve depressive disorder, without help from a professional. However, the therapist who proceeds carefully can lift the dejected mood of depressed adolescents by working around it and ferreting out whatever opportunities there may be to talk about positive emotional experiences they are still having. Depressed moods have been found to be self-remitting phenomena (Keller, Shapiro, Lavori, & Wolf, 1982), and they tend to diminish in time if the person can avoid dwelling on them. The more time and attention that is being devoted to thinking and talking about pleasant emotional experiences, both in and outside of the therapy, the less time and attention remains for brooding about the unpleasant ones, and the sooner their impact will fade.

Negative Attitudes

Regarding negative attitudes, progress toward less gloomy and more realistic perspectives ordinarily can be facilitated by techniques developed within the framework of cognitive models for formulating and treating depression (see Beck, 1979; Emery, Bedrosian, & Garber, 1983; Zeiss, Lewinsohn, & Munoz, 1979). As in efforts to improve the reality testing of schizophrenic adolescents, this involves discussing specific events and circumstances in the adolescent's life with an eye to identifying and resolving discrepancies between what actually is or was the case and whatever depressing impressions the young person has formed. These techniques help depressed adolescents recognize that they are feeling bad as a result of what they are thinking and saying to themselves, not because of insurmountable obstacles to their happiness in the real world.

Depleted Energy

In counteracting depleted energy, the therapist should regard the depressed adolescent as a wind-up clock that has run down and needs rewinding. The strategy here involves finding ways of getting lethargic, disinterested adolescents moving again; the tactics consist of identifying where their talents lie, what situations they have enjoyed or done well in previously, and what remaining embers of aspiration there are that can be fanned into some blaze of enthusiasm (see Glaser, 1978). Any step that depressed adolescents can be encouraged to take in a pleasurable direction creates an opportunity for reversing the downward cycle of their lethargy; becoming reengaged in rewarding pursuits has a potent reinforcing effect that helps to replace apathy with activity.

There are instances in which depressed young people attempt to ward off feeling sad, discouraged, and lethargic through problem behavior that suggests the presence of a conduct disorder or asocial personality orientation (see Gibbs, 1981; Inamdar, Siomopoulos, Osborn, & Bianchi, 1979). Therapists working with disruptive or delinquent adolescents need to make a careful differential diagnosis in this regard. Misbehaving adolescents whose primary psychological difficulty consists of being depressed may show little positive response to treatment focused on their conduct, at least as measured by the persistence of problem behavior (Exner & Weiner, 1982, Chap. 6). When accurately evaluated, however, and treated for depression in the manner discussed here, these young people are likely to curtail or discontinue entirely their problem behavior as soon as they become engaged in a treatment relationship.

INTERVENTION FOR SUICIDAL BEHAVIOR

Suicidal behavior in young people usually occurs as the end result of an unfolding process marked by four distressing kinds of life experience. First, suicidal adolescents are much more likely than their peers to have grown up in disrupted, disorganized homes characterized by long-standing family instability and discord. Second, there has usually been an escalation in family problems during the months prior to an adolescent's attempting or committing suicide, including a particularly sharp increase in parent-child conflicts that are causing the adolescent to feel powerless. Third, most suicidal adolescents have come to feel alienated from their parents and cut off from other personal relationships that have been important to them. Fourth, adolescents who engage in suicidal behavior have usually failed in a series of increasingly desperate efforts to resolve their escalating problems in other ways and have come to the conclusion that harming themselves is the only means they have left for getting through to other people, especially their parents, and bringing about some change in their circumstances (see Cantor, 1976; Garfinkel,

Froese, & Hood, 1982; Mehr, Zeltzer, & Robinson, 1981; Weiner, 1982, Chap. 12).

There is one overriding consideration in treating adolescents who have attempted suicide: *Every such attempt must be taken seriously.* Even the mildest suicidal gesture is intended to communicate some problem for which no other solution seems available. When no one responds, when the people to whom the suicidal adolescent is desperately trying to say something decline to listen or refuse to hear, then what is likely to follow are repeated suicide attempts, each one more damaging and life-threatening than its predecessor, until someone finally does pay attention—hopefully before it is too late to save the young person's life. Therapists working with suicidal adolescents should always assume that some unappreciated distress and some breakdown in interpersonal relationships have led to their self-destructive behavior. This calls in the treatment for seeking first to open lines of communication between suicidal young people and those around them and striving next to help these adolescents recognize and understand the motives underlying their suicidal actions (see Sheras, 1983; Toolan, 1984; Walker & Mehr, 1983).

Opening Lines of Communication

By being an interested and concerned person, eager to listen and understand, the therapist can begin to alter the typical conviction of suicidal adolescents that they are cut off from the affection, nurturance, and support of others. Beyond these customary benefits of building a positive treatment relationship, therapists seeing suicidal adolescents need to make an explicit and unqualified commitment to becoming, for as long as necessary, their "lifeline." This commitment includes being reachable around the clock to talk about troubling concerns, especially thoughts of another suicide attempt. By restoring hope that drastic action may not be necessary to get someone to pay attention and by creating opportunities to talk before acting on any further self-destructive urges, such determined intervention sharply reduces the immediate risk of recurring suicide attempts.

The therapist should also seek to establish similar lines of communication between suicidal adolescents and their family and friends. Working with the parents or meeting in family sessions is especially vital if therapy for these young people is to have any sustained effect (see Richman, 1984). The parents must be guided in becoming more alert and responsive to their child's problems, and the adolescent must be guided toward effective ways of communicating with his or her parents through words rather than actions. In individual sessions, the therapist should seek to help suicidal adolescents expand and enrich their friendships, both by encouraging them to seek new friends and by counseling them in more effective ways of handling their existing relationships. The more people there are with whom adolescents feel they can communicate and the more gratifying opportunities they have to share their feelings and concerns with others, the less likely they are to engage in suicidal behavior.

Identifying Underlying Motives

Along with establishing good lines of communication in the lives of suicidal adolescents, therapists should review with them the entire sequence of long-standing and mounting family problems, dissolving social relationships, and unsuccessful problem-solving that has preceded their suicide attempt. Suicide attempters who are feeling encouraged by supportive responses from the therapist and from their parents may resist this kind of discussion; often they would rather forget about their suicidal behavior than talk more about it. Nevertheless, they need very badly to vent the feelings associated with past unpleasant events in their lives and to see clearly how these events influenced their decision to attempt suicide. Suicidal risk tends to persist, no matter how good the young person is feeling about new or improved lines of communication, unless he or she can be helped to identify and acknowledge the motives underlying a suicide attempt.

Especially important in this regard is some exploration of the purposes the suicide attempt was intended to serve. What was the young person trying to communicate, and to whom? What changes was he or she hoping to bring about in whose behavior? Answers to such questions, openly discussed, provide a basis not only for eliminating suicidal behavior as a problem-solving technique, but also for resolving the problems that created an intolerable psychological impasse in the first place.

INTERVENTION FOR DRUG ABUSE

People who use drugs excessively, to the detriment of their physical and psychological well-being, typically show one of two patterns of drug abuse. In primary or addictive drug use, the person has become habituated to one or more drugs and comes to depend on their effects to feel good. Addictive drug use constitutes a chronic way of life and is characterized by the addict's susceptibility to withdrawal symptoms when deprived of drugs. In secondary or medicinal drug use, drugs are taken to relieve anxiety or tension or to enjoy a drug experience for its own sake. Secondary drug abuse occurs not as a chronic way of life, but as a reaction to distressing life events that the person is trying to avoid thinking or worrying about. These two patterns of drug abuse call for somewhat different strategies in working with drug-taking adolescents.

Treating Medicinal Drug Abuse

Because medicinal drug users are seeking to escape from feeling upset about circumstances in their lives, they usually respond well to psychotherapy aimed at easing their tensions and helping them find more effective ways of coping with whatever situations are giving them difficulty. As in the case of other behavior problems that are secondary to psychological concerns, such as neurotic delinquency and passive-aggressive underachievement, some resolution of the underlying concerns reduces the problem behavior by eliminating its basic cause.

Although medicinal drug abuse can thus be conceptualized and treated largely as an instance of individual psychopathology, some work with the young person's parent can also be helpful in minimizing symptomatic drug-taking. With respect to symptom selection, first, substantial relationships have been found between the likelihood of adolescents using drugs and the extent of their parents' use of alcohol, patent medicines, and both prescribed and illegal drugs (Johnson, Shontz, & Locke, 1984; Newcomb, Huba, & Bentler, 1983; Rees & Wilborn, 1983). Parents who present a "drug culture" at home for their children to emulate, even if they are not themselves using illegal drugs, should be encouraged to lessen if they can, their own "medicinal" orientation to life. Parents who can be helped to take a strong, explicit stand against using drugs, in what they say and what they do, can significantly influence their children to curb medicinal drug-taking (Griffin, 1981; Stanton, 1979).

Second, not uncommonly among medicinal drug-abusing adolescents, family discord is one of the major distressing events to which they are reacting symptomatically. Therapists need to explore the extent to which a negative family climate is contributing to youthful drug abuse and to focus their treatment efforts accordingly. Depending on the circumstances, a young person's motivation to abuse drugs may be decreased by successful efforts to improve the marital relationship between his or her parents or by effective family counseling in improved parent-child understanding and communication (see Millman, 1978).

Treating Addictive Drug Abuse

Whatever its original sources, addictive drug use has usually become a primary disorder in its own right. As an habitual, ego-syntonic pattern rather than an ego-alien reaction to specific circumstances, drug addiction poses many of the same kinds of obstacles to effective psychotherapy as characterological delinquency. Drug-addicted adolescents tend to deny needing any psychological help and to resist close or mutual relationships with a therapist. Office visits often prove insufficient to influence changes in what has become an ingrained life-style. For these reasons many authorities have concluded that addictive drug use can be successfully treated only in a residential setting that provides a total therapeutic community over an extended period of time (see Amini & Salasnek, 1975; Krug, 1983; Proskauer & Rolland, 1973).

As is widely known, however, even successful drug rehabilitation in a controlled environment frequently proves inadequate to buffer addicts against relapse when they return to the peer-group and neighborhood environment in which their drug problems initially emerged. Hence a treatment program should address as much as possible the interpersonal context of an addicted adolescent's life. To the extent that peer modeling, friendships based on shared drug involvement, and the lack of rewarding relationships with others have been contributing to the drug problem, they should be a central focus of individual discussions with the adolescent. In addition, group therapy and neighborhood counseling programs can be used to good advantage in efforts to reduce drug dependency. The more that socially influenced drug abusers can be helped to form friendships with peers and adults from similar backgrounds who do not abuse drugs, the better their prospects are for identifying and choosing a nondrug alternative life-style (see Bratter, 1973; Dembo & Burgos, 1976; Gullotta & Adams, 1982).

CONCLUSION

Implicit in this overview of psychological interventions with disturbed adolescents are two general principles of providing effective psychotherapy that should be made explicit in concluding the chapter. The first of these is that appropriate treatment strategies flow from careful diagnostic assessment, and the second is that optimal treatment effects flow from carefully crafted combinations of relationship-building, awareness-expanding, and behavior-shaping techniques.

With respect to the first principle, there is no sensible way to escape the fact that you can't treat something effectively if you don't know what it is. Interventions employed without regard to specific and distinctive characteristics of a person's disorder may in some fortuitous circumstances prove helpful; however, such unguided interventions are much less likely to yield benefits than are interventions thoughtfully chosen to address the particular psychological problems and personal needs of the person being treated. As elaborated in this chapter, diagnostically informed intervention with adolescents means not only identifying strategies applicable to this age group and to broad categories of disorder, but also differentiating subtypes or variations within a single kind of disorder that call for different treatment approaches.

Regarding the second principle, it very often proves the case that treatment approaches based solely on the expected benefits of a good relationship with the therapist, or on the anticipated salutary effects of promoting increased self-understanding, or on the predictable positive impact of appropriately designed schedules of reinforcement are less helpful to disturbed adolescents than are integrations of these strategies tailored to address specific clinical circumstances. The psychological interventions described in this chapter have accordingly incorporated aspects of all three approaches in formulating differential intervention planning.

REFERENCES

Adelman, H. S., Kaser-Boyd, N., & Taylor, L. (1984). Children's participation in consent for psychotherapy and their subsequent response to treatment. *Journal of Clinical Child Psychology, 13*, 170-178.

Adelman, H. S., & Taylor, L. (1983). Enhancing motivation for overcoming learning and behavior problems. *Journal of Learning Disabilities, 16*, 384-392.

Amini, F., & Salasnek, S. (1975). Adolescent drug abuse: Search for a treatment model. *Comprehensive Psychiatry, 16*, 379-389.

Arieti, S. (1974). *Interpretation of schizophrenia* (2nd ed.). New York: Basic Books.

Arieti, S., & Bemporad, J. (1978). *Severe and mild depression.* New York: Basic Books.

Awad, G. W. (1983). The middle phase of psychotherapy with antisocial adolescents. *American Journal of Psychotherapy, 37*, 190-201.

Baker, H. S. (1979). The conquering hero quits: Narcissistic factors in underachievement and failure. *American Journal of Psychotherapy, 33*, 418-427.

Bastien, R. T., & Adelman, H. S. (1984). Noncompulsory vs. legally mandated placement, perceived choice, and response to treatment among adolescents. *Journal of Consulting and Clinical Psychology, 52*, 171-179.

Beck, A. T. (1979). *Cognitive therapy of depression.* New York: Guilford Press.

Becker, W. C., & Carnine, D. W. (1980). Direct instruction: An effective approach to educational intervention with the disadvantaged and low performers. In B. B. Lahey & A. E. Kazdin (Eds.), *Advances in clinical child psychology* (Vol. 3, pp. 429-473). New York: Plenum Press.

Berman, S. (1964). Techniques of treating a form of juvenile delinquency, the antisocial character disorder. *Journal of the American Academy of Child Psychiatry, 3,* 24-52.

Blos, P. (1962). *On adolescence.* New York: Free Press of Glencoe.

Bratter, T. E. (1973). Treating alienated, unmotivated, drug abusing adolescents. *American Journal of Psychotherapy, 27,* 583-598.

Canavan-Gumpert, D., Garner, K., & Gumpert, P. (1978). *The success-fearing personality.* Lexington, Mass.: D. C. Heath.

Cantor, P. C. (1976). Personality characteristics found among youthful suicide attempters. *Journal of Abnormal Psychology, 85,* 324-329.

Chwast, J. (1977). Psychotherapy of disadvantaged acting out adolescents. *American Journal of Psychotherapy, 31,* 216-226.

Coates, R. B. (1981). Community-based services for juvenile delinquents. *Journal of Social Issues, 37,* 87-101.

Collingwood, T. R., & Genthner, R. W. (1980). Skills training as treatment for juvenile delinquents. *Professional Psychology, 11,* 591-598.

Dembo, R., & Burgos, W. (1976). A framework for developing drug abuse prevention strategies for young people in ghetto areas. *Journal of Drug Education, 6,* 313-325.

Emery, G., Bedrosian, R., & Garber, J. (1983). Cognitive therapy with depressed children and adolescents. In D. Cantwell & G. Carlson (Eds.), *Affective disorders in childhood and adolescence* (pp. 445-472). New York: Spectrum Publications.

Exner, J. E., & Weiner, I. B. (1982). *The Rorschach Comprehensive System: Vol. 3. Assessment of children and adolescents.* New York: John Wiley.

Feinstein, S. C. (1975). Adolescent depression. In E. J. Anthony & T. Benedek (Eds.), *Depression and human existence* (pp. 317-336). Boston: Little, Brown.

Freud, A. (1958). Adolescence. *Psychoanalytic Study of the Child, 13,* 255-278.

Gardner, R. A. (1971). *Therapeutic communication with children: The mutual storytelling technique.* New York: Science House.

Garfinkel, B. D., Froese, A., & Hood, J. (1982). Suicide attempts in children and adolescents. *American Journal of Psychiatry, 139,* 1252-1261.

Gibbs, J. C., Arnold, K. D., Ahlborn, H. H., & Cheesman, F. L. (1984). Facilitation of sociomoral reasoning in delinquents. *Journal of Consulting and Clinical Psychology, 52,* 37-45.

Gibbs, J. W. (1981). Depression and suicidal behavior among delinquent females. *Journal of Youth and Adolescence, 19,* 159-167.

Gibson, R. W. (1974). The intensive psychotherapy of hospitalized adolescents. *Journal of the American Academy of Psychoanalysis, 2,* 187-200.

Glaser, K. (1978). The treatment of depressed and suicidal adolescents. *American Journal of Psychotherapy, 32,* 252-269.

Griffin, J. B. (1981). Some psychodynamic considerations in the treatment of drug abuse in early adolescence. *Journal of the American Academy of Child Psychiatry, 20,* 159-166.

Gullotta, T., & Adams, G. R. (1982). Substance abuse minimization: Conceptualizing prevention in adolescent and youth programs. *Journal of Youth and Adolescence, 11,* 409-424.

Holmes, D. J. (1964). *The adolescent in psychotherapy.* Boston: Little, Brown.

Inamdar, S. C., Siomopoulos, G., Osborn, J., & Bianchi, E. C. (1979). Phenomenology associated with depressed moods in adolescents. *American Journal of Psychiatry, 136,* 156-159.

Johnson, G. M., Shontz, F. C., & Locke, T. P. (1984). Relationships between adolescent drug use and parental drug behaviors. *Adolescence, 19,* 295-299.

Josselyn, I. (1971). *Adolescence.* New York: Harper & Row.

Karon, B. P., & Vandenbos, G. R. (1981). *Psychotherapy of schizophrenia.* New York: Aronson.

Kazdin, A. E., & Petti, T. A. (1982). Self-report and interview measures of childhood and adolescent depression. *Journal of Child Psychology and Psychiatry, 23,* 437-457.

Keller, M. B., Shapiro, R. W., Lavori, P. W., & Wolf, N. (1982). Recovery in major depressive disorder. *Archives of General Psychiatry, 39,* 911-915.

Kimmel, D. C., & Weiner, I. B. (1985). Adolescence: A developmental transition. Hillsdale, N.J.: Lawrence Erlbaum.

Krug, R. S. (1983). Substance abuse. In C. E. Walker & M. C. Roberts (Eds.), Handbook of clinical child psychology (pp. 853-879). New York: John Wiley.

Laufer, M., & Laufer, M. E. (1984). Adolescence and developmental breakdown: A psychoanalytic view. New Haven, Conn.: Yale University Press.

Malmquist, C. P. (1976). The theoretical status of depressions in childhood. In E. J. Anthony & D. C. Gilpin (Eds.), Three clinical faces of childhood (pp. 173-204). New York: Halsted.

Marohn, R. C. (1981). Hospital treatment of the behaviorally disordered adolescent. In W. H. Reid (Ed.), The treatment of antisocial disorders (pp. 146-161). New York: Van Nostrand Reinhold.

McCaughan, D. L. (1985). Teaching and learning adolescent psychotherapy. Adolescent Psychiatry, 12, 414-433.

McIntyre, P. M. (1964). Dynamics and treatment of the passive-aggressive underachiever. American Journal of Psychotherapy, 18, 95-108.

Meeks, J. E. (1980). The fragile alliance: An orientation to the outpatient psychotherapy of the adolescent (2nd ed.). Malabar, Fla.: Krieger.

Mehr, M., Zeltzer, L. K., & Robinson, R. (1981). Continued self-destructive behaviors in adolescent suicide attempters: Part I. Journal of Adolescent Health Care, 1, 269-274.

Millman, R. B. (1978). Drug and alcohol abuse. In B. B. Wolman (Ed.), Handbook of treatment of mental disorders in childhood and adolescence (pp. 238-267). Englewood Cliffs, N.J.: Prentice-Hall.

Newcomb, M. D., Huba, G. J., & Bentler, P. M. (1983). Mothers' influence on the drug use of their children: Confirmatory tests of direct modeling and mediational theories. Developmental Psychology, 19, 714-726.

Noshpitz, J. D. (1957). Opening phase in the psychotherapy of adolescents with character disorders. Bulletin of the Menninger Clinic, 21, 153-164.

Nuechterlein, K. H., & Dawson, M. E. (1984). Information processing and attentional functioning in the development and course of schizophrenia. Schizophrenia Bulletin, 10, 160-203.

Parker, B. (1962). My language is me: Psychotherapy with a disturbed adolescent. New York: Basic Books.

Proskauer, S., & Rolland, R. S. (1973). Youth who use drugs: Psychodynamic diagnosis and treatment planning. *Journal of the American Academy of Child Psychiatry, 12,* 32–47.

Quay, H. C. (1965). Personality and delinquency. In H. C. Quay (Ed.), *Juvenile delinquency: Research and theory* (pp. 139–169). Princeton, N.J.: Van Nostrand.

Rees, C. D., & Wilborn, B. L. (1983). Correlates of drug abuse in adolescents: A comparison of families of drug abusers with families of nondrug abusers. *Journal of Youth and Adolescence, 12,* 55–64.

Richman, J. (1984). The family therapy of suicidal adolescents. In H. S. Sudak, A. B. Ford, & N. B. Rushforth (Eds.), *Suicide in the young* (pp. 393–406). Boston: Wright.

Rinsley, D. B. (Ed.). (1980). *Treatment of the severely disturbed adolescent.* New York: Aronson.

Rodick, J. D., & Henggeler, S. W. (1980). The short-term and long-term amelioration of academic and motivational deficiencies among low-achieving inner-city adolescents. *Child Development, 52,* 1126–1132.

Safer, D. J. (Ed.). (1982). *School programs for disruptive adolescents.* Baltimore: University Park Press.

Sarason, I. G., & Sarason, B. R. (1981). Teaching cognitive and social skills to high school students. *Journal of Consulting and Clinical Psychology, 49,* 908–918.

Shaw, W. J. (1983). Delinquency and criminal behavior. In C. E. Walker & M. C. Roberts (Eds.), *Handbook of clinical child psychology* (pp. 880–902). New York: John Wiley.

Sheras, P. L. (1983). Suicide in adolescence. In C. E. Walker & M. C. Roberts (Eds.), *Handbook of clinical child psychology* (pp. 759–784). New York: John Wiley.

Shore, M. F., & Massimo, J. L. (1973). After ten years: A follow-up study of comprehensive vocationally-oriented psychotherapy. *American Journal of Orthopsychiatry, 43,* 128–132.

Stanton, M. D. (1979). Family treatment approaches to drug abuse problems: A review. *Family Process, 18,* 251–258.

Strober, M. (1983). Clinical and biological perspectives on depressive disorders in adolescence. In D. Cantwell & G. Carlson (Eds.), *Affective disorders in childhood and adolescence* (pp. 97–105). New York: Spectrum Publications.

Sutker, P. B., Archer, R. P., & Kilpatrick, D. G. (1981). Sociopathy and antisocial behavior: Theory and treatment. In S. M. Turner, K. S. Calhoun, & H. E. Adams (Eds.), *Handbook of clinical behavior therapy* (pp. 665–712). New York: John Wiley.

Toolan, J. M. (1978). Therapy of depressed and suicidal children. *American Journal of Psychotherapy, 32,* 243-251.

——. (1984). Psychotherapeutic treatment of suicidal children and adolescents. In H. S. Sudak, A. B. Ford, & N. B. Rushforth (Eds.), *Suicide in the young* (pp. 325-344). Boston: Wright.

Tramontana, M. G. (1980). Critical review of research on psychotherapy outcome with adolescents: 1967-1977. *Psychological Bulletin, 88,* 429-450.

Ulrici, D. K. (1983). The effects of behavioral and family interventions on juvenile recidivism. *Family Therapy, 10,* 25-36.

Walker, B. A., & Mehr, M. (1983). Adolescent suicide—a family crisis: A model for effective intervention by family therapists. *Adolescence, 18,* 285-292.

Wallace, C. J. (1984). Community and interpersonal functioning in the course of schizophrenic disorders. *Schizophrenia Bulletin, 10,* 233-257.

Weiner, I. B. (1971). Psychodynamic aspects of learning disability: The passive-aggressive underachiever. *Journal of School Psychology, 9,* 246-251.

——. (1975a). Juvenile delinquencey. *Pediatric Clinics of North America, 22,* 673-684.

——. (1975b). Depression in adolescence. In F. F. Flach & S. C. Draghi (Eds.), *The nature and treatment of depression* (pp. 99-118). New York: John Wiley.

——. (1982). *Child and adolescent psychopathology.* New York: John Wiley.

White, K. R. (1982). The relationship between socioeconomic status and academic achievement. *Psychological Bulletin, 91,* 461-481.

Zeiss, A. M., Lewinsohn, P. M., & Munoz, R. F. (1979). Nonspecific improvement effects in depression using interpersonal skills training, pleasant activity schedules, or cognitive training. *Journal of Consulting and Clinical Psychology, 47,* 427-439.

7

ASSESSMENT AND TREATMENT CONSIDERATIONS FOR SEXUAL OFFENDERS AGAINST CHILDREN: BEHAVIORAL AND SOCIAL LEARNING APPROACHES

William D. Murphy

Susan J. Stalgaitis

The sexual abuse of children is a problem that has recently been receiving much needed increased public attention. It is difficult for a month to go by when one does not see a newspaper article, magazine article, or television show devoted to the topic. Finkelhor (1984) indicates that of a sample of 521 households in Boston, 93 percent of adults had been exposed in one way or another to the topic of child sexual abuse. Summit (1983) reports that in a short span of less than five years, over 30 books have appeared on the topic. Increased exposure of the problem has also led to an increase in reports of child sexual abuse to authorities. For example, in the first six months of 1982, the Child Protective Services Division of the State of Tennessee Department of Human Services received an average of 187 reports per month. In the first six months of 1985, this had increased to 670 reports per month (Wilson, 1985). It is likely that the Tennessee experience has been replicated or is being replicated across the country.

In response to the flood of reports of child sexual abuse, an explosion of treatment programs for victims and offenders has occurred. MacFarlane and Bulkley (1982) report that, in a 1976 survey (Brecher, 1978), only one program could be identified that was specifically designed for child sexual abuse perpetrators. In 1978 the National Center for Child Abuse and Neglect identified only 12 programs designed for treating intrafamily sexual abuse. However, by 1981, 300 such programs could be identified (MacFarlane & Bulkley, 1982).

Although there has been a rapid increase in treatment programs for perpetrators, there have been few good empirical studies to evaluate the effectiveness of the myriad programs that exist. Literature in this area is heavily weighted with clinical descriptions and clinical case studies, with a scattering of a few single-case experimental studies. Few large-scale program evaluations or well-controlled group outcome studies are available. In defense of the literature, the design of studies on the evaluation and treatment of sex offenders is difficult at best. There are major problems in gathering reliable and valid information from individuals who are many times mandated to receive services, especially when the information revealed may often be incriminating. The literature that does exist is many times biased by sampling techniques, since any one program may see only one type of offender against children. For example, a research program within a community study dealing with intrafamily child sexual abuse is likely to see a very different population than a program within a correctional setting dealing with large numbers of individuals who have molested children outside the home. Additionally, for obvious ethical reasons, the use of no-treatment controls or minimal contact controls in treatment studies is almost impossible. Finally, the collection of follow-up data, including the important variable of recidivism data, is fraught with difficulties that have been well reviewed previously (Tracy, Donnelly, Morgenbesser, & Macdonald, 1983).

Given the rapidly expanding reports of child sexual abuse, more clinicians will be faced with the evaluation and treatment of child molesters. The purpose of this chapter is to attempt to review and summarize the existing literature. A major focus will be on approaches derived from the behavioral and social learning literature, which have probably received more empirical investigations than other approaches. Additional approaches will be cited because of their historical importance or because they are receiving major attention in the current literature.

However, the first task at hand is to clarify the terminology that will be used throughout this chapter. Readers of the child abuse literature are faced with a variety of terms used to describe sex offenders such as child molesters, child rapists, pedophiles, incest offenders, intrafamilial offenders, extrafamilial abusers, and so forth. Most investigations, regardless of the terms employed, seem to make a distinction between individuals who have a primary sexual orientation to children versus those who do not. However, the distinction at times is confused with a familial relationship between the offenders and victims. For the purposes of this chapter, sexual offender against children or child molester will be used as a general description for any individual who sexually abuses children. Pedophile will be used (except where noted) as a term for those offenders against children who have a primary sexual orientation to children, while situational offender will refer to those whose primary sexual orientation is not to children. This distinction is made without regard to familial relationship. Intrafamily/incest offender will refer to those individuals who molest a relative, while extrafamily will refer to those offenders who molest children outside the family. The distinction between intrafamily and extrafamily offenders is made without regard to primary sexual orientation. Child sexual abuse itself will be defined simply as the exploitation of children by an individual at least five years older than the victim for sexual gratification or monetary reward (that is, child pornography). In this definition, child sexual abuse includes both touching and nontouching offenses. However, whether those individuals who expose to children are different from those who actually have sexual contact with children is not clear (Murphy, Abel, & Becker, 1980).

PREVALENCE OF CHILD SEXUAL ABUSE

One of the first questions asked by the general public, as well as by clinicians, when the area of child sexual abuse is addressed, is "How often does it occur?" Numerous studies have addressed the prevalence of child sexual abuse and several of these are summarized in Table 7.1.

In reviewing the table, it will quickly become obvious to the reader that prevalence rates vary to a great extent based on a number of factors. Some of these factors include whether one uses official statistics, samples of defined populations (such as college students), or samples of the general population, as well as the thoroughness of the survey technique. Additionally, rates will differ greatly depending on what is defined as abuse. For example, whether the survey includes both touching and nontouching offenses, such as exhibitionism, as cases of abuse or whether only touching offenses are counted. Regardless of which of these percentages actually turn out to be true, the data do seem to indicate clearly from multiple sources that child sexual abuse is a significant problem, affecting a significant portion of our population. This is especially important in light of the many studies suggesting that such abuse may have major psychological impact on children, both for the short term and the long term (Finkelhor, 1979; Gelinas, 1983; Gomes-Schwartz, Horowitz, & Sauzier, 1985).

The above studies also speak to a number of other issues related to child sexual abuse. One is the question of whether child sexual abuse is "a new problem" or "the rediscovery of an old problem." The study of Landis (1965) is based on surveys collected from college students between 1952 and 1955 and Gagnon's (1965) data are a reanalysis of the data collected by Kinsey between 1949 and 1952 on female sexuality. This makes it clear that the recent explosion in reports of child sexual abuse is not a relatively new phenomenon but that high percentages of individuals were reporting being victimized as early as 1950. These objective data are substantiated by the large number of adult women in their middle and elderly years who acknowledge to clinicians that they had been sexually

TABLE 7.1 Reported Prevalence of Child Sexual Abuse

Study	Sample	Method	Prevalence	Form of Abuse	Age at Time of Offense
Sarafino (1979)	Urban population	Surveyed official reports	74,725 cases nationwide/year	Touching and nontouching	
Fritz, Stoll, & Wagner (1981)	College students, N = 952	Anonymous questionnaires	9.7% of females 4.8% of males	Touching	Prior to puberty
Finkelhor (1979)	College students, N = 791	Anonymous questionnaires	19% of females 9% of males	Touching and nontouching	< 17 years
Landis (1965)	College students	Questionnaires	28% of females 19% of males	Touching and nontouching Touching and nontouching	< 17 years < 13 years
Gagnon (1965)	General population surveyed by Kinsey between 1949 and 1952	Interview	28% of females	Touching and nontouching	< 13 years
Russell (1983)	General population	Structured interview	28% of females 12% (intrafamilial) 20% (extrafamilial) 38% of females 48% of females 54% of females	Touching Touching Touching and nontouching Touching and nontouching	< 14 years < 18 years < 14 years < 18 years
Finkelhor (1984)	Families with children aged 7 to 14 in the home		15% of females 6% of males	Touching and nontouching Touching and nontouching	

abused as children. Another issue is the underreporting of
instances of child sexual abuse. In the Russell (1983) study
where 48 percent of females reported victimization prior to the
age of 14 and 54 percent reported victimization prior to the
age of 18, only 2 percent of the intrafamilial and 6 percent
of the extrafamilial cases were reported to the police. The
numbers cited in official reports are therefore most likely only
the tip of the iceberg.

A third question is related to the number of male victims.
Because clinicians very seldom saw male victims, it has been
assumed that boys are not frequent sexual abuse victims.
However, Finkelhor (1984), in a review of surveys of the general population, suggests that between 2.5 and 8.7 percent of
boys are victims of sexual abuse. Finkelhor also compares the
ratio of boys to girls across various studies. It is interesting
to note that in samples drawn from child protective service
agencies, the ratio varies from 11 to 15 males for each 100
females, while in general population surveys, the ratio is 27
to 48 per 100. This suggests that male victimization is probably greatly underreported. It may well be that the males
have an even more difficult time admitting to having been
sexually abused than females because not only is there a
taboo regarding sexual molestation but also a taboo against
homosexual behavior.

Available prevalence data also raise some questions about
the notion that the rate of intrafamilial sexual abuse is higher
than extrafamilial abuse. For example, during the first six
months of 1985, 56 percent of cases reported to child protective services in Tennessee were intrafamilial. However, in her
general population survey, Russell (1983) reported that 29 percent were abused intrafamilially. Again, depending on the
sample surveyed, very different pictures emerge of the "typical" child sexual abuse case. Therefore, the common belief
that most abuse occurs within the family is not clearly supported by available prevalence data.

In summary, the prevalence data suggest that sexual abuse
is occurring at a very high frequency. In addition, they suggest that at the current time the majority of known victims
are females, although there is some evidence to suggest that
there may be a large number of unidentified male victims.
Finally, although the majority of victims will know their offenders, the evidence is not clear that the majority of abuse occurring to children does occur within the family. These are areas
that will need further investigation to give us a clear picture
of the rate of abuse, the characteristics of victims, and the
circumstances under which abuse occurs.

MODELS

A number of typologies or models have been proposed as
attempts to more clearly understand the heterogeneity observed

among offenders against children (Finkelhor, 1984; Quinsey, 1977). Tradition has been to divide cases into intrafamily and extrafamily child sexual abuse and to divide extrafamily cases into those with male or female targets. Early data (Frisbee & Dondis, 1965) have shown differences in recidivism rates between such groups. Six-year recidivism rates were found to be 10.2 percent for daughter/stepdaughter incest cases, 21.5 percent for heterosexual pedophiles, and 34.5 percent for homosexual pedophiles. Such classification may be useful for predicting recidivism in groups. However, because they are based on historical data, they do not help the clinician determine assessment strategies or treatment needs for individual offenders.

A model more closely tied to assessment/treatment issues than past events is the behavioral or social learning model (Abel, Blanchard, & Becker, 1978; Murphy, Coleman, & Haynes, 1983). This model describes areas of deficits and excesses within each patient that need to be assessed and possibly targeted for treatment. These include deviant arousal, nondeviant arousal, social competence, sexual functioning, and cognitions/perceptions. The model posits that not all deficits or excesses will exist in any one offender and they may exist in varying degrees within offenders. It has heuristic value in terms of suggesting specific areas for assessment and treatment with many of the procedures being drawn from the general behavior therapy and social learning theory literature.

In general, the social learning model suggests that the accurate assessment of offenders needs to include measures of the degree of deviant sexual arousal or attraction to children, in addition to determining the extent to which appropriate sexual arousal patterns exist. Patients also are assessed in terms of general social competence, which is broadly defined to include not only heterosocial and assertiveness skills, but other skills that possibly are antecedents to acting out. Such factors include ability to cope with emotional states (anger, depression, anxiety), interpersonal conflict (rejection, marital discord), or environmental situations that could possibly expose an individual to children (shopping malls, video arcades, and such) (Pithers, Marques, Gibat, & Marlatt, 1983). A third area is an individual's general sexual functioning, including not only issues related to sexual knowledge or sexual dysfunction but also more complex sexual/social information such as male/female roles, female sexual functioning, and sexual stereotyping. Finally, there is a need for assessment and targeting of cognitions and perceptions, especially cognitive distortions, offenders often hold regarding children's behavior (the child rubbing my leg means the child is interested in "sex") and the meaning of the sexual abuse (that is, its sex education). Although many times such statements from offenders are dismissed as rationalizations or denials, it may also be that offenders have come to accept such false beliefs, similar to other irrational beliefs frequently described within the cognitive therapy literature (Beck, 1976; Ellis & Grieger, 1977).

The remainder of the chapter will focus mainly on techniques derived from the social learning model. However, there are other models that receive frequent mention in the literature. Groth (1982) describes a typology of pedophiles (defined as all offenders against children) based on the dynamics of offenders. In Groth's typology, the fixated offender is an individual whose primary sexual orientation is to children, has little sexual contact with agemates, identifies closely with the victim, is characterologically immature, and has poor socio-sexual relationships. For the fixated offender, the offense is seen as a maladaptive resolution of long-standing life issues. The regressed offender, on the other hand, is seen as having a primary sexual orientation to agemates, the child serves as a substitute for conflictual adult relationships, and the offender has a more traditional life-style although peer relationships are underdeveloped. From a dynamic standpoint, the regressed offender's offense is a maladaptive attempt to cope with specific life stresses.

A third, very recent model, the Four Factor Model (Finkelhor, 1984; Finkelhor & Araji, 1983) was designed and presented as a method of organizing and summarizing current theories of child sexual abuse. This model suggests that current explanations for pedophilia (defined broadly as all child sexual molestation) related to one of four factors: emotional congruence, sexual arousal, blockage, and disinhibition. Emotional congruence refers to the nonsexual or emotional needs, such as need for power or need for affection, that are derived from the sexual molestation of children. Sexual arousal is the degree to which an individual finds children sexually attractive. Blockage classifies those factors, such as lack of social skills or sexual skills, that interfere with an individual's ability to meet sexual and emotional needs in adult interactions. Finally, disinhibition describes factors, such as alcoholism, impulse control disorders, and so on, that allow an individual to overcome the normal inhibitions to sexual abuse.

An interesting aspect of this model is hypothesizing two levels of explanation for each of the factors. One level is an individual explanation and the other one is based on social-cultural factors. For example, at the individual level, sexual arousal to children might be explained by modeling or conditioning processes while, at the social-cultural level, it might be explained by the presence of child pornography in our culture, the tendency to sexualize children in advertisements, or the tendency of males to sexualize all emotional needs.

The three general models, although coming from different theoretical perspectives, do have some common ground. All three models suggest that offenders vary on degree of sexual orientation to children and all three suggest that offenders vary in terms of general social/sexual skills. Which of the three models will ultimately prove most useful in terms of predicting recidivism, generating treatment and assessment techniques, or generating hypotheses regarding etiology awaits further investigations.

ASSESSMENT

Within the social learning model presented as a theoretical framework to view assessment and treatment of child molesters, the following four basic areas of assessment are important: arousal, social competence, general sexual functioning, and cognitions/perceptions. Although the social learning model is the major approach delineated in this chapter, methods of basic personality assessment with child molesters have also been included because of the plethora of writings that have described the personality traits and characteristics of child molesters.

Personality Assessment

Early studies utilizing projective techniques (Hammer, 1954, 1957) appear to support the notion that child molesters are immature, threatened, and feel inadequate sexually. However, the studies have serious methodological problems, such as subjectivity of ratings of projective data, lack of control groups, heterogeneity of comparison groups, and generalization of results to all offenders. More objective assessment of personality characteristics of child molesters has been accomplished in the majority of cases through the use of Minnesota Multiphasic Personality Inventory (MMPI) testing and two approaches to analysis. The first approach is the development of specialized scales within the MMPI. Marsh, Hilliard, and Liechti (1955) developed a 100-item sexual deviation scale to attempt to differentiate individuals convicted of sexual offenses from presumably normal individuals with no history of sexual offenses. They were successful in differentiating offenders referred to a state psychiatric facility from college students but the scale did not discriminate hospitalized sexual offenders from other psychiatric offenders.

The second and most common approach utilized is to attempt to identify specific MMPI profiles for child molesters (Armentrout & Hauer, 1978; McCreary, 1975; Panton, 1978, 1979; Quinsey, Arnold, & Pruesse, 1980). A review of these studies suggests the presence of at least the three following general profiles: profiles with elevations on schizophrenia and psychopathic deviance scales; profiles with elevations on psychopathic deviance and mania; and profiles with elevations on hypochondriasis, depression, hysteria, and psychasthenia. Elevations on the depression scale, which is sensitive to situational feelings, varied in the above profiles. Although these general profiles were suggestive, clear-cut personality profiles have not been determined that might consistently correlate with various types of sexual offenders and offenses. Thus, there tends to be a heterogeneity of profiles and personality characteristics among offenders of various kinds.

Some of the variability reported may reflect the fact that samples were drawn from a variety of settings (outpatient, psychiatric facilities, forensic psychiatric facilities, general prisons). In addition variables such as amount of violence utilized, sex of victim, and relationship of offender to victim were not controlled. In the overall assessment of offenders, personality testing is probably best utilized on an individual basis to provide information to assist in treatment planning rather than in attempting to form typologies. Relevant psychopathology other than sexual deviation and modes of coping and problem solving (such as impulsivity, rebelliousness, worrisomeness, and aggressiveness) might be assessed and specific interventions to combat these assessed problems can be designed. Such testing can never be used, however, to predict or prove whether an individual is a child molester.

Assessment of Sexual Arousal

The measurement of deviant and nondeviant sexual arousal has played a major role in behavioral approaches to treating child molesters. A number of approaches have been suggested to measure sexual arousal but the most reliable and valid method is direct recording of penile tumescence to sexual stimuli (Zuckerman, 1971). The use of the technique and specifics of application have been well reviewed for a variety of sex offenders (Abel, 1976; Abel & Blanchard, 1976; Barlow & Abel, 1976; Laws & Osborn, 1983). Basically the technique involves the use of circumferential measures of penile tumescence via either a mercury and rubber strain gauge (Bancroft, Jones, & Pullman, 1966) or a metal band strain gauge (Barlow, Becker, Leitenberg, & Agras, 1970). These two devices are reliable and comfortable and operating characteristics are very similar. Other researchers employ a volumetric device (Freund, 1957, 1961; McConaghy, 1974) that encloses most of the penis. Although these devices are more sensitive, the device is much more obtrusive and complex to employ and, therefore, less applicable to most clinical researchers and clinicians (Abel & Blanchard, 1976). In the general procedure, the subject places the transducer on his penis and is then exposed to various forms of sexual stimuli, which usually include slides of males and females who vary in age or audiotaped descriptions that may vary in amount of violence (Abel, Becker, Murphy, & Flanagan, 1981; Laws & Osborn, 1983).

One of the first questions addressed in the use of these measurement procedures with offenders against children is their ability to discriminate offenders from nonoffenders. Freund (1965, 1967a, 1967b) was the first to provide controlled data that suggest that pedophiles respond more than normal controls to child stimuli. Quinsey, Steinman, Bergersen, and Holmes (1975) found that erection responses to child stimuli clearly differentiated 20 incarcerated sex offenders against children from a control group that included both nonsexual offending residents and nonincarcerated controls.

A second major issue in the area of sexual abuse of children concerns possible differences between pedophiles who are thought to be sexually attracted to children versus incest cases, who are considered situational offenders (Langevin, 1983; Quinsey, 1977). Two studies have attempted to address this issue using measured erection responses. Abel et al. (1981) compared 6 heterosexual incest cases, 10 heterosexual pedophiles, and 11 subjects with other sexual deviations. Subjects' responses were compared on a series of two-minute audiotaped descriptions of sexual interactions with children that varied in extent of sexual aggression from no aggression to a sadistic attack on a child. This study indicated no difference between incest cases and pedophilic cases. Both showed more arousal to children than the other offenders. However, Quinsey, Chaplin, and Carrigan (1979), using slides presented for 30 seconds, found that pedophiles showed sexual responding to slides of children more than did a daughter/stepdaughter incest group.

Because a number of factors differed in this study (that is, short slide presentation versus longer audiotaped presentation and inpatients in the Quinsey et al. 1979 study versus outpatients in the Abel et al. 1981 study) clear comparisons between the studies cannot be made. Therefore, the question of whether incest cases differ from pedophiles is yet to be determined. From a clinical standpoint, however, the important question is the degree of sexual arousal shown to child stimuli by an individual patient. This is especially relevant given that a larger number of offenders referred for incest offenses (usually considered situational offenders) have actually also molested children outside the home. The patients showing high sexual arousal to children, regardless of the familial relationship to their victim, will probably need specific treatment directed at altering that arousal pattern.

A third issue of concern to clinicians in evaluating sex offenders is the potential for physical violence. Although child molesters are generally seen as nondangerous in terms of physically hurting their victims, this has not always been supported by the literature. Christie, Marshall, and Lanthier (1978) report data for convicted offenders where presentencing reports, probation reports, transcripts from the courtroom testimony, and reports from the medical personnel who evaluated the victim were reviewed. When these sources were reviewed rather than reliance on offender self-report, surprisingly, it was found that 42 percent of the victims of child molesters sustained noticeable injury, a figure almost identical to the 39 percent of adult victims of rapists who sustained injury. Because of these findings, Abel et al. (1981) developed a series of audiotapes, as described above, varying on level of aggression that seemed to differentiate a small number of six nonaggressive child molesters from four more sadistic offenders against children. Avery-Clark and Laws (1984) expanded the study using a larger sample of 16 less dangerous and 15 more dangerous (defined clinically by level of physical coercion used in the offense) incarcerated offenders. Longer (four-minute) audiotapes varying on level of aggression were used because it was felt that the longer audiotapes would elicit more arousal. Although the tapes did elicit more sexual arousal than in the Abel et al. study, the results were very similar between the two studies. The erection responses to aggressive sexual inter-actions did clearly distinguish between the less dangerous and more dangerous offenders.

In summary, the measurement of penile tumescence with child molesters has proven effective in separating offenders from normal controls and nonsex offender patients. In addition, the technique also seems to show value in separating more physically aggressive from less physically aggressive offenders. Whether the technique will separate incestuous from noninces-tuous offenders awaits further investigation. Although the tech-nique is extremely valuable in the clinical assessment of sex offenders, there are certain limitations. Erection responses can be controlled and response faking has been well documented (Laws & Holmen, 1978; Quinsey & Carrigan, 1978). Therefore, lack of responding should never be considered proof of lack of arousal to children. On the other hand, the presence of erection responses to children, although possibly suggesting attraction to children, does not prove that an individual has acted on this arousal. Therefore, one cannot "prove" if an individual is a child molester based solely on erection data. The value of tumescence measures is in detailing specific arousal and attraction patterns for treatment planning and in monitoring the impact of treatment to determine effectiveness.

Social Competence

Throughout the literature on child molesters, these men have been almost universally described as socially introverted, regressed, inadequate socially, unassertive, and unable to relate to women. In spite of this clinical assumption and the indirect support through studies of personality assessment, amazingly little evaluation has been done in the area of assess-ment of social competence of child molesters. The social skills literature presents numerous methods to assess heterosocial skills and assertiveness including self-report questionnaires (Rathus, 1973), rated behavioral role plays (Eisler, Miller, & Hersen, 1973; McFall & Marston, 1970; Truax & Carkhuff, 1967), and assessment of cognitions (Glass & Merluzzi, 1981). These methods have been utilized with a variety of populations but few studies have involved child molesters. Josiassen, Fantuzzo, and Rosen (1980) present a successful case study of a pedophile in which aversive conditioning and graded social skills training were employed. However, social skills improvement was assessed only via self-report in an informal fashion.

Murphy, Abel, and Becker (1980) used a Heterosocial Behavior Checklist (Barlow, Abel, Blanchard, Bristow, & Young, 1977) to evaluate the heterosocial skills of 67 sexual deviates, including 21 pedophiles, during behavioral role plays. Components of heterosocial skills evaluated were voice, affect, form of conversation, and motor behavior. The means of all sexual deviate groups were much lower in these components than for the socially skilled groups reported by Barlow et al. (1977). This finding supports the notion that heterosocial skills deficits are present in sexual deviates, including pedophiles.

Segal and Marshall (1985) compared in vivo behavioral ratings of conversations with a female as well as questionnaire and cognitive assessments of social skills of rapists and child molesters with those of nonsexual offender inmates and nonincarcerated males. Child molesters in this sample presented a clearer profile of heterosocial inadequacy than did rapists and nonsexual offenders on questionnaire data. Child molesters also rated themselves as less skilled and more anxious in heterosexual interactions and less assertive in accepting positive feedback from others. Interestingly, this inadequacy was not perceived by judges or confederates in role plays and appeared related to the child molesters' cognitive views of themselves.

As part of our outpatient treatment program, we have done extensive psychosexual evaluations on a sample of male and female pedophiles and situational offenders. Because of the clinical cost of behavioral role plays, self-report questionnaires of social skills were utilized. Preliminary evaluation suggested that mean scores for our sample of sexual offenders were not statistically different from published norms on the Adult Self-Expression Scale (Gay, Hollandsworth, & Galassi, 1975; Hollandsworth, Galassi, & Gay, 1977), Survey of Heterosexual Interactions (Twentyman & McFall, 1975), Social Avoidance and Distress Scale (Watson & Friend, 1969, and Fear of Negative Evaluation Scale (Watson & Friend, 1969). Although group norms were not found to be statistically different from published norms, an analysis of the range of scores for offenders revealed vast variability between offenders. This suggests the need to assess various aspects of social skills in order to determine the individual offender's deficits and suggested areas for treatment intervention.

Furthermore, the controlled data on social competence that are available for child molesters appear to address a somewhat limited concept of social competence, which includes hetero-social skills and assertiveness. Pithers, Marques, Gibat, and Marlatt (1983) present a relapse prevention model for sexual aggressors. This approach emphasizes the importance both of determining high-risk, stressful situations, which so often lead to relapse, and of assisting the offender in developing realistic treatment expectations and learning successful coping responses to the high-risk stress situation. The authors suggest, among other things, the need to assess and instruct the client in various specific skills, such as stimulus control ability, anger management, decisionmaking, relaxation training, as well as general heterosocial skills and assertiveness. Unfortunately, they provide little empirical data or controlled investigation. Nevertheless, those suggestions for treatment are consistent with what our clinical experience suggests as important when dealing with child molesters.

Sexual Behavior

An area of particular relevance to child molesters that has been cited frequently in the literature is the area of sexual behavior, sexual knowledge, and attitudes associated with sexuality. Deficits in these areas may contribute to inappropriate sexual behavior. Again, few data are available in this area. Several questionnaires have been developed as adjuncts to clinical interviews. In 1966, Thorne developed the Sex Inventory, a 200-item, self-report questionnaire that had eight subscales felt to be related to sexual offenders. Cowden and Pacht (1969) found that the inventory scales assessing sexual maladjustment, loss of sexual controls, and homosexuality differentiated incarcerated sexual deviates from general incarcerants. The Clarke Sexual History Questionnaire (Paitich, Langevin, Freeman, Mann, & Handy, 1977) is a 225-item sexual history questionnaire that assesses frequency of, desire for, and disgust with erotic outlets. Twenty-four scales derived from factor analysis discriminated clinically relevant groups of sexual deviates, including child molesters, based on their reported frequency, disgust, and preference for specific sexual behavior. Questionnaires similar to the above can be helpful in developing a thorough sexual history on offenders and are especially important in light of the data of Abel and Becker (1985) and our own clinical observation that documents the polydeviant nature of many offenders in treatment.

More general measures are available for assessment of sexual functioning. For example, the Derogatis Sexual Functioning Inventory (Derogatis & Meyer, 1979) is a self-report scale designed to measure the current level of sexual functioning of individuals. It is composed of 245 items that reflect sexual functioning in the following areas: information, experience, drive, attitudes, symptoms, affect, gender role definition, fantasy, and global sexual satisfaction. Murphy (1985) has used this inventory in the psychosexual evaluation of outpatient male and female pedophiles and situational offenders. Preliminary data analysis reveals that the sample of 67 offenders was approximately one T-score lower on sexual information, attitudes of sexual conservatism, gender role definition, and body image scales when compared to the original means determined by Derogatis. Although the above suggests some trends, there was a wide range of scores arguing for the social learning theory notion of a continuum of various components and traits in child molesters rather than a typology with overall deficits.

Cognitions/Perceptions

As stated previously, the social learning theory model posits a need for assessment of cognitions and perceptions of offenders and a targeting of cognitive distortions and irrational beliefs regarding children's behavior and child-adult sexuality. Bandura (1977) in his social learning theory presents various ways by which self-evaluative consequences can be dissociated from censurable behavior. One set of methods is to portray the behavior as being in the service of moral ends, contrasting it with even more reprehensible conduct or euphemistic labeling of it. Another set of methods of disinhibition is by minimizing, ignoring, or miscontruing the consequences of the behavior of the victim. Dehumanizing victims or attributing blame to them also serves selectively to disengage self-evaluative cognitive processes. Finally, displacement or diffusion of responsibility for the conduct and its effects is often utilized. Those with clinical experience working with child molesters should quickly recognize many of these cognitive methods to disengage self-evaluations in the often-heard statements of child molesters. Examples include "I am preparing her for her husband" (in the service of moral ends), "but I never had intercourse with her" (palliative comparison), "fooling around, playing" (euphemistic labeling), "it didn't bother him" (ignoring the consequences), "she led me on" (attributing the blame to the victim), or "she was a whore anyway" (dehumanizing the victim). Thus far, little investigation has been conducted on assessing the cognitive distortions and the disinhibitions occurring for child molesters in spite of the recognition of the above processes. Abel and Becker (1984) have developed a scale (the Pedophile Cognition Checklist) that addresses some of the issues. Unfortunately, validity and reliability studies are not complete at this time.

Waterman and Foss-Goodman (1984) recently studied variables relating to attribution of fault to victims, child molesters, and nonparticipating parents in 180 male and 180 female college students. Male subjects were found to attribute significantly more fault than female subjects to 15-year-old male victims, and more fault to 15-year-old male victims than 15-year-old female victims. Subjects blamed 15-year-old victims more than 11- and 7-year old victims, respectively. Subjects' attitudes of sexual conservatism and acceptance of interpersonal violence were positively correlated with ratings of fault to the victim. Subjects who themselves had been molested as children blamed victims less than those who had not. Studies such as the Waterman and Foss-Goodman analogue, as well as studies of offenders, are needed in order to further illuminate these cognitive processes and to allow the development of treatment strategies to combat these processes.

General Assessment Issues

Although specific areas to be assessed have been reviewed, we would also like to present a general assessment framework used within the treatment/evaluation/research program at our center (Special Problems Unit, Department of Psychiatry, University of Tennessee, Memphis). Table 7.2 lists various areas of assessment and specific instruments used within our project. Although most of these areas have been reviewed previously, two have not been mentioned. One is the thorough psychosexual history. From a clinical standpoint, a thorough history is extremely important. It is only through the history that one can get a feel for the offender's attitudes toward the offense and get details of possible antecedents to offending as well as details of the offenses themselves. Second, and not clearly enunciated in the behavioral model, is marital-family functioning. For situational sexual abuse cases, marital-family distress may be a significant antecedent to sexual acting out.

The above assessment strategy serves two purposes. It provides a thorough clinical evaluation for treatment planning, and it provides a consistent set of data for research. The use of a standardized assessment battery is important for clinical research that is ongoing rather than "one shot." Standardized objective batteries allow comparisons across offender types and allow objective data for evaluation of treatment outcome and prediction of outcome.

However, regardless of the specific battery employed, a number of other issues will be faced by the clinician/researcher evaluating sexual offenders. One extremely important issue is the fact that sex offenders are frequently less than honest about their history and about the specific behaviors in which they have engaged. In general, the offender will be under some legal obligation to seek an evaluation or treatment and will most often, rightly so, see the evaluation as something that may impact on future prosecution and incarceration. At the same time, most of the assessment strategies reviewed can be falsified, at least to some extent, by the patient. Therefore, it is incumbent on the evaluator to gather as much collateral information as possible to validate the information collected from

TABLE 7.2 Components of Psychosexual Evaluation

I. Initial History
  A. General Social History
  B. General Sexual History
  C. Specific History of Deviant Sexual Behavior
II. Personality/Intellectual Assessment
  A. Otis Quick Scoring Mental Abilities Test
  B. Minnesota Multiphasic Personality Inventory
III. Social Competency
  A. Survey of Heterosexual Interactions
      (Twentyman & McFall, 1975)
  B. Adult Self-Expression Scale
      (Gay, Hollandsworth, & Galassi, 1975)
  C. Fear of Negative Evaluation Scale
      (Watson & Friend, 1969)
  D. Social Avoidance and Distress Scale
      (Watson & Friend, 1969)
IV. Sexual Functioning
  A. Derogatis Sexual Functioning Inventory
      (Derogatis & Meyer, 1979)
  B. Clarke Sexual History Questionnaire
      (Paitich, Langevin, Freeman, Mann, & Handy, 1977)
V. Cognitive/Perceptual
  A. Abel's Pedophile Cognition Checklist
      (Abel & Becker, 1984)
VI. Marital-Family Functioning
  A. Locke-Wallace Marital Functioning Inventory
      (Locke & Wallace, 1957)
  B. Family Adaptability and Cohesion Evaluation Scales
      (Olson & Portner, 1983)
VII. Psychophysiological Assessment of Sexual Arousal

---

the offender. This means that family members should be inter-
viewed and that police reports, victim's statements, child protective service reports, and other official documents should be
reviewed. Any evaluation that does not include collaborating
information should probably be considered incomplete.

Another major issue that faces the clinician is the referral
question. Many times district attorneys, judges, defense attorneys, or child protective service workers will want to know
whether the person "did it." To date, there are no known
psychological/physiological tests that "prove" whether anyone
has or has not sexually abused a child. Evaluators need to
educate referral sources regarding this and should be extremely

careful about not being "trapped" into answering inappropriate questions.

A question that often arises during the initial assessment of the offender is whether the individual is appropriate for outpatient treatment or needs to be in a more secure facility. In general, those asking the question many times are asking evaluators to address two factors: the potential for recidivism and the offender's dangerousness in terms of severely physically injuring victims. To date, there are few data related to either question to guide the evaluator. Recidivism rates tend to vary greatly across studies (Furby & Weinrott, in preparation). Individuals who molest young males outside the family have a much higher recidivism rate than those who molest young females outside the family, who in turn have a higher recidivism rate than those who molest within the family (Frisbee & Dondis, 1965; Quinsey, 1977). Other studies have shown that prior convictions for previous sex offenses greatly increase the risk of reoffending (Mohr, Turner, & Jerry, 1964; Tracy et al., 1983). Similarly, the presence of previous arrests for nonsexual offenses tends to some extent to increase the risks of recidivism (Mohr et al., 1964; Tracy et al., 1983). Also, Tracy et al. (1983) found that diagnosis of a "personality disorder" (usually sociopathy) was associated with higher recidivism. However, within their study, it was unclear how many of the recidivists were sex offenders against children. In addition, it may well be that the label sociopathy would be most often given to individuals who have had prior arrest records; therefore, this factor may be confounded with previous arrests.

Basically the data on recidivism rates of various types of offenders suggest that from an actuarial standpoint individuals who molest young males outside the home, who have had previous arrests, and who are considered sociopathic would be at more risk of recidivism than first-time incest offenders. However, the problem is that the clinician is not faced with predicting recidivism for a group but predicting recidivism for the individual offender. There is a strong need for research to examine individual deficits and assets that are predictive of recidivism rather than group membership. It seems possible that such factors as degree of deviant sexual arousal, or lack of nondeviant sexual arousal, degree of emotional congruence, and so on, may be more related to continued sexual acting out than whether the victim was a relative or not. However, few studies have addressed these issues. With a relatively small sample size, Quinsey, Chaplin, and Carrigan (1980) found a small but significant relationship between posttreatment objectively measured sexual arousal and recidivism. However, with a larger sample, Quinsey and Marshall (1983) found that initial psychophysiological arousal patterns were related to recidivism rather than posttreatment patterns. Therefore, the question of the role of arousal pattern in predicting recidivism is still open.

The prediction of dangerousness has been a major problem for the mental health professional. Quinsey (1977) has reviewed data related to this question and although a number of factors have been proposed to predict dangerousness, none have been appropriately validated. Therefore, from the research literature the clinician will find little help in making this decision. Clinically, most programs dealing with sexual offenders consider individuals who deny their charge, who have engaged in sadistic sexual behavior with a child, who have used a weapon in the commission of the offense, or who show no "remorse or guilt" (usually undefined) not to be appropriate outpatient treatment candidates. These guidelines have become standards of practice in the community that probably need to be followed until better data are available.

TREATMENT

Although the major focus of this chapter is on the behavioral treatment approaches, we will review briefly a second treatment model, the Child Sexual Abuse Treatment Program (Giaretto, 1981), that has been adoped for intrafamily sexual abuse cases in a number of communities. The program makes use of individual therapy for perpetrators, nonoffending spouses, and victims: mother-daughter dyadic counseling, marital therapy and family therapy. However, the unique component of this program is the use of self-help groups (with professional input) for parents (Parents United) and victims (Daughters and Sons United). These groups serve as a central component of the treatment program. A major purpose of Parent United groups is group therapy, but in addition they provide other services including a speakers' bureau, resources for parents with financial or employment problems, and support and crisis intervention to families immediately after disclosure.

The program has not been compared to other types of treatments, although it has been evaluated by an independent evaluator (Kroth, 1979, cited in Giaretto, 1981). The evaluation suggests an extremely low recidivism rate (.6 percent) with no recidivism for 600 families who have completed at least ten sessions of the program. However, it should be noted that the recidivism rate for intrafamily abuse is in general low so that these findings may not be surprising. However, results suggest a number of other positive outcomes that have arisen from this program, including maintenance of family structure, early return of the child to the home, and decreases in symptomatology in victims. Although not a controlled outcome study, the results do suggest that at least some components of the Child Sexual Abuse Treatment Program, especially the Parents United groups, should receive further empirical investigation. This program is not inconsistent with the social learning model, since self-help groups like Parents United might serve as useful adjuncts to more individual behavioral treatments for perpetrators. One caveat to the clinician, however, is that this program may not be appropriate to offenders whose primary sexual orientation is to children. This requires careful assessment, including the physiological assessment reviewed previously. As noted, some cases labeled "incest" have abused children outside the home. Given our current knowledge, a decision as to whether the case represents a situational offender or a true pedophile should be based on appropriate assessment rather than the familial relationship of the victim to the offender.

Reduction of Deviant Arousal

A number of authors have suggested that behavioral treatment for offenders against children should be individualized and include multiple treatments (Abel, Blanchard, & Becker, 1978; Crawford, 1979). However, the majority of studies have focused on the reduction of deviant sexual arousal. A number of procedures have been investigated to reduce deviant sexual arousal including biofeedback (Keltner, 1977; Laws, 1980) or shame aversion (Serber, 1972). However, the most frequently used procedures have been electrical aversion, covert sensitization, and various forms of masturbatory satiation (see Kelley, 1982; Langevin, 1983; Quinsey & Marshall, 1983 for other reviews of these techniques).

Traditionally, the first approaches applied to the treatment of sexual deviations were various forms of electrical aversion, that is, the pairing of painful electrical shock with slides or fantasies of children. A number of case studies have appeared in the literature alone (Rosenthal, 1973; Wijesinghe, 1977) or in combination with other treatment (Josiassen, Fantuzzo, & Rosen, 1980; Miller & Haney, 1976; Nolan & Sandman, 1978), which all report successful results. Quinsey, Bergersen, and Steinman (1976), using a classical conditioning paradigm, found very few changes that could be considered clinically significant. In the only controlled investigation in this population, Quinsey, Chaplin, and Varney (1981) found signaled punishment more effective than biofeedback, at least in terms of reduction of erection responses. However, it was not clear that long-term recidivism differed between groups.

Because of the ethical problems involved in the use of electrical aversion and questions regarding its effectiveness (Quinsey, 1973), there has been a search for other procedures to alter deviant arousal. One such procedure, covert sensitization, was originally described by Cautela and Wisocki (1971). In the covert sensitization procedure as originally proposed, the therapist describes in detail, to a relaxed subject, fantasies of molesting children and then pairs these with aversive imagery such as nausea and vomiting, or some natural consequence such as being arrested. Covert sensitization has been evaluated using appropriate single-case designs, either reversal (ABAB) or multiple baseline across behaviors with offenders against children or other offenders (Barlow, Leitenberg, & Agras, 1969; Brownell & Barlow, 1976; Brownell, Hayes, & Barlow, 1977; Levin, Barry, Gambaro, Wolfinsohn, & Smith, 1977). These studies, although with small numbers of subjects, have supported the effectiveness of covert sensitization based on self-report of urges, card-sort ratings of attraction to deviant and nondeviant stimuli, and in some cases penile tumescence measures. However, in general, long-term recidivism data are not reported. Callahan and Leitenberg (1973) report a comparison of electrical aversion to covert sensitization in a within-single-case design. Results tended to favor covert sensitization although only two pedophiles were included in the study.

The most thorough study of this technique with offenders is Maletzky's (1980) report comparing 23 court-referred to 15 self-referred pedophiles. Outcome measures included self-reports of urges and behaviors, penile tumescence measures, significant others' reports, and extensive review of legal records. Follow-up was for 30 months. In this study, assisted covert sensitization was employed, that is, an aversive odor was paired with the covert sensitization scenes, along with a variety of adjunctive behavioral therapies. Significant improvement was found in both groups with no difference between court-referred and self-referred patients. The multiple treatments, and the fact that groups did not differ, makes it difficult to determine what factors led to the effectiveness of treatment. However, this study is a model in terms of the multiple dependent variables used and extensive follow-up. The results do indicate that multiple behavior therapy techniques do seem to be effective in reducing recidivism over a 2.5-year period.

A third more recently developed technique is that of masturbatory satiation and variations on the technique. Marshall and Lippens (1977) first introduced the technique in the treatment of an individual with multiple fetishes and later showed the technique to be effective with a pedophilic subject in a controlled multiple baseline design across behaviors study (Marshall, 1979). As originally described, this procedure required subjects to masturbate to deviant fantasies for prolonged periods (60-90 minutes) including masturbation during the postejaculation phase. In addition, subjects verbalized the fantasies out loud into a tape recorder so that the clinician could check the accuracy of the fantasies. There have been a number of variations on this technique including reviewing the tape with the patient (Abel, Becker, & Skinner, 1980) or having the patient verbalize the deviant fantasies without masturbation (Laws & Osborn, 1983). In our own program, the patient is required initially to masturbate to orgasm using nondeviant fantasies (to reinforce appropriate fantasies) then to continue masturbating during the postorgasmic phase for 30 to 45 minutes. Although the original description of the procedure suggested that boredom or satiation was a key ingredient, our own experience suggests that the requirement to verbalize the fantasies actively and to listen to the fantasies with the therapist has a major impact on reducing the deviant arousal.

Although this procedure has not received the evaluation that other procedures have received, it has been adopted by numerous sex-offender treatment programs and our own clinical experience also supports the effectiveness of the procedure as one part of a comprehensive program. There is need for controlled research with this technique, especially research depicting which of the components are most effective—that is, the actual masturbation to the fantasies, the verbalizations, or the listening to the verbalizations.

Increasing Appropriate Arousal

It is a common assumption, even among undergraduates in learning classes, that suppression of behavior is more effective when alternative behaviors are available and reinforced. However, there have been surprisingly few studies, specifically with offenders against children, looking at methods to increase appropriate arousal. It should be noted that a number of patients will show an increase in appropriate arousal with suppression of deviant arousal, but this does not occur in all patients and should be assessed and not assumed. In terms of developing new arousal patterns, a number of procedures have been investigated for a variety of sex offenders and for homosexual males. Procedures have included classical conditioning, fading, exposure, systematic desensitization, and various forms of masturbatory reconditioning among others. Many of these procedures have been well-reviewed previously (Abel & Blanchard, 1976; Barlow, 1973) and the reader is referred to these sources for details. In general, support for these procedures has been limited and early studies focused mainly on homosexual males.

One of the most frequently used procedures for increasing arousal is some form of masturbatory or orgasmic reconditioning. Marquis (1970) originally described the procedure in a series of case studies that included a small number of pedophiles. Basically the technique involves a gradual shifting of fantasies from deviant to nondeviant. Initially subjects masturbate to deviant fantasies to the point of orgasm then switch to nondeviant stimuli. Gradually, the nondeviant fantasies are introduced earlier and earlier in the masturbatory sequence. Abel and Blanchard (1976), in a review of the literature, described numerous variations on this procedure and, in general, controlled studies have been lacking (Abel, Barlow, & Blanchard, 1973; Marshall, 1973). In a controlled single case study with homosexual males, improvements were found in subjects' self-reports but physiological measurements and behavioral measurements were unchanged (Conrad & Wincze, 1976). In addition, Kremsdorf, Holmen, and Laws (1980) found increases in nondeviant arousal and decreases in deviant arousal in a subject instructed to masturbate to nondeviant stimuli alone.

Because of difficulties in implementing the technique in terms of appropriate timing or switching of fantasies, Abel, Blanchard, Barlow, and Flanagan (1975) described a somewhat simplified technique. In this technique, subjects masturbated to one type of fantasy in blocks of trials, then switched to the alternative fantasy in a second block of time. That is, they masturbated for four days to deviant fantasies and then switched to four days of nondeviant fantasies with switching continuing until treatment was successful. VanDeventer and Laws (1978) present single-case-study data for a male pedophile treated with this procedure. Results clearly indicated increases in nondeviant arousal and unexpectedly decreases in deviant arousal. Foote and Laws (1981) report other evidence with single-case studies that daily alternations are as effective as weekly alternations.

In general, although further data are needed, the fantasy alternation procedure seems effective in increasing nondeviant arousal in at least some subjects. The technique has an advantage over orgasmic conditioning in that switching within sessions is not required, therefore making the technique easier to implement. Further studies need to address some of the hypotheses proposed (Laws, 1985; VanDeventer & Laws, 1978) as to why the technique works. Also, as noted with all the behavioral techniques, more data are needed with larger groups, longer-term follow-up, and appropriate recidivism data.

Social Competence, Sexual Functioning, and Cognitions/Perceptions

The last three components of the social learning model are included together because of the limited data regarding these techniques. It is surprising given the focus in the literature on social incompetence, passivity, nonassertiveness, and sexual inadequacy in this population that so few studies have addressed these issues. Controlled studies of social skills training, assertiveness training, sex education, and sex therapy are sorely needed. With such studies, the impact of training needs to be evaluated not only in terms of social functioning but also in terms of deviant arousal patterns. If such procedures did lead to decreases in deviant arousal, then the use of more aversive techniques could be avoided.

Basically, social skills and assertiveness training programs have been limited to case reports (Josiassen et al., 1980; Miller & Haney, 1976) which employed social skills training in combination with aversive therapy. Edwards (1972) reports a successful use of assertiveness training in the treatment of a male incest case, while Serber and Keith (1974) describe a unique program at Atascadero State Hospital (California) for teaching homosexual skills to homosexually oriented pedophiles using gay volunteers as part of the training program. However, the results of this program have not been reported.

Similarly, there have been no controlled studies of sex education or sexual dysfunction therapy with child molesters, at least known to the authors, although a sex education component is included in numerous treatment programs for offenders (Brecher, 1978).

Kohlenberg (1974) does describe the use of a program based on Masters and Johnson's techniques to reduce sexual anxiety with male adult partners in a male pedophile. Aversive therapy had not been effective in this case while the use of sensate focus and graduated sexual homework assignments did appear to reduce deviant behavior and fantasies while at the same time increasing interactions with adult males.

Similarly, attempts at mediating cognitive distortions, although considered important by almost all therapists, have received almost no empirical investigation, except for references to the use of confrontation in group therapy (Saylor, 1979). From a clinical standpoint, a comprehensive program for the treatment of sex offenders should include education regarding the impact of such abuse on victims and confrontation regarding the cognitive distortions employed by offenders. In our own program, we have found that the review of the deviant sexual fantasies generated during masturbatory satiation is an excellent means of confronting denial systems in offenders. The patient's self-generated fantasies are recorded on audio-tape. The tape allows observation of a "sample" of the patient's behavior and allows identification of some of the cognitions subjects use to justify their behavior. For example, on the tape, subjects may verbalize "that the child agreed to the sexual behavior." At that point, the tape can be stopped and the subject questioned as to how they knew the child agreed. Many subjects will verbalize because he or she "didn't say no." At that point, subjects can be confronted about the fact that the child did not say yes and that children find it very difficult to say no to adults. In careful review of the tapes, one can usually find numerous examples of cognitive distortions, justifications, and rationalizations employed by offenders. The evaluation of this confrontation procedure with some objective measures of cognitive distortions in offenders is needed.

General Treatment Issues

In the above discussion, a number of treatment techniques have been reviewed. However, the treatment of sex offenders, or, for that matter, the treatment of any problem, involves more than the application of techniques. Treatment occurs in the context of a patient-therapist relationship with the clinician and patient holding certain assumptions regarding the nature of treatment and what constitutes successful outcome. The purpose of this section is to outline some of these issues. Unlike the review of techniques, this section is not based on research literature but on the clinical experience and the assumptions held by the authors of this chapter. As such, it should be evaluated in that light.

The first assumption is that the major reason for treating sex offenders against children is to prevent other children from being abused. The second assumption is that the majority of patients will come to treatment under some external pressure and their motivation for change will be mixed at best. The third assumption is that at the present time there is no "cure" for child sexual abuse but that there are methods that help the patient control such behavior.

These assumptions suggest certain characteristics of the therapeutic relationship. For one, the therapist may need to be more authoritarian (Sgroi, 1982) than usually seen in patient-therapist relationships. Therapists may need to more clearly structure the patient's life in certain areas. For example, in outpatient treatment, offenders should be prohibited from any contact with children that would place them at risk for sexual acting out. Incestuous fathers need to move out of the home and pedophiles must change their employment or social activities when such activities place them with children (school teachers, camp counselors, soccer coaches, and such). When the therapist has knowledge that the patient is consistently placing himself in high-risk situations, this needs to be considered as noncompliance to the treatment program. For patients who are court-ordered into treatment where progress reports are required, the therapist must be willing to relay this information, even when the consequences for the patient may be negative. Like it or not, when a clinician agrees to treat a sex offender on an outpatient basis, they are assuming certain responsibilities for the protection of society. Clinicians who are not comfortable with this responsibility should probably consider carefully whether they want to be involved in treatment of this population.

The assumption of no "cure" suggests that all the treatment techniques outlined should be seen as methods to help the patients control their behavior and the major goal of treatment is to prevent relapse. Pithers et al. (1983) have presented an excellent description of the application of a relapse prevention model to sex offenders. This means that all treatment should be presented and described to the patient as self-control strategies. The patient should be informed that they will have occasional fantasies or urges and that these are not signs of treatment failure but only signals to employ various treatment strategies. Within this relapse prevention model, all treatments can be seen as serving one of two purposes. The first is to provide the patient with methods of reducing the intensity of or controlling their deviant urges (electrical aversion, masturbatory satiation, covert sensitization) or to provide skills to deal with antecedents to sexually acting out (increasing appropriate sexual arousal, social skills training, anger management, environmental manipulations, and so on). The therapist's task is to assess the offender appropriately and to teach and monitor needed treatment techniques; while the patient's task is to implement the techniques. Finally, the patients need to be aware that the implementation of techniques is a life-long endeavor, and not limited to a one- to two-year therapy program.

CONCLUSIONS

In this chapter, some of the basic literature related to behavioral and social learning approaches for the evaluation and treatment of child molesters has been reviewed. Additionally, attempts have been made to translate the literature into clinical practice. It is probably clear to the reader by this point that such literature is, at the present time, in its infancy. A number of high-priority research areas including studies directed at etiological factors in child sexual abuse, larger scale studies of treatment outcome, studies investigating factors related to recidivism, among others, are suggested throughout the chapter. In addition to research needs, there is also a need for better training of mental health professionals to deal with the problem of child sexual abuse. Graduate training programs need to include such training in their curriculums.

Such research and clinical training will be expensive, but the scope of the problem seems to warrant the financial investment. The prevalence data indicate that approximately 25 percent of women and 5 to 10 percent of men will have been sexually abused as children. There are few if any other mental health or health problems that affect this many children. It is time for mental health professionals, in greater numbers, to bring their expertise to bear on this national problem.

REFERENCES

Abel, G. G. (1976). Assessment of sexual deviation in the male. In M. Hersen & A. S. Bellack (Eds.), *Behavioral assessment: A practical handbook* (pp. 437-457). New York: Pergamon Press.

Abel, G. G., Barlow, D. H., & Blanchard, E. B. (1973). *Developing heterosexual arousal by altering masturbatory fantasies: A controlled study.* Paper presented at the meeting of the Association for the Advancement of Behavior Therapy, December, Miami.

Abel, G. G., & Becker, J. V. (1984). [Pedophile Cognition Checklist]. Unpublished test.

——. (1985). *Emerging findings on the assessment and treatment of sex offenders.* Paper presented at the NIMH Conference, "Next Steps in Research on Sex Offenders," February, St. Louis.

Abel, G. G., Becker, J. V., Murphy, W. D., & Flanagan, B. (1981). Identifying dangerous child molesters. In R. B. Stuart (Ed.), *Violent behavior: Special learning approaches to prediction, management, and treatment* (pp. 116-137). New York: Brunner/Mazel.

Abel, G. G., Becker, J. V., & Skinner, L. J. (1980). Aggressive behavior and sex. *Psychiatric Clinics of North America, 3,* 133-151.

Abel, G. G., & Blanchard, E. B. (1976). The measurement and generation of sexual arousal in male sexual deviates. In M. Hersen, R. Eisler, & P. M. Miller (Eds.), *Progress in behavior modification* (Vol. 2; pp. 99-136). New York: Academic Press.

Abel, G. G., Blanchard, E. B., Barlow, D. H., & Flanagan, B. (1975). *A case report of the behavioral treatment of a sadistic rapist.* Paper presented at the meeting of the Association for the Advancement of Behavior Therapy, December, San Francisco.

Abel, G. G., Blanchard, E. B., & Becker, J. V. (1978). An integrated treatment program for rapists. In R. T. Rada (Ed.), *Clinical aspects of the rapist* (pp. 161-224). New York: Grune & Stratton.

Armentrout, J. A., & Hauer, A. L. (1978). MMPIs of rapists of adults, rapists of children, and non-rapist sex offenders. *Journal of Clinical Psychology, 34,* 330-332.

Avery-Clark, C. A., & Laws, D. R. (1984). Differential erection response patterns of sexual child abusers to stimuli describing activities with children. *Behavior Therapy, 15,* 71-83.

Bancroft, J., Jones, H. C., & Pullman, B. P. (1966). A simple transducer for measuring penile erections with comments on its use in the treatment of sexual disorders. *Behavior Research and Therapy, 4,* 239-241.

Bandura, A. (1977). *Social learning theory.* Englewood Cliffs, N.J.: Prentice-Hall.

Barlow, D. H. (1973). Increasing heterosexual responsiveness in the treatment of sexual deviation: A review of the clinical and experimental evidence. *Behavior Therapy, 4,* 655-671.

Barlow, D. H., & Abel, G. G. (1976). Recent developments in assessment and treatment of sexual deviation. In W. E. Craighead, A. E. Kazdin, & M. J. Mahoney (Eds.), *Behavior modification: Principles, issues and application* (pp. 341-360). Houston: Houghton Mifflin.

Barlow, D. H., Abel, G. G., Blanchard, E. B., Bristow, A. R., & Young, L. D. (1977). A heterosocial skills behavior checklist for males. *Behavior Therapy, 8,* 229-239.

Barlow, D. H., Becker, R., Leitenberg, H., & Agras, W. D. (1970). A mechanical strain gauge for recording penile circumference change. *Journal of Applied Behavior Analysis, 3,* 73-76.

Barlow, D. H., Leitenberg, H., & Agras, W. S. (1969). The experimental control of sexual deviation through manipulation of the noxious scene in covert sensitization. *Journal of Abnormal Psychology, 74,* 596-601.

Beck, A. T. (1976). *Cognitive therapy and the emotional disorders.* New York: International Universities Press.

Brecher, E. M. (1978). *Treatment programs for six offenders.* Washington, D.C.: National Institute of Law Enforcement and Criminal Justice, Law Enforcement Assistance Administration, U.S. Department of Justice.

Brownell, K. D., & Barlow, D. H. (1976). Measurement and treatment of two sexual deviations in one person. *Journal of Behavior Therapy and Experimental Psychiatry, 7,* 349-354.

Brownell, K. D., Hayes, S. C., & Barlow, D. H. (1977). Patterns of appropriate and deviant sexual arousal: The behavioral treatment of multiple sexual deviations. *Journal of Consulting and Clinical Psychology, 45,* 1144-1155.

Callahan, E. J., & Leitenberg, H. (1973). Aversion therapy for sexual deviation: Contingent shock and covert sensitization. *Journal of Abnormal Psychology, 81,* 60-73.

Cautela, J. R., & Wisocki, P. A. (1971). Covert sensitization for the treatment of sexual deviations. *Psychological Record, 21,* 37-48.

Christie, M. M., Marshall, W. L., & Lanthier, R. D. (1978). *A descriptive study of incarcerated rapists and pedophiles.* Unpublished manuscript.

Conrad, S. R., & Wincze, J. P. (1976). Orgasmic reconditioning: A controlled study of its effects upon the sexual arousal and behavior of adult male homosexuals. *Behavior Therapy, 7*, 155-166.

Cowden, J. E., & Pacht, A. R. (1969). The sex inventory as a classification instrument for sex offenders. *Journal of Clinical Psychology, 25*, 53-57.

Crawford, D. A. (1979). Modification of deviant sexual behavior: The need for a comprehensive approach. *British Journal of Medical Psychology, 52*, 151-156.

Derogatis, L., & Meyer, J. (1979). A psychological profile of the sexual dysfunctions. *Archives of Sexual Behavior, 8*, 201-223.

Edwards, N. B. (1972). Case conference: Assertive training in a case of homosexual pedophilia. *Journal of Behavior Therapy and Experimental Psychiatry, 3*, 55-63.

Eisler, R. M., Miller, P. M., & Hersen, M. (1973). Components of assertive behavior. *Journal of Clinical Psychology, 29*, 295-299.

Ellis, A., & Grieger, R. (Eds.). (1977). *Handbook of rational-emotive therapy.* New York: Springer.

Finkelhor, D. (1979). *Sexually victimized children.* New York: Free Press.

——. (1984). *Child sexual abuse: New theory and research.* New York: Free Press.

Finkelhor, D., & Araji, S. (1983). *Explanations of pedophilia: A four-factor model.* Durham: University of New Hampshire Press.

Foote, W. D., & Laws, D. R. (1981). A daily alternation procedure for orgasmic reconditioning with a pedophile. *Journal of Behavior Therapy and Experimental Psychiatry, 12*, 267-273.

Freund, K. (1957). Diagnostika homosexuality u nuzu. *Ceskoslovenska Psychiatrie, 53*, 382-393.

——. (1961). A laboratory differential diagnosis of homo- and heterosexuality: An experiment with faking. *Review of Czechoslovak Medicine, 7*, 20-31.

——. (1965). Diagnosing heterosexual pedophilia by means of a test for sexual interest. *Behaviour Research and Therapy, 3*, 229-234.

——. (1967a). Diagnosing homo- or heterosexuality and erotic age-preference by means of a psychophysiological test. *Behaviour Research and Therapy, 5*, 209-228.

——. (1967b). Erotic preference in pedophilia. *Behaviour Research and Therapy, 5*, 339-348.

Frisbee, L. V., & Dondis, E. H. (1965). *Recidivism among treated sex offenders* (California Mental Health Research Monograph No. 5). Sacramento: Department of Mental Health.

Fritz, G. S., Stoll, K., & Wagner, N. N. (1981). A comparison of males and females who were sexually molested as children. *Journal of Sex and Marital Therapy, 7,* 54-59.

Furby, L., & Weinrott, M. (In preparation). *Recidivism among sex offenders: A review.*

Gagnon, J. (1965). Female child victims of sex offenders. *Social Problems, 13,* 176-192.

Gay, M. L., Hollandsworth, J. G., & Galassi, J. P. (1975). An assertiveness inventory for adults. *Journal of Counseling Psychology, 22,* 340-344.

Gelinas, D. J. (1983). The persisting negative effects of incest. *Psychiatry, 46,* 312-332.

Giaretto, H. (1981). A comprehensive child sexual abuse treatment program. *Child Abuse and Neglect, 6,* 263-278.

Glass, C. R., & Merluzzi, T. V. (1981). Cognitive assessment of social-evaluative anxiety. In T. V. Merluzzi, C. R. Glass, & G. M. Genest (Eds.), *Cognitive assessment* (pp. 388-438). New York: Guilford Press.

Gomes-Schwartz, B., Horowitz, J. M., & Sauzier, M. (1985). Severity of emotional distress among sexually abused preschool, school-age, and adolescent children. *Hospital and Community Psychiatry, 36,* 503-508.

Groth, A. N. (1982). The incest offender. In S. M. Sgroi (Ed.), *Handbook of clinical intervention in child sexual abuse* (pp. 215-239). Lexington, Mass.: D. C. Heath.

Hammer, E. F. (1954). A comparison of H-T-P's of rapists and pedophiles. *Journal of Projective Techniques, 18,* 346-354.

——. (1957). A psychoanalytic hypothesis concerning sex offenders. *Journal of Clinical and Experimental Psychopathology, 18,* 177-184.

Hollandsworth, J. G., Galassi, J. P., & Gay, M. L. (1977). The Adult Self-Expression Scale: Validation by the multitrait-multimethod procedure. *Journal of Clinical Psychology, 33,* 407-415.

Josiassen, R. C., Fantuzzo, J., & Rosen, A. C. (1980). Treatment of pedophilia using multistage aversion therapy and social skills training. *Behavior Research and Experimental Psychiatry, 11,* 55-61.

Kelley, R. J. (1982). Behavioral re-orientation of pedophiliacs. Can it be done? *Clinical Psychology Review, 2*, 387–408.

Keltner, A. A. (1977). The control of penile tumescence with biofeedback in two cases of pedophilia. *Corrective and Social Psychiatry and Journal of Behavior Technology, Methods and Therapy, 23*, 117–121.

Kohlenberg, R. J. (1974). Treatment of a homosexual pedophiliac using in vivo desensitization: A case study. *Journal of Abnormal Psychology, 83*, 192–195.

Kremsdorf, R. B., Holmen, M. L., & Laws, D. R. (1980). Orgasmic reconditioning without deviant imagery. *Behaviour Research and Therapy, 18*, 203–207.

Kroth, J. (1979). *Child sexual abuse: Analysis of a family therapy approach.* Springfield, Ill.: Thomas.

Landis, J. T. (1965). Experiences of 500 children with adult sexual deviants. *Psychiatric Quarterly Supplement, 30*, 91–109.

Langevin, R. (1983). *Sexual strands: Understanding and treating sexual anomalies in men.* Hillsdale, N. J.: Lawrence Erlbaum.

Laws, D. R. (1980). Treatment of bisexual pedophilia by a biofeedback-assisted self-control procedure. *Behaviour Research and Therapy, 18*, 207–211.

———. (1985). Sexual fantasy alternation: Procedural considerations. *Journal of Behavior Therapy and Experimental Psychiatry, 16*, 39–44.

Laws, D. R., & Holmen, M. L. (1978). Sexual response faking by pedophiles. *Criminal Justice and Behavior, 5*, 343–356.

Laws, D. R., & Osborn, C. A. (1983). How to build and operate a behavioral laboratory to evaluate and treat sexual deviance. In J. G. Greer & I. R. Stuart (Eds.), *The sexual aggressor: Current perspectives on treatment* (pp. 293–335). New York: Van Nostrand Reinhold.

Levin, S. M., Barry, S. M., Gambaro, S., Wolfinsohn, L., & Smith, A. (1977). Variations of covert sensitization in the treatment of pedophilic behavior: A case study. *Journal of Consulting and Clinical Psychology, 45*, 896–907.

Locke, H., & Wallace, K. (1957). Short marital adjustment and prediction tests: Their reliability and validity. *Marriage and Family Living, 21*, 251–255.

MacFarlane, K., & Bulkley, J. (1982). Treating child sexual abuse: An overview of current program models. In J. R. Conte & D. A. Shore (Eds.), *Social work and child sexual abuse* (pp. 69–89). New York: Haworth Press.

Maletzky, B. M. (1980). Self-referred versus court-referred sexually deviant patients: Success with assisted covert sensitization. *Behavior Therapy*, *11*, 306-314.

Marquis, J. N. (1970). Orgasmic reconditioning: Changing sexual object choice through controlling masturbation fantasies. *Journal of Behavior Therapy and Experimental Psychiatry*, *1*, 263-271.

Marsh, J. T., Hilliard, J., & Liechti, R. (1955). A sexual deviation scale for the MMPI. *Journal of Consulting Psychology*, *19*, 55-59.

Marshall, W. L. (1973). The modification of sexual fantasies: A combined treatment approach to the reduction of deviant sexual behavior. *Behaviour Research and Therapy*, *11*, 557-564.

——. (1979). Satiation therapy: A procedure for reducing deviant sexual arousal. *Journal of Applied Behavior Analysis*, *12*, 10-22.

Marshall, W. L., & Lippens, B. A. (1977). The clinical value of boredom: A procedure for reducing inappropriate sexual interests. *Journal of Nervous and Mental Disease*, *165*, 283-287.

McConaghy, N. (1974). Measurements of change in penile dimensions. *Archives of Sexual Behavior*, *3*, 381-388.

McCreary, C. P. (1975). Personality differences among child molesters. *Journal of Personality Assessment*, *39*, 591-593.

McFall, R. M., & Marston, A. R. (1970). An experimental investigation of behavioral rehearsal in assertiveness training. *Journal of Abnormal Psychology*, *76*, 295-303.

Miller, H. L., & Haney, J. R. (1976). Behavior and traditional therapy applied to pedophiliac exhibitionism: A case study. *Psychological Reports*, *39*, 1119-1124.

Mohr, J. W., Turner, R. E., & Jerry, M. B. (1964). *Pedophilia and exhibitionism: A handbook*. Toronto: University of Toronto Press.

Murphy, W. D. (1985). Characteristics of offenders against children. Unpublished manuscript.

Murphy, W. D., Abel, G. G., & Becker, J. V. (1980). Future research issues. In D. J. Cox & R. J. Daitzman (Eds.), *Exhibitionism: Description, assessment, and treatment* (pp. 339-392). New York: Garland Press.

Murphy, W. D., Coleman, E. M., & Haynes, M. R. (1983). Treatment and evaluation issues with the mentally retarded sex offender. In J. G. Greer & I. R. Stuart (Eds.), *The sexual aggressor: Current perspectives on treatment* (pp. 22-41). New York: Van Nostrand Reinhold.

Nolan, J. D., & Sandman, C. (1978). "Biosyntonic" therapy: Modification of an operant conditioning approach to pedophilia. *Journal of Consulting and Clinical Psychology, 46,* 1133-1140.

Olson, D. H., & Portner, J. (1983). Family Adaptability and Cohesion Evaluation Scales. In E. E. Filsinger (Ed.), *Marriage and family assessment: A sourcebook for family therapy* (pp. 299-315). Beverly Hills, Calif.: Sage Publications.

Paitich, D., Langevin, R., Freeman, R., Mann, K., & Handy, L. (1977). The Clarke SHQ: A clinical sex history questionnaire for males. *Archives of Sexual Behavior, 6,* 421-436.

Panton, J. H. (1978). Personality differences appearing between rapists of adults, rapists of children, and nonviolent sexual molesters of female children. *Research Communications in Psychology, Psychiatry, and Behavior, 3,* 385-393.

———. (1979). MMPI configurations associated with incestuous and non-incestuous child molesting. *Psychological Reports, 45,* 335-338.

Pithers, W. D., Marques, J. K., Gibat, C. C., & Marlatt, G. A. (1983). Relapse prevention with sexual aggressives: A self-control model of treatment and maintenance of change. In J. G. Greer & I. R. Stuart (Eds.), *The sexual aggressor: Current perspectives on treatment* (pp. 214-239). New York: Van Nostrand Reinhold.

Quinsey, V. L. (1973). Methodological issues in evaluating the effectiveness of aversion therapies for institutionalized child molesters. *Canadian Psychologist, 14,* 350-361.

———. (1977). The assessment and treatment of child molesters: A review. *Canadian Psychological Review, 18,* 204-220.

Quinsey, V. L., Arnold, L. S., & Pruesse, M. G. (1980). MMPI profiles on men referred for a pretrial psychiatric assessment as a function of offense type. *Journal of Clinical Psychology, 36,* 410-417.

Quinsey, V. L., Bergersen, S. G., & Steinman, C. M. (1976). Changes in physiological and verbal responses of child molesters during aversion therapy. *Canadian Journal of Behavioral Science, 8,* 202-212.

Quinsey, V. L., & Carrigan, W. F. (1978). Instructional control of penile responses to visual stimuli with and without auditory sexual fantasy correlates. *Criminal Justice and Behavior, 5,* 333-342.

Quinsey, V. L., Chaplin, T. C., & Carrigan, W. F. (1979).

Sexual preferences among incestuous and nonincestuous child molesters. *Behavior Therapy, 10,* 562-565.

Quinsey, V. L., Chaplin, T. C., & Carrigan, W. F. (1980). Biofeedback and signaled punishment in the modification of inappropriate sexual age preferences. *Behavior Therapy, 11,* 567-576.

Quinsey, V. L., Chaplin, T. C., & Varney, G. (1981). A comparison of rapists' and non-sex offenders' sexual preferences for mutually consenting sex, rape, and physical abuse of women. *Behavioral Assessment, 3,* 127-135.

Quinsey, V. L., & Marshall, W. L. (1983). Procedures for reducing inappropriate sexual arousal: An evaluation review. In J. G. Greer & I. R. Stuart (Eds.), *The sexual aggressor: Current perspectives on treatment* (pp. 267-289). New York: Van Nostrand Reinhold.

Quinsey, V. L., Steinman, C. M., Bergersen, S. G., & Holmes, T. F. (1975). Penile circumference, skin conductance, and ranking responses of child molesters and "normals" to sexual and nonsexual visual stimuli. *Behavior Therapy, 6,* 213-219.

Rathus, S. A. (1973). A 30-item schedule for assessing assertive behavior. *Behavior Therapy, 4,* 398-406.

Rosenthal, T. L. (1973). Response-contingent versus fixed punishment in aversion conditioning of pedophilia: A case study. *Journal of Nervous and Mental Disease, 156,* 440-443.

Russell, D. E. H. (1983). The incidence and prevalence of intrafamilial and extrafamilial sexual abuse of female children. *Child Abuse and Neglect, 7,* 133-146.

Sarafino, E. P. (1979). An estimate of nationwide incidence of sexual offenses against children. *Child Welfare, 58,* 127-134.

Saylor, M. (1979). *A guided self-help program to treatment of the habitual sexual offender.* Paper presented at the 12th Cropwood Conference, December, Cambridge, England.

Segal, Z. V., & Marshall, W. L. (1985). Heterosexual social skills in a population of rapists and child molesters. *Journal of Consulting and Clinical Psychology, 53,* 55-63.

Serber, M. (1972). Shame aversion therapy with and without heterosexual retraining. In R. D. Rubin, J. D. Henderson, H. Fensterheim, & L. P. Ullman (Eds.), *Advances in behavior therapy* (pp. 115-119). New York: Academic Press.

Serber, M., & Keith, C. G. (1974). The Atascadero Project: Model of a sexual retraining program for incarcerated homosexual pedophiles. *Journal of Homosexuality, 1,* 87-97.

Sgroi, S. M. (1982). *Handbook of clinical intervention in child sexual abuse.* Lexington, Mass.: D. C. Heath.

Summit, R. C. (1983). The child sexual abuse accommodation syndrome. *Child Abuse and Neglect, 7,* 177-193.

Thorne, F. C. (1966). The sex inventory. *Journal of Clinical Psychology, 22,* 367-374.

Tracy, F., Donnelly, H., Morgenbesser, L., & Macdonald, D. (1983). Program evaluation: Recidivism research involving sex offenders. In J. G. Greer and I. R. Stuart (Eds.), *The sexual aggressor: Current perspectives on treatment* (pp. 198-213). New York: Van Nostrand Reinhold.

Truax, C. B., & Carkhuff, R. R. (1967). *Toward effective counseling and psychotherapy: Training and practice.* Chicago: Aldine.

Twentyman, C. T., & McFall, R. M. (1975). Behavioral training of social skills in shy males. *Journal of Consulting and Clinical Psychology, 43,* 384-395.

VanDeventer, A. D., & Laws, D. R. (1978). Organic reconditioning to redirect sexual arousal in pedophiles. *Behavior Therapy, 9,* 748-765.

Waterman, C. K., & Foss-Goodman, D. (1984). Child molesting: Variables relating to attribution of fault to victims, offenders and non-participating parents. *The Journal of Sex Research, 20,* 329-349.

Watson, D., & Friend, R. (1969). Measurement of social-evaluative anxiety. *Journal of Consulting and Clinical Psychology, 33,* 448-457.

Wijesinghe, B. (1977). Massed aversion treatment of sexual deviance. *Journal of Behavior Therapy and Experimental Psychiatry, 8,* 135-137.

Wilson, C. (1985). Personal communication.

Zuckerman, M. (1971). Physiological measures of sexual arousal in the human. *Psychological Bulletin, 75,* 297-329.

8

BRIEF AND TIME-LIMITED PSYCHOTHERAPIES: PRESENT STATUS AND APPRAISAL

John P. Garske
Andrew L. Molteni
James M. Moore, Jr.

Brief interventions have long been in a minority among the mental health professions that have developed and practiced long-term psychotherapies. Now it appears that the tide has turned. Consider these data. In a recent survey of nearly 1 million psychiatric patients conducted by the National Center for Health Statistics, the average number of sessions with a therapist was less than five (Lorion, 1974). In an exhaustive review of psychotherapy outcome studies, Smith, Glass, and Miller (1980) found that, while the number of sessions ranged from one to over 300, the average duration was less than 16 hours and two-thirds of the effects came from studies in which the length was 12 hours or less. The therapy durations in both of these divergent samples are a far cry from the average of 855 sessions for psychoanalysis in the Menninger Foundation Psychotherapy Research Project (Kernberg, Burstein, Coyne, Appelbaum, Horwitz, & Voth, 1972). Psychotherapy, whether by plan or accident, does not appear to last long.

The mental health professions have responded to this reality by offering direct training in brief psychotherapy. For example, Clarkin, Frances, Taintor, and Warburg (1980) found that nearly 90 percent of the psychiatric residency programs incorporate brief therapy into their curricula and practica. The scholarship too has burgeoned. Mandel (1981) has compiled an annotated bibliography on brief therapy that contains 1,552 entries.

While many psychotherapies are brief, psychotherapists do not necessarily practice brief psychotherapy. Therapies might be abbreviated for a number of unplanned reasons. One major factor is client attrition. It is not uncommon for half of the clients who begin therapy to drop out prior to a successful completion of treatment (for example, Rogers, 1960). Another

factor is that clients frequently respond quickly to the nonspecific elements of the treatment situation, feel better emotionally,
and lose their motivation to continue (Frank, 1981). Therapists
also might prematurely shorten the therapy by showing their
clients the door because of early failures or successes. In
these instances, brevity is not a by-product of a successfully
planned treatment regimen.

The hallmark of any brief psychotherapy is that the duration of the intervention is limited intentionally. The strategy
is to produce the maximum benefit in the shortest time. The
therapist's task is to reduce the excesses of long-term, vaguely
defined approaches and thereby make the therapist's work efficient and the client's cost, in economic and emotional terms,
minimal. This objective is commonly accomplished in several
ways (Butcher & Koss, 1978):

- The time that the therapy lasts is limited, usually by
  mutual agreement of the therapist and client during the
  first session.
- The goals of the therapy are focused and circumscribed,
  and typically include increased effective coping strategies,
  insight into current life circumstances, symptomatic relief,
  and the acquisition of new, adaptive behaviors. Major
  alterations of character problems or of chronic behavior
  patterns are neither attempted nor hoped for.
- Because of the time constraints, the therapist must assess
  problems adeptly and quickly, and act. A premium is thus
  placed on therapist skills such as flexibility, directiveness,
  activity, time management, and a capacity to foster a good
  working relationship with the client.

Budman and Gurman (1983) contend that the practice of
brief, time-limited therapy is facilitated by a set of attitudes
and values that are distinctive from those that characterize
extended, time-unlimited therapy. Taken together, they define
a minimalist approach to psychotherapy in which the therapist
facilitates but does not guide the process of change for the
client. The priority is upon mobilizing the client's resources
and returning him or her to the environment somewhat strengthened. The most significant changes are assumed to take place
after the therapy is over. The "cure," by means of which the
client is recast in a perfected form with improved materials,
is seen as mythical. The bedrock of the brief therapy orientation is thus characterized as an attitudinal emphasis on health
rather than disorder. This value system, while probably desirable in an ideal form, is not embraced by all brief therapists,
especially those of the psychodynamic ilk (Strupp & Binder,
1984).

Brief therapy can be distinguished from crisis intervention
(Aguilera & Messick, 1982). Crisis intervention is a therapeutic
procedure by which, following a major upheaval in life circum-

stances, such as a suicide attempt, accident, divorce, job loss, or loss of a loved one, a person is restored to his or her level of functioning prior to the crisis. The focus is upon enhancing the client's coping ability and problem-solving skills with specific reference to the stressful situation or precipitating event. The crisis worker, who can be a paraprofessional with less training than a psychotherapist, is available at any time and meets the client for irregular sessions as needed. Contact is usually very brief, frequently only once, and typically involves referral to a professional service (Marmor, 1979). By contrast, brief therapy has the accouterments of standard psychotherapy. The brief therapist meets for regularly scheduled appointments with the client to explore present and past experiences. While focused, the therapy is not bound by the presenting situation and, hence, targets change primarily in the client and secondarily in environmental circumstances. The objective is the improvement of adaptive functioning and not simply its restoration.

This chapter discusses several aspects of brief and time-limited psychotherapies. The format consists of four primary sections. First, the emergence of brief therapy and the factors that contributed to its development are reviewed. Second, a sampler of the primary models of brief and time-limited psychotherapy is presented. Third, the issue of effectiveness is addressed by a critical examination of two research areas: the effects of duration on psychotherapy outcome and comparative studies of time-limited versus time-unlimited psychotherapies. Finally, some technical aspects of brief therapy practice are discussed. These include the concept of brevity, therapist variables, and client applicability.

HISTORY AND DEVELOPMENT

The early history of brief psychotherapy is intertwined with that of psychoanalysis. Unlike the marathon length of present-day psychoanalytic treatment, Freud's initial therapeutic efforts were quite modest. Brevity was the rule, not the exception. For example, he treated Katharina in a single session atop a mountain in the Austrian Alps while on holiday (Breuer & Freud, 1957). For the next decade, Freud maintained his short-term orientation and was apologetic regarding the duration of his treatments even if they lasted a few months or less (Strupp & Binder, 1984).

The subsequent historical development is well-known. As psychoanalytic theory evolved, the scope of psychoanalytic treatment expanded proportionally. Freud and his fellow psychoanalytic theorists eventually worked their way into an epistemological trap. Because the theory was constructed to explain neurosis in terms of a complex set of variables involving unconscious instinctual drives, psychosexual development, and intrapsychic conflict, the requirements of therapy were correspondingly toilsome. Complex causes of necessity require complex solutions. Brief interventions for Freud were hence relegated as insufficient and ineffective.

For the next half century or so, there was remarkably little deviance from this orthodox psychoanalytic view that long-term treatment is mandatory for effective results. There were two notable exceptions that presaged the modern emergence of brief psychodynamic methods. Ferenczi and Rank (1925) contended that therapeutic change did not require the repetitive, laborious analytic work of psychoanalysis. They brashly proposed that the patient's *present* experience of past conflicts rooted in psychological development was sufficient during psychotherapy and, moreover, that such a phenomenon was best facilitated by the active interventions of the therapist. This heretical diminution of the importance of, time and again, retracing the psychological past and the redefinition of the role of the therapist away from the blank-screen prototype of the psychoanalyst were critical for abbreviating the lengthy process of psychoanalytic treatment.

The work of Ferenczi and Rank lay dormant until Alexander and French (1946) rediscovered and extended their ideas. Alexander and French argued that therapeutic change was not proportionate to the duration of treatment but depended primarily on a "corrective emotional experience" brought about by the intense revival of neurotic conflict in therapy. Therapist flexibility was imperative in the service of this goal. Alexander and French were aware of the negative consequences of too much therapy, especially the risk of excessive dependency, and were the first to plan brevity as part of the therapy protocol by varying the frequency of sessions, introducing an occasional hiatus during treatment, and setting termination dates. The brief therapy approach of Alexander and French, like that of Ferenczi and Rank two decades earlier, had little immediate effect on practice. As a prominent psychoanalyst, Alexander was, however, able to create an intellectual climate that enabled therapeutic change to be viewed as feasible independent of treatment longevity.

In the 1960s and 1970s, the Zeitgeist shifted dramatically and the brief therapy movement moved from the periphery to the center of services available in the mental health professions. Within the psychoanalytic community, three models of brief psychodynamic psychotherapy emerged: brief focal therapy (Balint, Ornstein, & Balint, 1972; Malan, 1963, 1976), short-term anxiety-provoking psychotherapy (Sifneos, 1972, 1979), and time-limited psychotherapy (Mann, 1973; Mann & Goldman, 1982). These approaches, developed independently of each other, retained many psychoanalytic assumptions regarding theory and technique, but they departed radically from the standards of psychoanalytic treatment. All eschewed the task of overhauling the personality as a therapeutic objective and geared the work of brief therapy toward a focused problem that was treatable in a limited period of time.

A significant impetus to the development of brief therapies was the emergence of the use of behavioral techniques in the modification of behavior. Early work in learning theory applications to psychotherapy (Dollard & Miller, 1953) and the development of specific learning-based techniques (Wolpe, 1958) catapulted behavior therapy out of the laboratory and into the clinic. Throughout the 1960s and 1970s, behavior therapy matured theoretically and grew enormously as a treatment alternative to psychoanalysis and other long-term, insight-oriented therapies. Today the theories are complex and the techniques emphasize cognitive and social variables (Bandura, 1977) and self-regulatory capacities (Wilson & O'Leary, 1980). Practice has broadened to enlist a divergent array of effective procedures (compare Meichenbaum, 1985). From its origins to its present form, behavior therapy has placed a premium on specific well-defined treatment objectives and efficient, rapidly acting procedures.

The psychoanalytic and behavioral paradigms, while rivals theoretically, have given rise to brief therapy hybrids such as cognitive therapy (Beck, 1976) and cognitive behavior modification (Meichenbaum, 1985). These therapies meld the psychoanalytic emphasis on inner experience with the behavioral emphasis on action to develop approaches that make stubborn and slow-changing disorders, such as depression and complex phobias, more amenable to efficient, time-limited interventions.

An important principle is evident in the history of brief psychotherapy: Therapies in their infancy are typically short and focused, and tend to lengthen as they develop. This has obviously been true with psychoanalysis. Even behavior therapy, a treatment modality that has as its hallmark specificity and efficiency, can last 100 hours or more (Wilson, 1981). This tendency toward longevity might also await the newly developed cognitive therapies. The reasons are complex. One might be that clients are helped more as they receive more treatment from a more sophisticated therapeutic system. We shall discover later in this chapter, however, that longevity is not associated with greater improvement. Another explanation might be that therapists prefer extended contact. Appelbaum (1981) speculates that any client, even if improved after a short time in treatment, can always use more. Under these conditions, "Parkinson's Law" operates and the therapy continues to fill the time that is available. Theoretically, then, the emergence of brief methods can be seen jointly as a rediscovery of a fundamental, straightforward therapeutic orientation at the foundation of many therapies and a struggle within a therapeutic approach to counter a tendency for it to overtreat its clients.

Because there appears to be resistance within established therapeutic orientations to practice brief therapy, it is not surprising that the impetus is generated from outside the psychotherapy professions. The first influence comes from the social system and its need for mental health services. Brief therapies are efficient means for extending limited professional services to greater numbers. It is no accident that Alexander and French (1946) developed their brief dynamic approach at a time when psychiatric services were strained by an influx of emotional problems during World War II. In the 1960s and 1970s, the flurry of activity in brief psychodynamic psychotherapy and the emergence of behavior therapy also corresponded with manpower shortages for mental health services documented by the Joint Commission of Mental Illness and Health in 1961. Mann's (1973) time-limited psychotherapy was developed specifically to reduce the long client waiting lists at his clinic at the Boston University Medical School.

Despite the impact of brief, efficient therapeutic methods on increasing available mental health services, the demand for such services appears to be expanding rather than shrinking (Budman & Gurman, 1983). The availability of psychotherapy has increased dramatically because of the rapid growth of community clinics that offer affordable fees-for-service and the inclusion of mental health coverage in most private and public health care provisions. The psychotherapy professions also have acquired a halo of credibility and attractiveness due in large order to our society's tendency to consider many problems of living as psychological (Zilbergeld, 1983).

Another factor leading to an emphasis on brief and time-limited therapies is cost-effectiveness. Those who pay for psychotherapeutic services—insurance companies, legislatures, policymakers, and clients themselves—have become concerned with burgeoning costs. Limiting costs limits the amount of service. Many insurance policies and health maintenance organizations now specify dollar amounts or limit the number of sessions per calendar year. The effect is to time-limit the therapy. It appears that brief therapy may save money in two ways: It is less expensive than extended, long-term therapies and it also reduces the utilization of expensive medical services (Schlesinger, Mumford, & Glass, 1980).

The emergence of brief therapy approaches has been buoyed up by the elevated level of scholarship in the psychotherapy field, especially psychotherapy research. Following Szasz's (1961) classic analysis of mental illness and critique of the medical model, concepts of psychopathology and mental disorders have undergone considerable revision. Many emotional problems are no longer considered pathognomic and intractable. Rather they are understandable in terms of transient personal states and environmental circumstances such as stress, marital dissatisfaction, and situational anxieties. Conceptualized without the encumbrances of the medical model, many psychological problems are suitable for and amenable to brief, time-limited therapies. Most importantly, as we shall discuss in some detail later in this chapter, there is an absence of evidence that long-term therapies are superior to short-term therapies.

REPRESENTATIVE MODELS AND METHODS

The last three decades or so have witnessed the emergence and development of many brief and time-limited psychotherapies. This section presents a selective sample of methods from the major psychological paradigms. Our intent is not a survey but merely a smattering of the representative approaches to brief therapy.

Brief Psychodynamic Psychotherapies

There are a variety of brief psychodynamic psychotherapies that share common features with each other and with traditional psychoanalytic psychotherapy (Davanloo, 1980; Malan, 1976; Mann, 1973; Sifneos, 1972). All of these therapies conceptualize behavior problems from the psychoanalytic perspective, with particular emphasis on the presence of intrapsychic conflict and its relationship to critical interpersonal events in psychological development. Moreover, they rely on interpretation as the main therapeutic technique. In the brief approaches, interpretations are made earlier and more frequently than in traditional psychoanalytic psychotherapy. These approaches all differ from each other and from psychoanalysis, to some degree, on how these interpretations should link the present and the past. All of the brief approaches are time-limited, although they set time limits in different ways (compare Garske & Molteni, 1985).

Sifneos's (1972, 1979) short-term anxiety-provoking psychotherapy attempts to make lasting changes by resolving the basic neurotic conflict. As do many of the other brief dynamic therapists, Sifneos has specific guidelines to indicate who is appropriate for therapy. He requires the patient to be of above-average intelligence, to be motivated to change, and to have a circumscribed chief complaint of a neurotic nature. The patient must also be able to tolerate the anxiety that is catalyzed by the early and frequent interpretations of resistance, transference, and impulse that mark Sifneos's approach. Even while the therapist is formulating a psychodynamic hypothesis, he is making interpretations of resistance to working in therapy, in addition to vigorous clarification and interpretation of positive transference reactions in order to limit regression. Through these active and vigorous interpretations of resistance and transference, the therapist causes the patient to examine how he or she recreates the neurotic conflict in present relationships.

The termination date is set fairly late in the course of therapy when there is some resolution of the neurosis. Therapy duration is typically 12 to 15 weeks. During termination, the therapist works through resistance to termination, but not all of the conflicts associated with separation.

Davanloo (1980), extending the pioneering work of Malan (1963, 1976), also recommends that the therapist be active and make early interpretations of transference and resistance. Early confrontation of resistance and transference is thought to produce less dependency and allow for early working through of conflict. Although Davanloo works with a broader range of problems than Sifneos, including characterological problems and obsessive neuroses, he is still selective in accepting patients. The prospective patients must be motivated and able to tolerate the anxiety, anger, and other emotions aroused by uncovering and working through long-standing problems. The patient must have had at least one meaningful relationship, and, most importantly, must have positive responses to the rather confrontive trial interpretations made during the evaluation.

In addition to being ambitious in patient selection, Davanloo is also ambitious in terms of the goals of therapy: The aim of his therapy is the amelioration of symptoms and change in maladaptive behavior. This change occurs through active interpretation and the linkage of interpersonal conflicts between the present and past and between the therapist and significant others.

Termination is generally uneventful, although sometimes problems with separating from the therapist must be worked through. Davanloo is explicit about his time limits at the beginning of therapy. The number of sessions required ranges from 5 to 15 for patients with a circumscribed neurotic conflict and from 20 to 30 for patients with a long-standing character problem.

Mann's (1973) time-limited psychotherapy catalyzes the separation-individuation issue at the heart of many conflicts by the continual reminder of the limited number of sessions. Patient selection is geared around the separation issue, and young adults in a developmental crisis are the ideal candidates for Mann's approach. Similarly, the separation-individuation issue determines how the central issue is defined. Once the central issue is delineated, Mann imposes a 12-session limit on therapy. This explicit limit gives rise to rapid mobilization of positive transference, which is quickly followed by the realization that separation from the therapist is inevitable. This impending separation, and the negative transference reaction that accompanies it, is then related to the central issue; it is here that interpretations of transference link current and past loss and provide the opportunity for correcting and working through distortions.

Despite the claims of their adherents, the brief psychodynamic psychotherapies are more alike than different (Garske &

Molteni, 1985). They all share a psychodynamic flavor, emphasize a focal conflict or issue, and proceed within a limited
temporal framework. There have been recent attempts to integrate brief psychodynamic therapies (Garske & Molteni, 1985;
Gustafson, 1984) and new approaches have emerged that are
based jointly on psychoanalytic heritage, concerns for brevity
and efficiency, and psychological research (Horowitz, Marmor,
Krupnick, Wilner, Kaltreider, & Wallerstein, 1984; Strupp &
Binder, 1984).

Cognitive Therapy

One of the more popular forms of brief therapy that has
appeared in the past two decades is the cognitive therapy
developed by Aaron Beck and his associates (Beck, Rush,
Shaw, & Emery, 1979). Initially developed for use in treating
depression, cognitive therapy is an active, time-limited, structured therapy that is now being used to treat anxiety, phobias,
and pain problems as well as depression.

Based on the assumption that a person's affect and behavior are to a large degree influenced by how he or she per-
ceives and construes his or her world, cognitive therapy
attempts to correct these maladaptive constructs and assumptions and thereby change behavior and feelings. Cognitive
therapy focuses on maladaptive cognitions in the here and now
rather than on reconstruction of the past as in dynamic therapies, but cognitive therapy is introspective, requiring the
patient to examine the way he or she appraises events.

Cognitive therapy, according to Beck (1976), follows an
orderly, structured approach that begins with the establishment of a therapeutic alliance and the establishment of a
mutually agreed upon focus and goals. The next step involves
examination and clarification of external events and the subsequent maladaptive, automatic thoughts that lead to characteristic affective or behavioral reactions. Examination of these
thoughts leads to questioning the patient's subjective distortions and systematic errors in appraising external events.
The patient is then directed to make rational interpretations
or appraisals free of distortions and irrational assumptions.
The cognitive therapist is both active and directive in helping
the patient to identify and challenge these patterns of distorted and irrational beliefs. Change is seen as occurring
through the persistent, constructive confrontation of these
maladaptive beliefs.

Beck has compiled a fairly comprehensive list of patterns
of distorted thinking (for example, arbitrary and dichotomous
thinking, or sorting all events into one of two mutually exclusive categories such as all good or all bad), and different
logical arguments are used to modify each of these patterns.

Cognitive therapy is generally limited to 25 sessions or
fewer. Therapy initially may be twice weekly and then once

weekly, and by the termination phase, sessions may be on only a monthly basis. This tapering off at the end of therapy is thought to facilitate working through, consolidate changes in thinking, and ease the separation process.

Behavior Therapy

Behavior therapy, which emerged in the 1950s and 1960s partly as a reaction to the length of the traditional psychodynamic therapies, may be conceptualized as a brief therapy. Wilson's (1981) review of behavior therapy as a short-term intervention indicates that therapies lasting from 25 to 50 sessions are common with occasional, albeit rare, therapies exceeding 100 sessions, and that many disorders can be treated in brief periods of time using behavioral techniques. Specific phobias appear to respond in about six sessions using graduated in vivo techniques, and more complex phobias such as agoraphobia also appear to respond to brief interventions. Obsessive-compulsive disorders have been improved significantly by brief (15 sessions) interventions using in vivo flooding and modeling (Rachman & Wilson, 1980). Addictive disorders such as alcoholism, obesity, and cigarette smoking also appear to be treated successfully by brief behavioral interventions.

The length of treatment varies and is in part influenced by the complexity of the problem: Cases of sexual dysfunction not complicated by other marital problems, for example, often respond to self-help behavioral interventions of less than 15 sessions, but if behavioral marital therapy is required in addition to sex therapy, as many as 50 sessions may be required.

The focus of brief behavioral interventions tends to be circumscribed and specific, with tangible and measurable indexes of improvement. The grist for the behavioral mill has changed drastically since Wolpe's (1958) narrow stimulus-response (S-R) approach. Less emphasis is placed on environmental influences and more emphasis is put on cognitive processes that mediate behavior. Social learning theory has had increasing influence on behavior therapy as well, casting behavior and personal experience in a reciprocal role with environmental influences where behavior influences and is in turn influenced by the environment (Bandura, 1977).

No specific set of techniques is part of all behavioral interventions although some, such as modeling, flooding, and relaxation training, are common. Rather, the style and procedure of the behavior therapists set them apart from other therapists: Active, direct interventions follow close on the heels of the behavioral assessment, and continued assessment of the focal problem is part of therapy. Interventions are tailored to fit the unique needs of the patient to a large degree, but Wilson (1981) is critical of behavior therapists' reliance on tradition rather than empirical data in staying with the weekly or twice weekly 50-minute treatment format.

Termination of treatment and the therapeutic relationship is not abrupt in behavior therapy. The focus in the termination phase is on generalization and maintenance of therapeutic change rather than on separation and dependency on the therapist. As the focal problems in therapy improve, successive sessions are often scheduled further apart until the patient is seen on only a monthly basis, and these later sessions are apt to be briefer than the earlier ones. Posttreatment contacts or crisis sessions after termination are not discouraged by the behavior therapist. The possibility of dependency on the therapist is of less concern to the behavior therapist than is sustaining therapeutic change, and booster or follow-up sessions may be planned as part of therapy.

Brief Strategic Therapy

Another brief interactional approach to psychotherapy has been developed by Watzlawick, Weakland, and their associates (Watzlawick & Coyne, 1980; Watzlawick, Weakland, & Fisch, 1974; Weakland, Fisch, Watzlawick, & Bodin, 1974). Their brief strategic interactional approach, which developed out of their experience working with families at the Mental Research Institute in Palo Alto, California, tries to change the behaviors that maintain a problem rather than the initial causes of the problem. They contend that many problems are the result of misguided attempts to solve everyday dilemmas, including developmental hurdles such as marriage, divorce, and issues associated with growing older. Well-meaning attempts to remedy these dilemmas often perpetuate the problem, and people all too often persevere in applying these well-intentioned but maladaptive remedies.

Five frequently observed metapatterns of maladaptive remedies have been described (Fisch, Weakland, Watzlawick, Segal, Hoebell, & Deardoff, 1975). They include trying to be deliberately spontaneous, trying to get others to voluntarily do as one wants, looking for a risk-free method where some risk is inevitable, attempting to argue until an agreement has been reached, and trying to change a problem by withdrawing from the setting. Brief strategic therapy attempts to make small but significant changes in how these problems are approached with the assumption that the small changes and initial gains will generalize.

Brief strategic therapy is somewhat unconventional in identifying the patient. Rather than working with just the one person who calls for or comes to the appointment, the brief strategic therapist assumes that problems, including more severe forms of psychopathology, occur in an interpersonal context, and hence attempts to influence the interpersonal context within which the problem occurs.

The first step in brief strategic therapy is for the therapist to obtain a thorough and specific description of how the problem manifests itself in daily interpersonal interactions. It is also important to find out what attempts have been made to solve the problem and how these attempts tend to maintain the situation they seek to resolve. At this point, the brief strategic therapist assists the patient in formulating a goal for therapy. This is usually a small but meaningful strategy that will start the patient on a gradual path of change.

There is virtually no limit to the type of interventions a brief strategic therapist may use, but the interventions, whether suggestions, prescriptions, or paradoxical suggestions, tend to be in a completely different tack than what the patient has been trying. The intervention is designed to "reframe" the problem, or create a different perspective on the problem so that different solutions and ways of behaving are more apparent and accessible to the patient. The brief strategic therapist tends to operate in a way to minimize resistance rather than to analyze or confront it. The therapist may appear pessimistic about change, which may cause the patient to give up his or her pessimistic position in opposition, or the brief strategic therapist may tell the patient to go slowly in changing, thus alleviating the pressure to improve quickly that patients sometimes feel.

The number of sessions varies with the type of problem and intervention. Seven is average, and single-session treatments are not uncommon (Watzlawick et al., 1974).

The brief strategic approach shares many of the principles and techniques of therapeutic interventions based upon the work of Milton Erickson (1980; see Feldman, 1985), who pioneered and popularized the use of brief hypnosuggestive techniques. In both, the interventions are minimal and emphasize utilizing the complexities and paradoxes of communication within and among systems of interpersonal behavior.

Conclusions

The brief therapies reviewed above are by no means either exclusive or exhaustive. These therapies, while they have seemingly different theoretical frameworks and emphases, most likely share common features in addition to their short-term orientation (compare Garske & Lynn, 1985; Garske & Molteni, 1985). The particular model of brief therapy that is adopted in clinical work is probably more important for therapist comfort than client improvement, in light of the comparable effects of major therapeutic approaches (Smith et al., 1980).

Moreover, brief therapy is not limited to primary theoretical orientations of individual psychotherapy. Technique-oriented approaches, such as gestalt therapy (Grayson, 1979) and hypnosis (Barber, 1985), are geared toward specific and swift changes in the client, and supportive and relationship-based interventions, such as counseling, are typically brief and circumscribed by virtue of the problems and settings in which they take place (compare Bordin, 1980). Other modalities that implement change in the social environment, such as group therapy (Budman, Bennett, & Wineski, 1981) and family therapy (Kinston & Bentovim, 1981), are likewise adaptable to a time-limited framework.

EFFECTIVENESS OF BRIEF AND TIME-LIMITED PSYCHOTHERAPIES

How effective are brief psychotherapies? The answer is important for practical and academic reasons. Since brief therapies by definition are shorter in duration than their long-term counterparts, the professional wisdom has been that they are less effective. More is presumed to be better. If, however, comparable outcomes can be obtained with shorter interventions, brevity is likely to be preferred by the consumers of psychotherapeutic services and most definitely by the payers (supportive public programs, private insurance companies, and so on). It will also be embraced by some efficiency-minded professionals. Comparable effectiveness would also strengthen the theoretical positions of brief models and provide validity for their respective methods, as well as stimulate a reexamination of the prevalent concepts of maladaptive behaviors and their change that underlie long-term approaches to psychotherapy and counseling.

The general question of the effectiveness of brief therapies, like that of any therapy, is composed of several specific questions: Are brief therapies more effective than no therapy at all? Are they better than or equivalent to long-term therapies? Is one short-term approach superior to another? What are the effects of time limits? Are certain clients more responsive to brief interventions than other clients? The effectiveness question and its components can be addressed by reviewing the findings from two areas of research: the effects of duration on psychotherapy outcomes and the comparative effects of time-limited versus time-unlimited therapies.

Effects of Psychotherapy Duration

The length of treatment can be specified in at least three ways: the number of sessions, the number of weeks, and a joint index of the two: the number of sessions per week. Since the correlations among the three are high (Smith et al., 1980), only the findings for the total number of sessions will be considered here. Sessions are typically one hour long and occur once per week.

An overall assessment of the effects of treatment length can be obtained from the Smith et al. (1980) review, which is based upon the meta-analyses of nearly 500 psychotherapy studies. When effect sizes were analyzed as a function of duration, no clear pattern of differences was revealed. Longer psychotherapies were not more successful than shorter ones. In fact, a trend emerged in the data that suggested that the reverse might be true. The strongest effects appeared to be associated with therapies of 7 hours or less, whereas the weakest effects occurred in those 15 to 20 hours long! The authors contend that this finding does not indicate that brief therapies are superior to extended therapies. Rather, it appears to be an artifact of the substantial reduction of specific fears and anxieties with behavioral therapies. Comparable long-term therapies were not carried out. Smith et al. suggest also that the longer therapies typically treat problems of greater severity and therefore less tractability.

The comparison of the magnitude of effects *across* studies or meta-analysis, such as that by Smith et al. (1980), has problems in terms of methodological rigor and interpretability (compare Garske, 1982). While effect sizes did not appear to vary as a function of length, specific differences *within* studies were not assessed. Others have reviewed studies in which relationships were established between the length of therapy and outcome. The results of two such narrative reviews (Luborsky, Chandler, Auerbach, Cohen, & Bachrach, 1971; Meltzoff & Kornreich, 1970) suggest that these studies have found a direct link between time and effectiveness; the longer the therapy, the greater its benefits.

Johnson and Gelso (1980) contend that the apparent relationship between the length of psychotherapy and client improvement is moderated by the source of the outcome measurement. In their critical analysis of 36 studies, only one class of outcome measure—therapist ratings—was related consistently to therapy duration. This measure was the most reliable predictor and showed that, through the therapist's eyes, duration and improvement were related. Since no other source of outcome evaluation (client ratings, ratings of independent observers, behavioral indexes, and psychological tests) bore as consistent a relationship with duration, the authors suggest that the therapist evaluations were anomalous and probably biased. They prefer an explanation for this phenomenon derived from cognitive dissonance theory; the more time one invests in his or her work, the greater the perceived benefits. Even if this circumscribed difference were robust and meaningful, it appears that it does not last. Two to five years after therapy, the effects of brief and extended therapies are indiscriminable and both show more positive effects than were evident immediately at the cessation of treatment. Johnson and

Gelso conclude that once the process of change is initiated by a minimal number of therapy sessions, the passage of time enables the client independently to consolidate the therapeutic learning and to strengthen the improvement. Thus, in terms of the expenditure of therapist time, more is not necessarily better.

Comparisons of Time-Limited versus Time-Unlimited Therapies

The findings reviewed above have implications for gauging the effects of brief therapy, but they are inconclusive. The major shortcoming is that while research literature has investigated the impact of therapy length, the issue of whether the therapies of less duration were *purposely* brief is confounded. Many therapies are abbreviated without the length necessarily being agreed to by the therapist and the client at the beginning of treatment. Therapies might be shortened by factors such as unexpected dropouts, poor therapist-client relationships, and rapid client improvement.

The clearest evaluation of the effects of planned, short-term therapies is provided by studies in which time-limited and time-unlimited therapies are compared. In time-limited therapies, the therapist and client agree on the maximum number of sessions, usually during the initial hour. In time-unlimited therapies, the number of sessions remains unspecified. The typical research design of such studies is to vary only the prescription of duration (time-limited versus time-unlimited) and to otherwise equate the therapeutic procedures. Ideally, client and therapist variables, outcome measures, data collection methods, and so forth are matched for both conditions.

While the research literature on time-limited versus time-unlimited therapies is small, the results in general have shown that there are no consistent differences in effectiveness (Butcher & Koss, 1978; Luborsky & Singer, 1975). However, a close look at the pattern of results suggests that brief, time-limited therapies produce different effects under certain conditions.

In an intensive review of 12 comparative studies of time-limited versus time-unlimited therapies, Johnson and Gelso (1980) note that while therapists tend to rate the two approaches as similarly effective, the clients consistently judge themselves, in terms of ratings and self-report psychological tests, to be more improved in the time-limited therapies. This is especially noteworthy because not only are these therapies time-limited, but indeed they are significantly shorter. Across studies, the median duration for the time-limited therapies was 7.5 sessions whereas that for the time-unlimited studies was 26 sessions. There is also less attrition with the time-limited protocols and time-limited clients are less likely

to seek additional therapy after termination. The superior outcomes from the clients' perspective for time-limited therapies
are sustained when evaluated at the time when the longer,
time-unlimited therapies would be terminated (a median time
of about four months later). However, long-term follow-ups,
ranging from six months to two and a half years after termination, show that the circumscribed advantages of time-limited
therapies have diminished and that both procedures appear to
be comparably effective in the long run.

The conservative implications of the Johnson and Gelso
(1980) review are that briefer, time-limited therapies are as
effective as longer, time-unlimited therapies. This conclusion
is based upon a motley group of investigations that all met a
minimal set of criteria in terms of providing a direct comparison of time-limited versus time-unlimited therapies. If, however,
we accentuate the findings of the Reid and Shyne (1969) study,
the only one of those reviewed that incorporated the currently
acceptable rigors of psychotherapy research design and methodology (compare Gottman & Markman, 1978), the implications
broaden. Using clients with family problems and practicing
therapists in a community setting, Reid and Shyne found that
not only did the clients view time-limited therapy as more
effective than time-unlimited therapy, but so did the therapists
and independent observers who evaluated the progress of the
treatments. A recent study by Molteni, Garske, and Stedman
(1984), using a similar design and procedures with students
at a university counseling center, replicated and extended
Reid and Shyne's findings; *both* client and therapist measures
of outcome showed that the time-limited therapy resulted in
significantly better outcomes. The findings of these studies
clearly demonstrate that the positive effects of brief, time-
limited therapies need not be restricted only to the client's
self-evaluation. The outcomes appear to be sufficiently robust
to be observed as well by sources other than the client (that
is, therapists and independent observers).

Some specific aspects of the Reid and Shyne (1969) and
Molteni et al. (1984) studies are noteworthy. Reid and Shyne
attained their results with a time-limited therapy of 8 sessions
that was much shorter than the time-unlimited therapy. The
average durations were 8 and 26 sessions, respectively. Why
was a much shorter therapy more effective? One explanation
might be that change in terms of emotional relief and symptom
reduction takes place quickly for many clients (Garske, 1982).
In the absence of temporal restraints, clients in open-ended
therapies continue nevertheless, perhaps being uncertain if
the apparent change is real and developing a gratifying relationship with the therapist as the hours go by. Over time,
the objectives of the therapy broaden, more perceived problems
and complexity emerge, and dependency on the therapist
increases.

Another explanation for this brief-is-better phenomenon is suggested by the Molteni et al. study. They established a five-session time limit based upon the average duration of therapy in the university counseling center in which they collected their data. Unlike Reid and Shyne, they were consequently able to equate the durations for the time-limited and time-unlimited therapies and evaluate the effects of time limits unconfounded by the length of therapy. All previous studies investigated time-limited therapies that were also shorter in duration than time-unlimited therapies (compare Johnson & Gelso, 1980, Table 2, p. 86). Molteni et al. thereby showed that time limits themselves were instrumental in producing effects that were superior to a therapy that was equivalent in duration with no such temporal constraint formally structured into the treatment plan. The apparent paradox of brief therapies being more effective than longer therapies is best understood in terms of the potent impact of time limits.

Mann and Goldman (1982) provide a theoretical explanation for the therapeutic impact of time limits in terms of the client's increased motivation to change. They contend first that imposition of a time limit requires that a client confront fears and conflicts about dependency and act autonomously to individuate and separate himself or herself from the therapist and symbolically from significant others. Empirical evidence suggests that, to the contrary, time limits appear to affect therapists more than clients. Stedman, Garske, and Molteni (1984) found that therapists were more active, focused, and directive when working with time limits than without. Clients behaved similarly under time-limited and time-unlimited conditions. In time-limited therapies it therefore appears that clients improve more because the therapists act differently than they do in time-unlimited therapies; they are probably more active and more focused. Limited contact with clients, prescribed at the outset of treatment, apparently intensifies the therapists' efforts.

Despite some speculation about what clients might prove most suitable for time-limited therapy (compare Johnson and Gelso, 1980), client variables have not been investigated systematically with one exception. Molteni et al. (1984) found that clients with a high dependence upon the approval of others benefited most from time-limited therapy. These clients are likely to be sensitive to therapist expectations (Mosher, 1965) and likely to follow therapist directives (McLaughlin & Hewitt, 1972). Such attributes make approval-dependent clients especially good candidates for time-limited therapy because the therapists provided them with an expectation that the five-session limit was sufficient for change and, in the time-limited conditions, the therapists were more directive (compare Stedman et al., 1984).

Conclusions

Our review of the effects of duration on psychotherapy outcomes and of comparisons of time-limited versus time-unlimited therapies warrants several conclusions. Despite the lore and beliefs of the psychotherapy professions, there is little evidence that extended therapies produce better results than brief therapies. Longer therapies are perceived to be more effective only by the therapists conducting them.

Brief, time-limited therapies are at least as effective as extended, time-unlimited therapies. They appear to be especially helpful from the client's perspective. Some evidence suggests that the implementation of time limits increases therapist activity and directiveness, and produces greater improvement in shorter periods of time. Such improvements are durable and correspond to those obtained with much longer therapies 6 to 30 months after therapy is completed. It appears that in the long run more time from the onset of psychotherapy predicts improvement better than more therapy itself.

Like other areas of psychotherapy research, there is no evidence that one particular type of brief therapy is superior to another. Moreover, client variables have been virtually unexplored despite a platform of presumptive criteria. One study has shown that approval-dependent clients improve the most in brief, time-limited therapy.

SOME TECHNICAL ASPECTS OF BRIEF PSYCHOTHERAPY

This section includes a short discussion of three technical aspects of brief psychotherapy that have implications for its practice. The first involves the issue of brevity. How few sessions qualify a therapy as brief? How many are enough? The second pertains to the range of applicability. What clients are suitable for brief approaches? The last considers the therapist characteristics and behaviors that are necessary for the practice of brief psychotherapy.

The Concept of Brevity

We noted at the beginning of this chapter that the typical duration for psychotherapy is in fact quite brief, in the range of 5 to 15 sessions. Among brief psychotherapists who plan at the beginning of treatment to limit its duration, the numbers are comparable although the recommended range is broader. Quite predictably, the upper end is defined by brief therapists with psychoanalytic orientations who extend time limits as long as 40 hours (for example, Malan, 1963; Sifneos, 1979; Strupp, 1981). Behavior therapies also frequently last this long (compare Wilson, 1981). The lower end is a single session (Bloom, 1981). The most widely used time limit appears to be 12 sessions, such as that set by Mann and his followers (Mann & Goldman, 1982). Twelve sessions is also the maximum duration of therapies that have been researched (Smith et al., 1980).

Is there a clear basis for defining time limits? The most likely criterion, the characteristics of the client's problem, is not consistently associated with a specific time limit. For example, the treatment of quite severe psychopathology ranges from 4 (Bellak & Small, 1965) to 40 sessions (Malan, 1976). Also from a behavioral perspective, Wilson (1981) makes the point that problem severity does not necessarily extend the duration of brief treatment. In our view, just how brief a therapy is depends primarily on the modus operandi of the therapist. Therapist behaviors are multiply determined by an array of variables including theoretical predilection, general clinical skill and training, and experience with time-constrained therapy formats.

Given the inconsistency in time limits and the arbitrary bases for their determination, increased knowledge of the issues pertaining to how brief a brief therapy should be seems to be a first order of business for the field. Empirically, the effects of different time limits have gone virtually uninvestigated. The few studies that have been carried out have shown no significant differences between different time limits. For example, Gelso and Johnson (1983) found that 8 and 16 session limits produce comparable outcomes.

In the absence of any systematic bases for determining time limits in brief psychotherapies, we suggest two interim solutions. First, the establishment of time limits might be empirically based upon the typical duration of psychotherapy for a particular setting or practitioner. Molteni et al. (1984) selected a five-session limit based upon an average duration for psychotherapy at the university counseling center where they collected their data. This time limit was thus keyed to the usual temporal framework of the therapist and the expected counseling duration of the client. Selecting time limits in this way is especially crucial when introducing a brief, time-limited approach into a service delivery system in which the therapists and clients are unaccustomed to such temporal constraints.

Another means by which to arrive at time limits for brief therapy in the absence of guidelines from research is to implement them based upon the counterintuitive assumption that the shortest feasible duration will be at least as effective as a longer one. In essence this amounts to assuming that the null hypothesis with regard to the effects of time on psychotherapy cannot be rejected. While this assumption might seem radical from the perspective of the long-term psychotherapist, there is considerable interest among many brief therapists in taking this notion to the extreme and practicing brief therapies of a single session. Bloom (1981) has articulated a scheme and procedures for single-session psychotherapy, and Rockwell and Pinkerton (1982) reviewed evidence supportive of the effectiveness and efficacy of single-session therapy contacts. One of the most compelling sources of data comes from one of the most unlikely sources. Malan, Heaton, and Bacal (1975) found that many patients received symptomatic relief from a single consultation and furthermore that a subset of this clientele changed on so-called dynamic criteria. That is, they made significant changes on very stringent indexes of intrapsychic experience derived from psychoanalytic theory in *only* a single session. For these patients, the changes were not unlike those resulting from hundreds of hours of intensive psychoanalysis (compare Kernberg et al., 1972).

Client Suitability

Malan (1976) delineates two opposing views of client suitability for brief psychotherapy that he terms conservative and radical. The conservative position stems from traditional notions of psychotherapy and psychopathology. It suggests that seriously disturbed clients are inappropriate for brief psychotherapy and that its range of clients is narrowly limited to a select group with a halo of good characteristics such as intelligence, psychological mindedness, good interpersonal skills, and motivation to change (compare Garske & Molteni, 1985). This view, somewhat moderated, characterizes the mainstream of brief therapies. Abbreviated methods of therapy in the main have been limited to the more adaptive end of the psychopathology spectrum. The dilemma is that good clients have a good prognosis for change irrespective of the type or duration of the psychotherapy (Luborsky et al., 1971).

The so-called radical position, by contrast, proposes the extension of brief therapeutic methods to a much broader range of clients. Malan (1976) describes his view after three decades of work in brief therapy as shifting from conservative to radical. Other theorists also have contended that brief methods can be applied to many of the same clientele that are treated more lengthily (for example, Bellak & Small, 1965; Davanloo, 1980; Wilson, 1981). Brief methods have been applied to complex disorders that present a challenge even to long-term therapists such as borderline syndromes (Nurnberg & Suh, 1982), narcissistic disturbances (Lazarus, 1982), and addictive disorders (Wilson, 1981). The broad applicability of brief methods appears to be bolstered by two assumptions: psychological symptoms, though severe, need not be viewed as intractable illnesses; and behavior change, whether great or minuscule, is produced quickly during psychotherapy. The overriding treatment strategy is first to plan the therapy to be time-limited and rethink it only if necessary.

Perhaps the best indexes of client suitability are functional rather than diagnostic. One such index that cuts across theoretical lines is the client's motivation for treatment (compare Strupp & Binder, 1984; Wilson, 1981). The client must have the will and capacity to take part in a therapeutic regimen that is brief, intensive, and emotionally arousing. This requires most significantly the rapid development of a working alliance with the therapist (Garske & Molteni, 1985; Strupp & Binder, 1984), in which the client collaborates with the therapist on the goals and tasks of the therapy (Bordin, 1979).

We noted before that the effects of client variables on brief, time-limited psychotherapy outcomes have been virtually uninvestigated. One finding is that approval-dependent clients respond very well to brief therapy formats (Molteni et al., 1984), perhaps because motivation for approval solidifies the working alliance with the therapist. Until the informational void regarding client predictors of success in brief therapy is filled, it seems that suitability is most appropriately defined by professional ethics and good judgment. At present, it appears that most candidates for long-term psychotherapies are likewise candidates for short-term psychotherapies.

Therapist Variables

What are the techniques of the brief therapist like? The answer to this straightforward question is not so straightforward for several reasons. First, what therapists theorize about and prescribe versus what they actually do are not necessarily the same. We have very little research-based knowledge about what psychotherapists in general do and even less about what brief psychotherapists do. Second, even if we were to ascertain some direct knowledge of therapist activities in brief therapy, it would be difficult to discern whether such behaviors were unique to a time-limited format or likewise characteristic of time-unlimited psychotherapies. It appears that the essential ingredients in psychotherapy are common and not specific (Garske & Lynn, 1985).

With these limitations in mind, let us proceed to discuss a few of the prominent, if not unique, characteristics of therapist behavior in brief psychotherapy that are gleaned from the references we have reviewed thus far. We will narrow our discussion in two ways: First, we will not reiterate therapist techniques and procedures that are part of the general system of psychotherapy from which a brief model was derived. For example, all psychoanalytic therapies, brief and long-term, emphasize the interpretation of resistance and transferences. Second, we will attempt to identify only therapist variables that pertain across different theoretical models and techniques and are not limited to a specific approach.

Because of the brevity of the approach, the brief therapist must perform a thorough assessment immediately. The assessment is highly structured and is aimed jointly at the gathering of pertinent clinical information and the articulation of a specific focus for the therapy (compare Garske & Molteni, 1985). The assessment process is not merely data collection as it is in many therapies, but it also provides the therapist with a forum by which to preview the therapy by making trial interventions and observing the client's response (compare Davanloo, 1980), and to establish a working alliance with the client (compare Strupp & Binder, 1984). This rapid, early assessment process enables the therapist, implicitly or explicitly, to forge an arrangement or contract with the client to work on a focused therapeutic objective for a limited period of time.

A critical cluster of therapist operations involves the maintenance of the therapeutic focus and the enforcement of the time-limited format. These operations have been collectively termed contract management by Garske and Molteni (1985). The therapeutic focus, though agreed to by the client, can easily be lost or diluted. Because of the emotional arousal associated with rapid behavior change, resistance is commonplace. Clients might seek to broaden the focus, or introduce new problems. Whatever the detour, it is the therapist's responsibility to keep the treatment on track. The temporal dimension might also prove stressful for the client. Since the number of sessions is explicitly agreed to by the therapist and client, variations such as coming late for sessions, leaving early, missing appointments, and frequently rescheduling require monitoring and intervention.

The implementation of therapeutic procedures is characterized by heightened therapist activity and directiveness. This intensification of therapist operations is prescribed consistently by virtually all brief therapy models. Therapists do not merely talk more but they are more actively involved in carrying out the therapeutic plan. The limited duration of brief psychotherapy seems to infuse energy into the therapist's behavior. Therapists seem to work better under the pressure of deadlines. As we noted previously, the increased activity level and directiveness of the therapist's behavior in time-limited versus time-unlimited therapy is one of the few unique operations in the brief therapist's repertoire to have received empirical support (Stedman et al., 1984).

The brevity of the therapy requires that much of the client's change will take place in the therapist's absence. The brief therapist therefore actively attempts to facilitate the client making changes in the environment.

SUMMARY AND CONCLUSIONS

This chapter reviewed several aspects of brief and time-limited psychotherapies: definitions of and issues pertaining to therapies of limited duration; the emergence of brief and time-limited therapies and the social and economic issues that provided an impetus for their development; representative models and methods of brief psychotherapy; research evidence for the effectiveness of abbreviated therapy approaches; and some technical aspects of brief therapy centering about brevity and time limits, client applicability, and therapist variables.

While most psychotherapies do not last long, brief psychotherapies have several defining characteristics. The objectives are focused and well-defined; the duration is limited, usually at the beginning of the therapy by the mutual agreement of the therapist and client; and the therapist must be especially adept at quickly sizing up the client's problem, fostering a good therapist-client relationship, maintaining the therapeutic focus, monitoring time, and intervening actively and directively. A broad range of clients appears to be suitable as long as they have the motivation and wherewithal to participate actively in the time-limited procedures.

A number of models and procedures have emerged that are oriented toward brief, focused interventions. These procedures appear to be as effective as their long-term counterparts and do not appear to differ significantly from each other. Preliminary evidence suggests that from the client's perspective, brief, time-limited therapies might even be perceived as more beneficial. Moreover, it appears that the presence of time limits might be an active ingredient in the apparently positive outcomes associated with brief therapies.

Since brief, time-limited therapies appear to be at least as effective as extended, time-unlimited therapies, they offer an efficient, cost-effective alternative to other mental health services. The chief resistance to the widespread adoption of such procedures derives from the theoretical, ethical, and economic concerns of the psychotherapy professions.

REFERENCES

Aguilera, D. C., & Messick, J. M. (1982). *Crisis intervention: Theory and methodology* (4th ed.). St. Louis: Mosby.

Alexander, F., & French, T. M. (1946). *Psychoanalytic therapy: Principles and application.* New York: Ronald Press.

Appelbaum, S. A. (1981). *Effective change in psychotherapy.* New York: Aronson.

Balint, M., Ornstein, P., & Balint, E. (1972). *Focal psychotherapy.* London: Tavistock.

Bandura, A. (1977). *Social learning theory*. Englewood Cliffs, N.J.: Prentice-Hall.

Barber, T. X. (1985). Hypnosuggestive procedures as catalysts for psychotherapies. In S. J. Lynn & J. P. Garske (Eds.), *Contemporary psychotherapies: Models and methods* (pp. 333-375). Columbus, Ohio: Merrill.

Beck, A. T. (1976). *Cognitive therapy and the emotional disorders*. New York: International Universities Press.

Beck, A. T., Rush, A. J., Shaw, B., & Emery, G. (1979). *Cognitive therapy of depression*. New York: Guilford Press.

Bellak, L., & Small, L. (1965). *Emergency psychotherapy and brief psychotherapy*. New York: Grune & Stratton.

Bloom, B. L. (1981). Focused single-session therapy: Initial development and evaluation. In S. H. Budman (Ed.), *Forms of brief therapy* (pp. 167-216). New York: Guilford Press.

Bordin, E. S. (1979). The generalizability of the psychoanalytic concept of the working alliance. *Psychotherapy: Theory, research, and practice, 16*, 252-260.

——. (1980). *Of human bonds that bind or free*. Presidential address at the meeting of the Society for Psychotherapy Research, June, Pacific Grove, Calif.

Breuer, J., & Freud, S. (1957). *Studies on hysteria*. New York: Basic Books. (Original work published in 1895.)

Budman, S. H., Bennett, M. J., & Wineski, M. J. (1981). An adult developmental model of short-term group psychotherapy. In S. H. Budman (Ed.), *Forms of brief therapy* (pp. 305-342). New York: Guilford Press.

Budman, S. H., & Gurman, A. S. (1983). The practice of brief therapy. *Professional Psychology: Research and Practice, 14*, 277-292.

Butcher, J. N., & Koss, M. P. (1978). Research on brief and crisis-oriented psychotherapies. In S. L. Garfield & A. E. Bergin (Eds.), *Handbook of psychotherapy and behavior change* (2nd ed., pp. 725-767). New York: John Wiley.

Clarkin, J. F., Frances, A., Taintor, Z., & Warburg, M. (1980). Training in brief therapy: A survey of psychiatric residency programs. *American Journal of Psychiatry, 137*, 978-979.

Davanloo, H. (Ed.). (1980). *Short-term dynamic therapy* (Vol. 1). New York: Aronson.

Dollard, J., & Miller, N. E. (1953). *Personality and psychotherapy*. New York: McGraw-Hill.

Erickson, M. (1980). *The collected papers of Milton H. Erickson on hypnosis* (Vols. 1-4, E. Rossi, Ed.). New York: Irvington.

Feldman, J. B. (1985). The work of Milton Erickson: A multi-system model of eclectic therapy. *Psychotherapy: Theory, research, and practice, 22,* 154-162.

Ferenczi, S., & Rank, O. (1925). *Development of psychoanalysis* (C. Newton, Trans.). New York: Nervous and Mental Disease Publishing.

Fisch, R., Weakland, J., Watzlawick, P., Segal, L., Hoebell, F., & Deardoff, M. (1975). *Learning brief therapy: An introductory training manual.* Palo Alto, Calif.: Mental Research Institute.

Frank, J. D. (1981). Therapeutic components shared by all psychotherapies. In J. H. Harvey & M. M. Parks (Eds.), *Psychotherapy research and behavior change* (pp. 5-37). Washington, D.C.: American Psychological Association.

Garske, J. P. (1982). Issues regarding effective psychotherapy: A research perspective. In J. R. McNamara & A. G. Barclay (Eds.), *Critical issues, developments, and trends in professional psychology* (pp. 152-189). New York: Praeger.

Garske, J. P., & Lynn, S. J. (1985). Toward a general scheme for psychotherapy: Effectiveness, common factors, and integration. In S. J. Lynn & J. P. Garske (Eds.), *Contemporary psychotherapies: Models and methods* (pp. 497-516). Columbus, Ohio: Merrill.

Garske, J. P., & Molteni, A. L. (1985). Brief psychodynamic psychotherapy: An integrative approach. In S. J. Lynn & J. P. Garske (Eds.), *Contemporary psychotherapies: Models and methods* (pp. 69-115). Columbus, Ohio: Merrill.

Gelso, C. J., & Johnson, D. H. (1983). *Explorations in time-limited counseling and psychotherapy.* New York: Columbia University Press.

Gottman, J. M., & Markman, H. J. (1978). Experimental designs in psychotherapy research. In S. L. Garfield & A. E. Bergin (Eds.), *Handbook of psychotherapy and behavior change* (2nd ed., pp. 23-62). New York: John Wiley.

Grayson, H. (Ed.). (1979). *Short-term approaches to psychotherapy.* New York: Human Sciences Press.

Gustafson, J. P. (1984). An integration of brief dynamic psychotherapy. *American Journal of Psychiatry, 141,* 935-944.

Horowitz, M., Marmor, C., Krupnick, J., Wilner, H., Kaltreider, N., & Wallerstein, R. (1984). *Personality styles and brief psychotherapy.* New York: Basic Books.

Johnson, D. H., & Gelso, C. J. (1980). The effectiveness of time limits in counseling and psychotherapy: A critical review. *The Counseling Psychologist, 9,* 70-83.

Kernberg, O. F., Burstein, E. D., Coyne, L., Appelbaum, A., Horwitz, L., & Voth, H. (1972). Psychotherapy and psychoanalysis: Final report of the Menninger Foundation's psychotherapy research project. *Bulletin of the Menninger Clinic, 36,* 1-276.

Kinston, W., & Bentovim, A. (1981). Creating a focus for brief marital or family therapy. In S. H. Budman (Ed.), *Forms of brief therapy* (pp. 361-386). New York: Guilford Press.

Lazarus, L. W. (1982). Brief psychotherapy of narcissistic disturbances. *Psychotherapy: Theory, research, and practice, 19,* 228-236.

Lorion, R. P. (1974). Patient and therapist variables in the treatment of low income patients. *Psychological Bulletin, 81,* 344-354.

Luborsky, L., Chandler, M., Auerbach, A. H., Cohen, J., & Bachrach, H. M. (1971). Factors influencing the outcome of psychotherapy: A review of quantitative research. *Psychological Bulletin, 75,* 145-185.

Luborsky, L., & Singer, B. (1975). Comparative studies of psychotherapies. *Archives of General Psychiatry, 32,* 995-1008.

Malan, D. H. (1963). *A study of brief psychotherapy.* New York: Plenum Press.

——. (1976). *Frontiers of brief psychotherapy.* New York: Plenum Press.

Malan, D. H., Heaton, E., & Bacal, H. (1975). Psychodynamic changes in untreated neurotic patients: Apparently genuine improvements. *Archives of General Psychiatry, 32,* 110-143.

Mandel, H. P. (Ed.). (1981). *Short-term psychotherapy and brief therapy techniques: An annotated bibliography 1920-1980.* New York: Plenum Press.

Mann, J. (1973). *Time-limited psychotherapy.* Cambridge, Mass.: Harvard University Press.

Mann, J., & Goldman, R. (1982). *A casebook in time-limited psychotherapy.* New York: McGraw-Hill.

Marmor, J. (1979). Short-term dynamic psychotherapy. *American Journal of Psychiatry, 136,* 149-155.

McLaughlin, D., & Hewitt, J. (1972). Need for approval and

perceived openness. *Journal of Experimental Research in Personality, 6,* 255–258.

Meichenbaum, D. (1985). Cognitive-behavioral therapies. In S. J. Lynn & J. P. Garske (Eds.), *Contemporary psychotherapies: Models and methods* (pp. 261–286). Columbus, Ohio: Merrill.

Meltzoff, J., & Kornreich, M. (1970). *Research in psychotherapy.* New York: Atherton.

Molteni, A. L., Garske, J. P., & Stedman, J. L. (1984). *Effects of time-limits on psychotherapy outcomes.* Paper presented at the meeting of the Society for Psychotherapy Research, June, Banff, Canada.

Mosher, D. L. (1965). Approval motive and acceptance of "fake" personality interpretations which differ in favorability. *Psychological Reports, 17,* 395–402.

Nurnberg, H. G., & Suh, R. (1982). Time-limited psychotherapy of the hospitalized borderline patient. *American Journal of Psychotherapy, 36,* 90–92.

Rachman, S. J., & Wilson, G. T. (1980). *The effects of psychological therapy.* New York: Pergamon Press.

Reid, W., & Shyne, A. (1969). *Brief and extended casework.* New York: Columbia University Press.

Rockwell, W., & Pinkerton, R. (1982). Single-session psychotherapy. *American Journal of Psychotherapy, 36,* 32–40.

Rogers, J. S. (1960). Drop-out rates of psychotherapy in government mental hygiene clinics. *Journal of Clinical Psychology, 16,* 89–92.

Schlesinger, H. J., Mumford, E., & Glass, G. V. (1980). Mental health services and medical utilization. In G. R. Vandenbos (Ed.), *Psychotherapy: Practice, research, and policy* (pp. 71–102). Beverly Hills, Calif.: Sage.

Sifneos, P. E. (1972). *Short-term psychotherapy: Evaluation and technique.* New York: Plenum Press.

——. (1979). *Short-term psychotherapy and emotional crisis.* Cambridge, Mass.: Harvard University Press.

Smith, M. L., Glass, G. V., & Miller, T. I. (1980). *The benefits of psychotherapy.* Baltimore: Johns Hopkins Press.

Stedman, J. L., Garske, J. P., & Molteni, A. L. (1984). *Psychotherapy process as a function of time-limits.* Paper presented at the meeting of Society for Psychotherapy Research, June, Banff, Canada.

Strupp, H. H. (1981). Toward a refinement of time-limited dynamic psychotherapy. In S. H. Budman (Ed.), *Forms of brief therapy* (pp. 219–242). New York: Guilford Press.

Strupp, H. H., & Binder, J. (1984). *Psychotherapy in a new key*. New York: Basic Books.

Szasz, T. (1961). *The myth of mental illness*. New York: Harper.

Watzlawick, P., & Coyne, J. C. (1980). Depression following stroke: Brief, problem-focused family treatment. *Family Process, 19*, 13–18.

Watzlawick, P., Weakland, J., & Fisch, R. (1974). *Change: Principles of problem formation and problem resolution*. New York: Norton.

Weakland, J., Fisch, R., Watzlawick, P., & Bodin, A. (1974). Brief therapy: Focused problem resolution. *Family Process, 13*, 141–168.

Wilson, G. T. (1981). Behavior therapy as a short-term therapeutic approach. In S. H. Budman (Ed.), *Forms of brief therapy* (pp. 131–166). New York: Guilford Press.

Wilson, G. T., & O'Leary, K. D. (1980). *Principles of behavior therapy*. Englewood Cliffs, N.J.: Prentice-Hall.

Wolpe, J. (1958). *Psychotherapy by reciprocal inhibition*. Stanford, Calif.: Stanford University Press.

Zilbergeld, B. (1983). *The shrinking of America: Myths of psychological change*. Boston: Little, Brown.

AUTHOR INDEX

SUBJECT INDEX

ABOUT THE EDITORS AND CONTRIBUTORS

J. REGIS McNAMARA is Professor of Psychology and Associate Director of the Institute for Health and Behavioral Sciences at Ohio University. He was previously Chairman of Continuing Education for the Ohio Psychological Association. Dr. McNamara has published extensively on the ethical and methodological bases of clinical psychology and behavior therapy, and he was Senior Editor on the two previous volumes of *Critical Issues, Developments, and Trends in Professional Psychology*. His current major areas of interest include organizational–behavior modification, program evaluation, and health psychology. He earned his Ph.D. in 1972 from the University of Georgia and previously served on the faculty of the University of Missouri School of Medicine, Kansas City.

MARGRET A. APPEL is Associate Professor and Assistant Chair for Undergraduate Affairs in the Department of Psychology at Ohio University. She received her Ph.D. from the University of Denver in 1971 and was a postdoctoral fellow at the San Fernando Valley Child Guidance Clinic. She is currently interested in the area of behavioral medicine, particularly cardiovascular psychophysiology and behavioral factors in hypertension.

CRAIG A. BLUMER received his Ph.D. in clinical psychology from Ohio University in 1984. His research and publications have been on role plays, with emphasis on the ecological validity of role-play assessment. His clinical activities have been primarily in the assessment and treatment of psychiatric inpatients. He is the team leader for inpatient psychiatry at the Forsyth-Stokes Mental Health Center, Winston-Salem, North Carolina.

HERBERT J. CROSS is Professor of Psychology and Director of the Human Relations Center at Washington State University. He is chair/secretary of the Association of Directors of Psychology Training Clinics and is past-chair of the Psychology Board of Examiners for the state of Washington. He has published extensively in personality research, social problems, and professional issues. His current major interests include health psychology, personality assessment, professional issues, and hypnosis. He received his Ph.D. from Syracuse University in 1965 and served on the faculty of the University of Connecticut at Storrs.

ABOUT THE EDITORS AND CONTRIBUTORS

WILLIAM W. DEARDORFF is a staff psychologist at Kaiser Permanente Medical Center in Los Angeles. He received his Ph.D. from Washington State University in 1985. He interned at the University of Washington Medical School and is interested in psychotherapy, diagnosis, behavioral medicine, and program evaluation.

DENNIS DROTAR received his Ph.D. in clinical psychology in 1970 from the University of Iowa, where he was also trained in pediatric psychology. Following internship at Boston Children's Hospital and a postdoctoral fellowship at the University of Colorado School of Medicine, he took a position as a staff psychologist at the Department of Pediatrics, Case Western Reserve University School of Medicine and Rainbow Babies and Childrens Hospital, and is now an Associate Professor of Psychology. His interests are psychological consultation-liaison, training of psychologists to work in medical settings, and research concerning the psychological aspects of chronic physical illness in children and failure to thrive, and he has regularly contributed to professional journals in these areas. He is a past president of the Society of Pediatric Psychology.

JOHN P. GARSKE received his Ph.D. in clinical psychology at the University of California, Berkeley, in 1972 and is Professor of Psychology at Ohio University. He has coauthored *Psychological Theories of Motivation* (2nd ed., Brooks/Cole, 1982) and coedited *Contemporary Psychotherapies: Models and Methods* (Merrill, 1985). His current research interests include time-limited psychotherapy, psychotherapy integration, and experimental psychopathology.

LUCIA ALBINO GILBERT received her Ph.D. in 1974 from the University of Texas at Austin. After two years on the faculty and counseling center staff at Iowa State University, she returned to the University of Texas where she is now Associate Professor of Educational Psychology and teaches in the department's doctoral program in counseling psychology. Her interests include the psychology of women, sexuality and gender issues in psychotherapy, and stress and coping in dual-earner and dual-career families, and she has published numerous articles and chapters in these areas. Her book *Men in Dual-Career Families: Present Realities and Future Prospects* was published in 1985 by Erlbaum.

STEPHEN N. HAYNES received his Ph.D. from the University of Colorado in 1971 and is Professor and Director of Graduate Studies in clinical psychology at the Illinois Institute of Technology. He has published a number of books and articles in the areas of behavioral medicine, experimental psychopathology, behavioral assessment, and marital distress.

ABOUT THE EDITORS AND CONTRIBUTORS

CAROLYN LEMSKY received her B.S. degree from the University of Illinois, Urbana-Champaign. She is a graduate student in clinical psychology at Illinois Institute of Technology.

ANDREW L. MOLTENI received his Ph.D. in clinical psychology at Ohio University in 1984. He is Director of the Psychology Clinic, Department of Psychology, University of Maine at Orono. His research interests include brief psychotherapy and eating disorders.

JAMES M. MOORE, JR. is a doctoral student in the clinical psychology program at Ohio University. He received a B.A. in psychology from Appalachian State University and an M.A. in psychology from Western Kentucky University. His interests include brief psychotherapy, psychotherapeutic treatment of schizophrenia, and empirical investigation of psychodynamic conflict.

WILLIAM D. MURPHY is an Associate Professor in the Department of Psychiatry, University of Tennessee, Memphis, where he directs the Special Problems Unit, an outpatient treatment program for sex offenders. He received his Ph.D. in clinical psychology from Ohio University in 1976. He completed his clinical psychology internship at Mendota Mental Health Institute in Madison, Wisconsin, where he was involved in the sex offender treatment program. He completed a post-doctoral fellowship in the Department of Psychiatry at the University of Tennessee in the area of sexual deviation. He has published a number of chapters and articles in the area of sexual deviation. Dr. Murphy also currently serves as the chairman of the Memphis and Shelby County Child Sexual Abuse Council and chairs the Treatment Subcommittee of the State of Tennessee Task Force on Child Sexual Abuse.

KATHLEEN SEXTON-RADEK received her B.A. degree from Augustana College and earned her M.S. degree in Rehabilitation from Illinois Institute of Technology. She is a graduate student in the clinical psychology program at Illinois Institute of Technology.

SUSAN J. STALGAITIS received her Ph.D. in clinical psychology at Memphis State University in 1983. She is employed in the private practice of a clinical psychologist in the Memphis area. She is also an Assistant Clinical Professor in the Department of Psychiatry at the University of Tennessee and an affiliate staff member of several local psychiatric hospitals. She serves as a consultant to the Sexual Abuse Unit at the Tennessee Department of Human Services and is a member of the Memphis and Shelby County Child Sexual Abuse Council.

ABOUT THE EDITORS AND CONTRIBUTORS

IRVING B. WEINER is Vice President for Academic Affairs and Professor of Psychology at Fairleigh Dickinson University. He received his Ph.D. in clinical psychology from the University of Michigan in 1959 and has previously held positions as Head of the Division of Psychology at the University of Rochester Medical Center, Chairman of the Department of Psychology and Dean of the School of Graduate Studies at Case Western Reserve University, and Vice Chancellor for Academic Affairs and Professor of Psychology at the University of Denver. He is a Fellow of the American Psychological Association, a Diplomate of the American Board of Professional Psychology, a past president of the Society for Personality Assessment, and a recipient of the Society for Personality Assessment Distinguished Contribution Award. Dr. Weiner is currently editor of the *Journal of Personality Assessment* and advisory editor in clinical psychology to John Wiley and Sons. His own writings include numerous articles and chapters and the following books: *Psychodiagnosis in Schizophrenia* (Wiley, 1966), *Psychological Disturbance in Adolescence* (Wiley-Interscience, 1970), *Rorschach Handbook of Clinical and Research Applications* (Prentice-Hall, 1971), *Principles of Psychotherapy* (Wiley, 1975), *Development of the Child* (Wiley, 1978), *Child and Adolescent Psychopathology* (Wiley, 1978), *The Rorschach Comprehensive System: Vol. 3. Assessment of Children and Adolescents* (Wiley, 1982), and *Adolescence: A Developmental Transition* (Erlbaum, 1985).

PROFESSIONAL PSYCHOLOGY UPDATE: PRAEGER STUDIES FOR CONTINUING EDUCATION

CRITICAL ISSUES, DEVELOPMENTS, AND TRENDS IN
PROFESSIONAL PSYCHOLOGY, Volume 2, edited by
J. Regis McNamara

Chapter

A SELF-ASSESSMENT OPTION FOR
CONTINUING-EDUCATION CREDIT IN PSYCHOLOGY

The publication of this edition provides professional psychologists with the opportunity to acquire new knowledge about their field as well as to obtain continuing-education credit for their reading by means of a self-assessment examination. Praeger, in conjunction with the School of Professional Psychology at Wright State University, is supporting this endeavor.

The self-assessment examination is keyed to the information presented in this book, is objective in nature, and follows a format similar to that of other self-assessment examinations. Questions on the examination are written to assess a person's knowledge and comprehension of the material presented in the text.

Individuals who take the self-assessment examination will receive prompt feedback on their performance. Individuals who pass the examination will be awarded 5 continuing-education credits, approved by the American Psychological Association, through a program sponsored by the School of Professional Psychology at Wright State University. A fee of $50.00 is charged for the examination service. Individuals who are interested in taking the self-assessment examination should complete the order form below.

Please send me the Self-Assessment Examination for CRITICAL ISSUES, DEVELOPMENTS, AND TRENDS IN PROFESSIONAL PSYCHOLOGY, Vol. 3.

To receive the Self-Assessment Examination, your Check, Money Order, or Postal Money Order for the full amount of $50.00 must accompany this order.

WE MUST HAVE YOUR SIGNATURE TO PROCESS THIS ORDER.

SIGN HERE: _____

Please send me _____ copies of the Self-Assessment Examination for McNamara & Appel/CRITICAL ISSUES, DEVELOPMENTS, AND TRENDS IN PROFESSIONAL PSYCHOLOGY, $50.00 each. Make all checks or money orders payable to: Professional Assessment and Development Services.

Name _____

Address _____

City _____ State _____ Zip _____

Mail order and payment to: Professional Assessment and Development Services, P.O. Box 822, Athens, Ohio 45701